JOHN WEBSTER
AND
CYRIL TOURNEUR

JOHN WEBSTER
AND
CYRIL TOURNEUR

(Four Plays)

With an Introduction and Notes by

JOHN ADDINGTON SYMONDS

A MERMAID DRAMABOOK

HILL AND WANG, INC. · NEW YORK

The Introduction and texts in this volume are those of the Mermaid
Series of English dramatists. Published by special arrangement with
Ernest Benn, Ltd.

Standard Book Number: 8090-0703-7

Library of Congress Catalog Card Number: 56-10715

FIRST DRAMABOOK EDITION AUGUST 1956

12 13 14 15 16

Manufactured in the United States of America

CONTENTS

	Page
JOHN WEBSTER AND CYRIL TOURNEUR	7
THE WHITE DEVIL	19
THE DUCHESS OF MALFI	121
THE ATHEIST'S TRAGEDY	219
THE REVENGER'S TRAGEDY	301

THE GLOBE THEATRE

THE first Globe Theatre, on the Bankside, Southwark, "the summer theatre of Shakespeare and his fellows," is believed to have been built in 1594, partly of materials removed from the Theatre in Shoreditch, "the earliest building erected in or near London purposely for scenic exhibitions." Outside, the Globe was hexagonal in shape, and, like all the theatres of that epoch, was open at the top, excepting the part immediately over the stage, which was thatched with straw. The interior of the theatre was circular. The performances took place by daylight, and while they were going on a flag with the cross of St. George upon it was unfurled from the roof. Originally, in place of scenery, the names of the localities supposed to be represented were inscribed on boards or hangings for the information of the audience. The sign of the theatre was a figure of Hercules supporting the globe, beneath which was written "Totus mundus agit Histrionem."

In 1601, the Globe Theatre was used as a place of meeting by the conspirators engaged in Essex's rebellion, and next year Shakespeare's *Hamlet,* following upon other of his plays, was here produced for the first time. In subsequent years plays by Shakespeare, Webster, Ford, and contemporary dramatists were performed at the Globe, until in 1613 the theatre was burnt to the ground owing to some lighted paper, thrown from a piece of ordnance used in the performance, igniting the thatch. The theatre was rebuilt in the following spring with a tiled roof, and according to Howes's MS., quoted by Collier in his life of Shakespeare, "at the great charge of King James and many noblemen and others." Ben Jonson styled the new theatre "the glory of the Bank and the fort of the whole parish."

The Globe Theatre was pulled down in 1644 by Sir Matthew Brand with the view to tenements being erected upon its site.

JOHN WEBSTER AND
CYRIL TOURNEUR

NOTHING is known about the lives of John Webster and
Cyril Tourneur. We are ignorant when they were born and
when they died. We possess only meagre hints of what
contemporaries thought of them. One allusion to Tourneur
survives, which shows that he was not popular in his life-
time as a dramatist:—

> His fame unto that pitch so only raised
> As not to be despised nor too much praised.

A superficial critic speaks of "crabbed Webster, the
playwright, cart-wright," and proceeds, at some length, to
deride his laborious style and obscurity. Commendatory
verses by S. Sheppard, Th. Middleton, W. Rowley, and
John Ford prove, however, that Webster's tragedies won
the suffrage of the best judges. None such are printed
with Tourneur's plays.

Webster began to write for the stage as early as 1601.
Between that date and 1607 he worked upon Marston's
Malcontent, and is supposed to have collaborated with
Dekker in the *History of Sir Th. Wyatt, Northward Ho,*
and *Westward Ho.* Tourneur began his literary career by
a satire called *Transformed Metamorphosis,* in 1600, which
was followed in 1609 by a *Funeral Poem on the Death of
Sir Francis Vere.* Both he and Webster published Elegi·s
in 1613 upon the death of Prince Henry.

In this year he was employed upon some business for
the Court, as appears from this passage in the Revels Accounts (ed. Cunningham, p. xliii.):

> To Cyrill Turner, upon a warraunte signed by the Lord
> Chamberleyne and Mr. Chaunccellor, dated at Whitehall, 23rd
> December, 1613, for his chardges and paines in carrying l'res for
> his Ma^{ts} service to Brussells . . . . X^{li}.

The amount of this payment renders it improbable that

Tourneur's mission was of any political or diplomatical im,
portance.

We do not know when he commenced playwright; but
The Revenger's Tragedy was licensed in 1607 and printed
in the same year. *The Atheist's Tragedy* was printed in
1611; it had been written almost certainly at some earlier
period. Webster's *White Devil* was printed and probably
produced in 1612; his *Duchess of Malfi,* produced perhaps
in 1616, was printed in 1623.

It is needful to dwell on the comparison of these dates,
since they give Tourneur the priority of authorship in a
style of tragedy which both poets cultivated with marked
effect. Not to class them together as the creators of a singular type of drama would be uncritical. They elaborated
similar motives, moved in the same atmosphere of moral
gloom, aimed at the like sententious apothegms, affected
the same brevity and pungency, handled blank verse and
prose on parallel methods, and owed debts of much the
same kind to Shakespeare. That Webster was the greater
writer, as he certainly possessed a finer cast of mind, and
surveyed a wider sphere of human nature in his work, will
be admitted. Yet it seems not impossible that he may have
followed Tourneur's lead in the peculiar form and tone of
his two masterpieces.

Speaking broadly, the two best tragedies of Webster and
the two surviving tragedies of Tourneur constitute a dis-
tinct species of the genus which has been termed Tragedy
of Blood.[1] It was Kyd, in his double drama called *The
Spanish Tragedy,* who first gave definite form to this type.
Those two plays exhibit the main ingredients of the Tragedy of Blood—a romantic story of crime and suffering, a
violent oppressor, a wronged man bent upon the execution
of some subtle vengeance, a ghost or two, a notorious villain
working as the tyrant's instrument, and a whole crop of
murders, deaths, and suicides to end the action. What use
Shakespeare made of the type, and how he glorified it in
Hamlet, is well known. Both Tourneur and Webster, writing after Shakespeare, had of necessity felt his influence,
and their handling of the species was modified by that of
their great master. Yet they reverted in many important

[1] See J. A. Symonds' *Shakespeare's Predecessors,* chap. xii., for a definition and
description of this dramatic genus.

particulars from the Shakespearean method to Kyd's. The use they both made of the villain, a personage which Shakespeare discarded, might be cited as distinctive. Kyd described the villain in the character of his Lazarrotto thus:—

> I have a lad in pickle of this stamp,
> A melancholy, discontented courtier,
> Whose famished jaws look like the chap of death;
> Upon whose eyebrow hangs damnation;
> Whose hands are washed in rape and murders bold;
> Him with a golden bait will I allure,
> For courtiers will do anything for gold.

The outlines sketched by Kyd were filled in with touches of diseased perversity and crippled nobleness by Tourneur in his Vendice, and were converted into full-length portraits of impressive sombreness by Webster in his Flamineo and Bosola.

When we compare Tourneur with Webster as artists in the Tragedy of Blood, the former is seen at once to stand upon a lower level. His workmanship was rougher and less equal; his insight into nature less humane, though hardly less incisive; his moral tone muddier and more venomous; his draughtsmanship spasmodic and uncertain. Tourneur seems to have invented his own plots; they have the air of being fabricated after a recipe. This flaw—an apparent insincerity in the choice of motives—corresponds to the more painful moral flaw which makes his occasional good work like that of a remorseful and regretful fallen angel. While we read his plays, the line of Persius rises to our lips:—

> Virtutem videant intabescantque relictâ.

Webster, as man and artist, never descends to Tourneur's level. He selects his two great subjects from Italian story, deriving thence the pith and marrow of veracity. These subjects he treats carefully and conscientiously, according to his own conception of the dreadful depths in human nature revealed to us by sixteenth century Italy. He does not use the vulgar machinery of revenge and ghosts in order to evolve an action. In so far as this goes, he may even be said to have advanced a step beyond *Hamlet* in the evolution of the Tragedy of Blood. His dramatic issues are worked out, without much alteration, from the matter given in the two Italian tales he used. Only he claims the right to view human fates and fortunes with despair, to paint a broad black background for his figures, to detach them sharply in sinister or pathetic relief, and to leave us at the last without a prospect over hopeful things. "One great Charybdis swallows all," said the Greek Simonides; and this motto might be chosen for the work of Shakespeare's greatest pupil in the art of tragedy. Yet Webster never fails to touch our hearts, and makes us remember a riper utterance upon the piteousness of man's ephemeral existence:—

> Sunt lacrimæ rerum, et mentem mortalia tangunt.

It is just this power of blending tenderness and pity with the exhibition of acute moral anguish by which Webster is so superior to Tourneur as a dramatist.

Both playwrights have this point in common, that their forte lies not in the construction of plots, or in the creation of characters, so much as in an acute sense for dramatic situations. Their plots are involved and stippled in with slender touches; they lack breadth, and do not rightly hang together. Their characters, though forcibly conceived, tend to monotony, and move mechanically. But when it is needful to develop a poignant, a passionate, or a delicate situation, Tourneur and Webster show themselves to be masters of their art. They find inevitable words, the right utterance, not indeed always for their specific personages, but for generic humanity, under the *peine forte et dure* of intense emotional pressure. Webster, being the larger, nobler, deeper in his touch on nature, offers a greater variety of situations which reveal the struggles of the human soul with sin and fate. He is also better able to sustain these situations at a high dramatic pitch—as in the scene of Vittoria before her judges, and the scene of the Duchess of Malfi's assassination. Still Tourneur can display a few such moments by apocalyptic flashes—notably in the scenes where Vendice deals with his mother and sister.

Both playwrights indulge the late Elizabethan predilection for conceits. Webster, here as elsewhere, proves himself the finer artist. He inserts Vittoria's dream, Antonio's dia-

logue with Echo, Bosola's Masque of Madmen, accidentally
and subserviently to action. Tourneur enlarges needlessly,
but with lurid rhetorical effect, upon the grisly humours
suggested by the skull of Vendice's dead mistress. Using
similar materials, the one asserts his claim to be called
the nobler poet by more steady observance of the Greek
precept "Nothing overmuch." Words to the same effect
might be written about their several employment of blank
verse and prose. Both follow Shakespeare's distribution of
these forms, while both run verse into prose as Shakespeare
never did. Yet I think we may detect a subtler discrimina-
tive quality in Webster's most chaotic periods than we can
in Tourneur's; and what upon this point deserves notice is
that Webster, of the two, alone shows lyrical faculty. His
three dirges are of exquisite melodic rhythm, in a rich
low minor key; much of his blank verse has the ring of
music; and even his prose suggests the colour of song by its
cadence. This cannot be said of the sinister and arid Muse
of Tourneur. She wears no evergreens of singing, nay, no
yew-boughs even, on her forehead. Her dusky eyes sparkle
with sharp metallic scintillations, as when Castiza says to
her mother:—

Come from that poisonous woman there.

The Revenger's Tragedy is an entangled web of lust,
incest, fratricide, rape, adultery, mutual suspicion, hate, and
bloodshed, through which runs, like a thread of glittering
copper, the vengeance of a cynical plague-fretted spirit.
Vendice emerges from the tainted crew of Duke and
Duchess, Lussurioso, Spurio and Junior, Ambitioso and
Supervacuo, with a kind of blasted splendour. They are
curling and engendering, a brood of flat-headed asps, in
the slime of their filthy appetites and gross ambitions. He
treads and tramples on them all. But he bears on his own
forehead the brands of Lucifer, the rebel, and of Cain, the
assassin. The social corruption which transformed them
into reptiles, has made him a fiend incarnate. Penetrated
to the core with evil, conscious of sin far more than they
are, he towers above them by his satanic force of purpose.
Though ruined, as they are ruined, and by like causes,
he maintains the dignity of mind and of volition. The right
is on his side; the right of a tyrannicide, who has seen

his own mistress, his own father, the wife of his friend, done to death by the brutalities of wanton princelings. But Tourneur did not choose to gift Vendice with elevation of nature. In the strongest scene of the play he showed this scorpion of revenge, stooping to feign a pander's part, tempting his mother and his sister as none but a moral leper could have done. In the minor scene of the duke's murder, he made him malicious beyond the scope of human cruelty and outrage. It was inherent apparently in this poet's conception of life that evil should be proclaimed predominant. His cynicism stands self-revealed in the sentence he puts into Antonio's mouth, condemning Vendice to death:—

You that would murder him would murder me.

Even justice, in his view, rests on egotism. And yet Tourneur has endowed Vendice with redeeming qualities. The hero of this crooked play is true to his ideal of duty, true to his sense of honour. He dies contented because he has perfected his revenge, preserved his sister's chastity, and converted his mother at the poniard's point. Where all are so bad and base, Vendice appears by comparison sublime. If we are to admire tone and keeping in a work of art, we certainly find it here; for the moral gradations are relentlessly scaled within the key of sin and pollution. The only character who stirs a pulse of sympathy is vicious. Castiza is a mere lay figure, and her mother one of the most repulsive personages of the Jacobean drama.

Webster presents a larger mass of dramatic work to the critic. Beside the tragedies included in this volume, he wrote another tragedy, *Appius and Virginia,* a tragi-comedy entitled *The Devil's Law-case,* and is said to have had a share in the history-play of *Sir Thomas Wyatt,* and in three comedies, *Northward Ho, Westward Ho,* and *A Cure for a Cuckold. The Devil's Law-case* shows how much this playwright depended on material supplied him, and how little he could trust his own inventive faculty. It starts with an involved plot of Italian deceit and contemplated crime, which Webster develops in his careful but not very lucid manner. We feel that we are working toward some sinister *dénouement,* when suddenly, by a twist of the hand, a favourable turn is given to events, and the play ends happily—violating probability, artistic tone, and the ethical integrity of the chief character, Romelio. From *The Famous History of Sir Thomas Wyatt* in its present mangled and misshapen form it is impossible to disengage Webster's handiwork with any certainty. The same may be said about the brisk and well-wrought pieces *Northward Ho* and *Westward Ho.* Yet I see no reason to dispute Webster's share in these three plays. *A Cure for a Cuckold* requires more particular comment. This comedy was ascribed by the publisher Kirkman to John Webster and William Rowley. But the ascription stands for absolutely nothing, unless we can discover corroborative internal evidence of Webster's collaboration. Such evidence I do not find, although there is certainly nothing in the play to disprove Kirkman's assertions. It should be added that a delicate little piece of serio-comic workmanship lies embedded in the otherwise trashy *Cure for a Cuckold.* Mr. Edmund Gosse early saw and twice pointed out how easily this play within the play could be detached from the rest; and the Honourable S. E. Spring Rice has recently printed, at Mr. Daniel's private press, a beautiful edition of what, following Mr. Gosse's suggestion, he calls *Love's Graduate.* I should like to believe that "piece of silver-work," as Mr. Gosse has aptly called it, to be truly the creation of Webster, "the sculptor whose other groups are all in bronze." Indeed, there are no reasons why the belief should not be indulged, except that Kirkman's ascription carries but a feather's weight, and that there is nothing special in the style to warrant it. *Love's Graduate,* rescued from *A Cure for a Cuckold* by pious hands, is one of the unclaimed masterpieces of this fruitful epoch.

The great length of Webster's two Italian tragedies rendered it impossible to print *Appius and Virginia* in this volume. That is much to be regretted; for without a study of his Roman play, justice can hardly be done to the scope and breadth of Webster's genius. Of *Appius and Virginia* Mr. Dyce observed with excellent judgment: "this drama is so remarkable for its simplicity, its deep pathos, its unobtrusive beauties, its singleness of plot, and the easy, unimpeded march of its story, that perhaps there are readers who will prefer it to any other of our author's productions." Webster, who was a Latin scholar, probably studied the

fable in Livy; but its outlines were familiar to English
people through Painter's "Palace of Pleasure." He has drawn
the mutinous camp before Algidum, the discontented city
ruled by a licentious noble, the stern virtues of Icilius and
Virginius, and the innocent girlhood of Virginia with a
quiet mastery and self-restraint which prove that the violent
contrasts of his Italian plays were calculated for a peculiar
effect of romance. When treating a classical subject, he
aimed at classical severity of form. The chief interest of
the drama centres in Appius. This character suited Webster's vein. He delighted in the delineation of a bold, imperious tyrant, marching through crimes to the attainment
of his lawless ends, yet never wholly despicable. He also
loved to analyse the subtleties of a deep-brained intriguer,
changing from open force to covert guile, fawning and
trampling on the objects of his hate by turns, assuming the
tone of diplomacy and the truculence of autocratic will at
pleasure, on one occasion making the worse appear the
better cause by rhetoric, on another espousing evil with
reckless cynicism. The variations of such a character are
presented with force and lucidity in *Appius*. Yet the whole
play lacks those sudden flashes of illuminative beauty, those
profound and searching glimpses into the bottomless abyss
of human misery, which render Webster's two Italian tragedies unique. He seems to have been writing under self-
imposed limitations, in order to obtain a certain desired
effect—much in the same way as Ford did when he composed the irreproachable but somewhat chilling history of
Perkin Warbeck.

The detailed criticism of Webster as a dramatist, and
the study of his two chief tragedies in relation to their
Italian sources, would lead me beyond the limits of this
Introduction. He is not a poet to be dealt with by any
summary method; for he touches the depths of human nature in ways that need the subtlest analysis for their
proper explanation. I am, however, loth to close this introduction without a word or two concerning the peculiarities
of Webster's dramatic style.[2] Owing to condensation of
thought and compression of language, his plays offer considerable difficulties to readers who approach them for the

[2] It ought, perhaps, to be mentioned that the remarks which follow are adapted
in part from an essay on Webster published in my *Italian By-ways*.

first time. So many fantastic incidents are crowded into a single action, and the dialogue is burdened with so much profoundly studied matter, that the general impression is apt to be blurred. We rise from the perusal of his Italian tragedies with a deep sense of the poet's power and personality, an ineffaceable recollection of one or two resplendent scenes, and a clear conception of the leading characters. Meanwhile the outlines of the fable, the structure of the drama as a complete work of art, seem to elude our grasp. The persons, who have played their part upon the stage of our imagination, stand apart from one another, like figures in a *tableau vivant*. *Appius and Virginia,* indeed, proves that Webster understood the value of a simple plot, and that he was able to work one out with conscientious firmness. But in *Vittoria Corombona* and *The Duchess of Malfi,* each part is etched with equal effort after luminous effect upon a murky background; and the whole play is a mosaic of these parts. It lacks the breadth which comes from concentration on a master-motive. We feel that the author had a certain depth of tone and intricacy of design in view, combining sensational effect and sententious pregnancy of diction in works of laboured art. It is probable that able representation upon the public stage of an Elizabethan theatre gave them the coherence, the animation, and the movement which a chamber-student misses. When familiarity has brought us acquainted with Webster's way of working, we perceive that he treats terrible and striking subjects with a concentrated vigour special to his genius. Each word and trait of character has been studied for a particular effect. Brief lightning flashes of acute self-revelation illuminate the midnight darkness of the lost souls he has painted. Flowers of the purest and most human pathos, like Giovanni de Medici's dialogue with his uncle in *Vittoria Corombona,* bloom by the charnel-house on which the poet's fancy loved to dwell. The culmination of these tragedies, setting like stormy suns in blood-red clouds, is prepared by gradual approaches and degrees of horror. No dramatist showed more consummate ability in heightening terrific effects, in laying bare the inner mysteries of crime, remorse, and pain combined to make men miserable. He seems to have had a natural bias toward the dreadful stuff with which he deals so powerfully. He was drawn to comprehend and reproduce abnormal elements of spiritual anguish. The materials with which he builds are sought for in the ruined places of abandoned lives, in the agonies of madness and despair, in the sarcasms of reckless atheism, in slow tortures, griefs beyond endurance, the tempests of sin-haunted conscience, the spasms of fratricidal bloodshed, the deaths of frantic hope-deserted criminals. He is often melodramatic in the means employed to bring these psychological elements of tragedy home to our imagination. He makes free use of poisoned engines, daggers, pistols, disguised murderers, masques, and nightmares. Yet his firm grasp upon the essential qualities of diseased and guilty human nature, his profound pity for the innocent who suffer shipwreck in the storm of evil passions not their own, save him, even at his gloomiest and wildest, from the unrealities and extravagances into which less potent artists— Tourneur, for example—blundered. That the tendency to brood on what is ghastly belonged to Webster's idiosyncrasy appears in his use of metaphor. He cannot say the simplest thing without giving it a sinister turn—as thus:

> You speak as if a man
> Should know what fowl is *coffined* in a baked meat,
> Afore you cut it open.

When knaves come to preferment, they rise *as gallowses are raised* in the Low countries, one upon another's shoulders.

Pleasure of life! what is't? only the *good hours of an ague*.

I would sooner *eat a dead pigeon taken from the soles of the feet of one sick of the plague* than kiss one of you fasting.

In his dialogue, people bandy phrases like—"O you screech-owl!" and "Thou foul black cloud!" A sister warns her brother to think twice before committing suicide, with this weird admonition:—

> I prithee, yet remember
> Millions are now in graves, which at last day
> Like mandrakes shall rise shrieking.

But enough has now been said about these peculiarities of Webster's dramatic style. It is needful to become acclimatised to his specific mannerism, both in the way of working and the tone of thinking before we can appreciate his real greatness as a dramatic poet and moralist. Then we recognise the truth of what has recently been written of him by an acute and sympathetic critic: "There is no poet morally nobler than Webster." [3]

JOHN ADDINGTON SYMONDS.

[3] Readers of this volume who are anxious to obtain more light upon Webster's art must be referred to Lamb's notes in the *Specimens from English Dramatic Poets*, to Mr. Swinburne's article on John Webster in *The Nineteenth Century* for June, 1886, and to my own essay upon *Vittoria Accoramboni* in *Italian Byways* (Smith and Elder, 1883).

The text adopted for Webster's two tragedies is that of Dyce's edition. His arrangement of scenes has been followed, except in the case of the *Vittoria Corombona*, which Dyce left undivided. The notes, too, are in the main extracted from the same source. With reference to Cyril Tourneur's plays, the text of *The Atheist's Tragedy* has been modernised from Mr. Churton Collins's edition; that of *The Revenger's Tragedy* is based upon the modernised version in Hazlitt's edition of Dodsley, collated throughout with Mr. Collins's text. Students of the English drama owe a debt of gratitude to Mr. Churton Collins for his scholarly issue of the complete works of Tourneur.

THE WHITE DEVIL;

or, Vittoria Corombona

THE *White Devil; or, the Tragedy of Paulo Giordano Ursini, Duke of Brachiano, With the Life and Death of Vittoria Corombona, the famous Venetian Curtizan,* was printed in 1612, as acted by the Queen's servants, and again in 1631, 1665, and 1672. In 1707 Nahum Tate published an alteration called *Injured Love; or, the Cruel Husband.*

Webster founded this play directly on the history of the Duke di Brachiano and his two wives, of whom the second, Vittoria Accorambaoni, was the widow of the nephew of Cardinal Montalto, afterwards Pope Sixtus V.

TO THE READER

IN publishing this tragedy, I do but challenge to myself that liberty which other men have ta'en before me: not that I affect praise by it, for *nos hæc novimus esse nihil;*[1] only, since it was acted in so dull a time of winter, presented in so open and black a theatre, that it wanted (that which is the only grace and setting-out of a tragedy) a full and understanding auditory; and that, since that time, I have noted most of the people that come to that play-house resemble those ignorant asses who, visiting stationers' shops, their use is not to inquire for good books, but new books; I present it to the general view with this confidence,—

> Nec ronchos metues maligniorum,
> Nec scombris tunicas dabis molestas.[2]

If it be objected this is no true dramatic poem, I shall easily confess it; *non potes in nugas dicere plura meas ipse ego quam dixt.*[3] Willingly, and not ignorantly, in this kind have I faulted: for, should a man present to such an auditory the most sententious tragedy that ever was written, observing all the critical laws, as height of style, and gravity of person, enrich it with the sententious Chorus, and, as it were, liven death in the passionate and weighty Nuntius; yet, after all this divine rapture, *O dura messorum ilia,*[4] the breath that comes from the uncapable multitude is able to poison it; and, ere it be acted, let the author resolve to fix to every scene this of Horace,

> Hæc porcis hodie comedenda relinques.[5]

To those who report I was a long time in finishing this tragedy, I confess, I do not write with a goose quill winged with two feathers; and if they will needs make it my fault, I

---

[1] Martial, xiii. 2.
[2] Martial, iv. 87.
[3] Martial, xiii. 2.
[4] Horace, *Epod.* iii.
[5] *Epist.* i. 7.

must answer them with that of Euripides to Alcestides,[6] a tragic writer. Alcestides objecting that Euripides had only, in three days, composed three verses, whereas himself had written three hundred, "Thou tellest truth," quoth he, "but here's the difference, —thine shall only be read for three days, whereas mine shall continue three ages."

Detraction is the sworn friend to ignorance: for mine own part, I have ever truly cherished my good opinion of other men's worthy labours; especially of that full and heightened style of Master Chapman; the laboured and understanding works of Master Jonson; the no less worthy composures of the both worthily excellent Master Beaumont and Master Fletcher; and lastly (without wrong last to be named), the right happy and copious industry of Master Shakespeare, Master Dekker, and Master Heywood; wishing what I write may be read by their light; protesting that, in the strength of mine own judgment, I know them so worthy, that though I rest silent in my own work, yet to most of theirs I dare (without flattery) fix that of Martial,

Non norunt hæc monumenta mori.[7]

[6] Valerius Maximus, Lib. iii. 7.
[7] Martial, x. 2.

DRAMATIS PERSONÆ

MONTICELSO, a Cardinal, afterwards Pope.

FRANCISCO DE MEDICIS, Duke of Florence.

BRACHIANO, otherwise Paulo Giordano Ursini, Duke of Brachiano, Husband of ISABELLA.

GIOVANNI, his Son.

COUNT LODOVICO.

CAMILLO, Husband of VITTORIA.

FLAMINEO, Brother of VITTORIA, Secretary to BRACHIANO.

MARCELLO, Brother of VITTORIA, Attendant on FRANCISCO DE MEDICIS.

HORTENSIO.

ANTONELLI.

GASPARO.

FARNESE.

CARLO.

PEDRO.

Doctor.

Conjurer.

Lawyer.

JAQUES.

JULIO.

CHRISTOPHERO.

Ambassadors, Physicians, Officers, Attendants, &c.

ISABELLA, Sister of FRANCISCO DE MEDICIS, Wife of BRACHIANO.

VITTORIA COROMBONA, married first to CAMILLO, afterwards to BRACHIANO.

CORNELIA, Mother of VITTORIA.

ZANCHE, a Moor, Waiting-woman to VITTORIA.

Matron of the House of Convertites.

SCENE—ROME and PADUA.

THE WHITE DEVIL;

or, Vittoria Corombona

ACT THE FIRST

SCENE I—*A Street in Rome*

Enter Count LODOVICO, ANTONELLI, *and* GASPARO.

Lod. Banished!
   Ant. It grieved me much to hear the sentence.
   Lod. Ha, ha! O Democritus, thy gods
That govern the whole world! courtly reward
And punishment. Fortune's a right whore:
If she give aught, she deals it in small parcels,
That she may take away all at one swoop.
This 'tis to have great enemies:—God quit[1] them!
Your wolf no longer seems to be a wolf
Than when she's hungry.
   Gasp. You term those enemies
Are men of princely rank.
   Lod. O, I pray for them:
The violent thunder is adored by those
Are pashed[2] in pieces by it.
   Ant. Come, my lord,
You are justly doomed: look but a little back
Into your former life; you have in three years
Ruined the noblest earldom.
   Gasp. Your followers
Have swallowed you like mummia[3] and, being sick
With such unnatural and horrid physic,
Vomit you up i' the kennel.
   Ant. All the damnable degrees
Of drinkings have you staggered through: one citizen

---

[1] Requite.
[2] Violently dashed.
[3] Different kinds of mummy were formerly used in medicine. "Mummie is become merchandise," says Sir Thomas Browne, "Mizraim cures wounds, and Pharaoh is sold for balsams." *Urn-Burial.*

Is lord of two fair manors called you master
Only for caviare.

   Gasp. Those noblemen
Which were invited to your prodigal feasts
(Wherein the phœnix scarce could scape your throats)
Laugh at your misery; as fore-deeming you
An idle meteor, which, drawn forth the earth,
Would be soon lost i' the air.

   Ant. Jest upon you,
And say you were begotten in an earthquake,
You have ruined such fair lordships.

   Lod. Very good.
This well goes with two buckets: I must tend
The pouring out of either.

   Gasp. Worse than these;
You have acted certain murders here in Rome,
Bloody and full of horror.

   Lod. 'Las, they were flea-bitings.
Why took they not my head, then?

   Gasp. O, my lord,
The law doth sometimes mediate, thinks it good
Not ever to steep violent sins in blood:
This gentle penance may both end your crimes,
And in the example better these bad times.

   Lod. So; but I wonder, then, some great men scape
This banishment: there's Paulo Giordano Ursini,
The Duke of Brachiano, now lives in Rome,
And by close panderism seeks to prostitute
The honour of Vittoria Corombona;
Vittoria, she that might have got my pardon
For one kiss to the duke.

   Ant. Have a full man within you.
We see that trees bear no such pleasant fruit
There where they grew first as where they are new set:
Perfumes, the more they are chafed, the more they render
Their pleasing scents; and so affliction
Expresseth virtue fully, whether true
Or else adulterate.

   Lod. Leave your painted comforts:
I'll make Italian cut-works[4] in their guts,
If ever I return.

⁴ Open-work embroidery.

Gasp. O, sir!

Lod. I am patient.
I have seen some ready to be executed
Give pleasant looks and money, and grown familiar
With the knave hangman: so do I: I thank them,
And would account them nobly merciful,
Would they despatch me quickly.

Ant. Fare you well:
We shall find time, I doubt not, to repeal
Your banishment.

Lod. I am ever bound to you:
This is the world's alms; pray, make use of it.
Great men sell sheep thus to be cut in pieces,
When first they have shorn them bare and sold their fleeces.

[*Exeunt.*

SCENE II—*An Apartment in* CAMILLO's *House*

Sennet.[5] *Enter* BRACHIANO, CAMILLO, FLAMINEO, VITTORIA
COROMBONA, *and* Attendants.

Brach. Your best of rest!

Vit. Cor. Unto my lord, the duke,
The best of welcome!—More lights! attend the duke.

[*Exeunt* CAMILLO *and* VITTORIA COROMBONA.

Brach. Flamineo,—

Flam. My lord?

Brach. Quite lost, Flamineo.

Flam. Pursue your noble wishes, I am prompt
As lightning to your service. O, my lord,
The fair Vittoria, my happy sister,   [*Whispers.*
Shall give you present audience.—Gentlemen,
Let the caroche[6] go on; and 'tis his pleasure
You put out all your torches, and depart.

[*Exeunt* Attendants.

Brach. Are we so happy?

Flam. Can't be otherwise?
Observed you not to-night, my honoured lord,
Which way soe'er you went, she threw her eyes?

[5] A sounding (but not a flourish) of trumpets or other wind instruments.
[6] Coach. Fr. *Carrosse.*

I have dealt already with her chambermaid,
Zanche the Moor; and she is wondrous proud
To be the agent for so high a spirit.

Brach. We are happy above thought, because 'bove merit.

Flam. 'Bove merit!—we may now talk freely—'bove merit! What is't you doubt? her coyness? that's but the superficies of lust most women have: yet why should ladies blush to hear that named which they do not fear to handle? O, they are politic: they know our desire is increased by the difficulty of enjoying; whereas satiety is a blunt, weary, and drowsy passion. If the buttery-hatch at court stood continually open, there would be nothing so passionate crowding, nor hot suit after the beverage.

Brach. O, but her jealous husband.

Flam. Hang him! a gilder that hath his brains perished with quick-silver is not more cold in the liver: the great barriers moulted not more feathers[7] than he hath shed hairs, by the confession of his doctor: an Irish gamester that will play himself naked, and then wage all downwards at hazard, is not more venturous: so unable to please a woman, that, like a Dutch doublet, all his back is shrunk into his breeches.
Shrowd you within this closet, good my lord:
Some trick now must be thought on to divide
My brother-in-law from his fair bedfellow.

Brach. O, should she fail to come!

Flam. I must not have your lordship thus unwisely amorous. I myself have loved a lady, and pursued her with a great deal of under-age protestation, whom some three or four gallants that have enjoyed would with all their hearts have been glad to have been rid of: 'tis just like a summer birdcage in a garden; the birds that are without despair to get in, and the birds that are within despair, and are in a consumption, for fear they shall never get out. Away, away, my lord!   [*Exit* BRACHIANO.
See, here he comes. This fellow by his apparel
Some men would judge a politician;
But call his wit in question, you shall find it
Merely an ass in's foot-cloth.[8]

---

[7] *i.e.* More feathers were not dislodged from the helmets of the combatants at the great tilting-match.—*Steevens.*
[8] Housings.

Re-enter CAMILLO.[9]

                                        How now, brother!
What, travelling to bed to your kind wife?

Cam. I assure you, brother, no; my voyage lies
More northerly, in a far colder clime:
I do not well remember, I protest,
When I last lay with her.

Flam. Strange you should lose your count.

Cam. We never lay together, but ere morning
There grew a flaw[10] between us.

Flam.   'Thad been your part
To have made up that flaw.

Cam. True, but she loathes
I should be seen in't.

Flam. Why, sir, what's the matter?

Cam. The duke, your master, visits me, I thank him;
And I perceive how, like an earnest bowler,
He very passionately leans that way
He should have his bowl run.

Flam. I hope you do not think—

Cam. That noblemen bowl booty? [11] faith, his cheek
Hath a most excellent bias; it would fain
Jump with my mistress.[12]

Flam.   Will you be an ass,
Despite your Aristotle? or a cuckold,
Contrary to your Ephemerides,
Which shows you under what a smiling planet
You were first swaddled?

Cam. Pew-wew, sir, tell not me
Of planets nor of Ephemerides:
A man may be made a cuckold in the day-time,
When the stars' eyes are out.

Flam. Sir, God b' wi' you;

---

[9] It is hardly possible to mark with any certainty the stage-business of this play. Though Brachiano, who has just withdrawn into a "closet," appears again when Flamineo calls him (*See* p. 31), it would seem that the audience were to *imagine* that a change of scene took place here to another apartment, as Flamineo says (p. 29): "Sister, my lord attends you in the banqueting-house." —Dyce.

[10] Quarrel.

[11] *i.e.* Allow an adversary to aim in order to draw him on to continue playing.

[12] The jack at bowls.

I do commit you to your pitiful pillow
Stuffed with horn-shavings.

Cam. Brother,—

Flam. God refuse me,
Might I advise you now, your only course
Were to lock up your wife.

Cam. 'Twere very good.

Flam. Bar her the sight of revels.

Cam. Excellent.

Flam. Let her not go to church, but like a hound
In lyam[13] at your heels.

Cam. 'Twere for her honour.

Flam. And so you should be certain in one fortnight
Despite her chastity or innocence,
To be cuckolded, which yet is in suspense:
This is my counsel, and I ask no fee for't.

Cam. Come, you know not where my night-cap wrings
me.

Flam. Wear it o' the old fashion; let your large ears
come through, it will be more easy:—nay, I will be bitter:
—bar your wife of her entertainment: women are more
willingly and more gloriously chaste when they are least
restrained of their liberty. It seems you would be a fine
capricious mathematically jealous coxcomb; take the height
of your own horns with a Jacob's staff[14] afore they are
up. These politic inclosures for paltry mutton make more
rebellion in the flesh than all the provocative electuaries
doctors have uttered[15] since last jubilee.

Cam. This doth not physic me.

Flam. It seems you are jealous: I'll show you the error
of it by a familiar example. I have seen a pair of spectacles
fashioned with such perspective art, that, lay down but one
twelve pence o' the board, 'twill appear as if there were
twenty; now, should you wear a pair of these spectacles,
and see your wife tying her shoe, you would imagine twenty
hands were taking up of your wife's clothes, and this would
put you into a horrible causeless fury.

Cam. The fault there, sir, is not in the eyesight.

Flam. True; but they that have the yellow jaundice think

13 Leash.
14 A measuring instrument.
15 Vended.

all objects they look on to be yellow. Jealousy is worser;
her fits present to a man, like so many bubbles in a bason
of water, twenty several crabbed faces; many times makes
his own shadow his cuckold-maker. See, she comes.

Re-enter VITTORIA COROMBONA.

What reason have you to be jealous of this creature? what
an ignorant ass or flattering knave might he be counted,
that should write sonnets to her eyes, or call her brow the
snow of Ida or ivory of Corinth, or compare her hair to
the blackbird's bill, when 'tis liker the blackbird's feather!
This is all; be wise, I will make you friends; and you shall
go to bed together. Marry, look you, it shall not be your
seeking; do you stand upon that by any means: walk you
aloof; I would not have you seen in't. [CAMILLO *retires*.]
Sister, my lord attends you in the banqueting-house. Your
husband is wondrous discontented.

Vit. Cor. I did nothing to displease him: I carved to him
at supper-time.[16]

Flam. You need not have carved him, in faith; they say
he is a capon already. I must now seemingly fall out with
you. Shall a gentleman so well descended as Camillo,—a
lousy slave, that within this twenty years rode with the
black guard [17] in the duke's carriage, 'mongst spits and
dripping-pans—

Cam. Now he begins to tickle her.

Flam. An excellent scholar,—one that hath a head filled
with calves-brains without any sage in them,—come crouch-
ing in the hams to you for a night's lodging?—that hath
an itch in's hams, which like the fire at the glass-house
hath not gone out this seven years.—Is he not a courtly
gentleman?—when he wears white satin, one would take
him by his black muzzle to be no other creature than a
maggot.—You are a goodly foil, I confess, well set out—
but covered with a false stone, yon counterfeit diamond.[18]

Cam. He will make her know what is in me.

Flam. Come, my lord attends you; thou shalt go to bed
to my lord—

16 A mark of good-will.
17 The lowest menials who rode in the vehicles which carried the domestic
utensils from mansion to mansion.
18 Flamineo's speeches are half-asides.

Cam. Now he comes to't.

Flam. With a relish as curious as a vintner going to taste new wine.—I am opening your case hard.   [*To* CAMILLO.

Cam. A virtuous brother, o' my credit!

Flam. He will give thee a ring with a philosopher's stone in it.

Cam. Indeed, I am studying alchymy.

Flam. Thou shalt lie in a bed stuffed with turtles' feathers; swoon in perfumed linen, like the fellow was smothered in roses. So perfect shall be thy happiness, that, as men at sea think land and trees and ships go that way they go, so both Heaven and earth shall seem to go your voyage. Shall't meet him; 'tis fixed with nails of diamonds to inevitable necessity.

Vit. Cor. How shall's rid him hence?

Flam. I will put the breeze in's tail,—set him gadding presently.—[*To* CAMILLO] I have almost wrought her to it, I find her coming: but, might I advise you now, for this night I would not lie with her; I would cross her humour to make her more humble.

Cam. Shall I, shall I?

Flam. It will show in you a supremacy of judgment.

Cam. True, and a mind differing from the tumultuary opinion; for, *quæ negata, grata.*

Flam. Right: you are the adamant[19] shall draw her to you, though you keep distance off.

Cam. A philosophical reason.

Flam. Walk by her o' the nobleman's fashion, and tell her you will lie with her at the end of the progress.[20]

Cam. [*Coming forward*]. Vittoria, I cannot be induced, or, as a man would say, incited—

Vit. Cor. To do what, sir?

Cam. To lie with you to-night. Your silkworm useth to fast every third day, and the next following spins the better. To-morrow at night I am for you.

Vit. Cor. You'll spin a fair thread, trust to't.

Flam. But, do you hear, I shall have you steal to her chamber about midnight.

Cam. Do you think so? why, look you, brother, because

---

[19] Magnet.
[20] State journey.

you shall not think I'll gull you, take the key, lock me into
the chamber, and say you shall be sure of me.

Flam. In troth, I will; I'll be your gaoler once. But have
you ne'er a false door?

Cam. A pox on't, as I am a Christian. Tell me to-morrow
how scurvily she takes my unkind parting.

Flam. I will.

Cam. Didst thou not mark the jest of the silkworm?
Good-night: in faith, I will use this trick often.

Flam. Do, do, do. [*Exit* CAMILLO; *and* FLAMINEO *locks
the door on him.*] So now you are safe.—Ha, ha, ha! thou
entanglest thyself in thine own work like a silkworm.
Come, sister; darkness hides your blush. Women are like
curst dogs: civility keeps them tied all daytime, but they
are let loose at midnight; then they do most good, or most
mischief.—My lord, my lord!

Re-enter BRACHIANO. ZANCHE *brings out a carpet,
spreads it, and lays on it two fair cushions.*

Brach. Give credit, I could wish time would stand still,
And never end this interview, this hour:
But all delight doth itself soon'st devour.

Enter CORNELIA *behind, listening.*

Let me into your bosom, happy lady,
Pour out, instead of eloquence, my vows:
Loose me not, madam; for, if you forego me,
I am lost eternally.

Vit. Cor. Sir, in the way of pity,
I wish you heart-whole.

Brach. You are a sweet physician.

Vit. Cor. Sure, sir, a loathèd cruelty in ladies
Is as to doctors many funerals;
It takes away their credit.

Brach. Excellent creature!
We call the cruel fair: what name for you
That are so merciful?

Zan. See, now they close.

Flam. Most happy union.

Cor. My fears are fall'n upon me: O, my heart!
My son the pander! now I find our house
Sinking to ruin. Earthquakes leave behind,

Where they have tyrannised, iron, lead, or stone;
But, woe to ruin, violent lust leaves none!
 Brach. What value is this jewel?
 Vit. Cor. 'Tis the ornament
Of a weak fortune.
 Brach. In sooth, I'll have it; nay, I will but change
My jewel for your jewel.
 Flam. Excellent!
His jewel for her jewel:—well put in, duke.
 Brach. Nay, let me see you wear it.
 Vit. Cor. Here, sir?
 Brach. Nay, lower, you shall wear my jewel lower.
 Flam. That's better; she must wear his jewel lower.
 Vit. Cor. To pass away the time, I'll tell your grace
A dream I had last night.
 Brach. Most wishedly.
 Vit. Cor. A foolish idle dream.
Methought I walked about the mid of night
Into a church-yard, where a goodly yew-tree
Spread her large root in ground. Under that yew,
As I sate sadly leaning on a grave
Chequered with cross sticks, there came stealing in
Your duchess and my husband: one of them
A pick-axe bore, the other a rusty spade
And in rough terms they gan to challenge me
About this yew.
 Brach. That tree?
 Vit. Cor. This harmless yew:
They told me my intent was to root up
That well-grown yew, and plant i' the stead of it
A withered blackthorn; and for that they vowed
To bury me alive. My husband straight
With pick-axe gan to dig, and your fell duchess
With shovel, like a Fury, voided out
The earth, and scattered bones. Lord, how, methought,
I trembled! and yet, for all this terror,
I could not pray.
 Flam. No; the devil was in your dream.
 Vit. Cor. When to my rescue there arose, methought,
A whirlwind, which let fall a massy arm
From that strong plant;
And both were struck dead by that sacred yew,

In that base shallow grave that was their due.

    Flam. Excellent devil! she hath taught him in a dream
To make away his duchess and her husband.

    Brach. Sweetly shall I interpret this your dream.
You are lodged within his arms who shall protect you
From all the fevers of a jealous husband;
From the poor envy of our phlegmatic duchess.
I'll seat you above law, and above scandal;
Give to your thoughts the invention of delight,
And the fruition; nor shall government
Divide me from you longer than a care
To keep you great: you shall to me at once
Be dukedom, health, wife, children, friends, and all.

    Cor. [*Coming forward*]. Woe to light hearts, they still
      fore-run our fall!

    Flam. What Fury raised thee up?—Away, away!
                           [*Exit* ZANCHE.

    Cor. What make you here, my lord, this dead of night?
Never dropped mildew on a flower here
Till now.

    Flam. I pray, will you go to bed, then,
Lest you be blasted?

    Cor. O, that this fair garden
Had with all poisoned herbs of Thessaly
At first been planted; made a nursery
For witchcraft, rather than a burial plot
For both your honours!

    Vit. Cor. Dearest mother, hear me.

    Cor. O, thou dost make my brow bend to the earth,
Sooner than nature! See, the curse of children!
In life they keep us frequently in tears;
And in the cold grave leave us in pale fears.

    Brach. Come, come, I will not hear you.

    Vit. Cor. Dear, my lord,—

    Cor. Where is thy duchess now, adulterous duke?
Thou little dreamd'st this night she is come to Rome.

    Flam. How! come to Rome!

    Vit. Cor. The duchess!

    Brach. She had been better—

    Cor. The lives of princes should like dials move,
Whose regular example is so strong,
They make the times by them go right or wrong.

Flam. So; have you done?

Cor. Unfortunate Camillo!

Vit. Cor. I do protest, if any chaste denial,
If anything but blood could have allayed
His long suit to me—

Cor. I will join with thee,
To the most woeful end e'er mother kneeled:
If thou dishonour thus thy husband's bed,
Be thy life short as are the funeral tears
In great men's—

Brach. Fie, fie, the woman's mad.

Cor. Be thy act, Judas-like,—betray in kissing:
Mayst thou be envied during his short breath,
And pitied like a wretch after his death!

Vit. Cor. O me accursed!   [*Exit.*

Flam. Are you out of your wits, my lord?
I'll fetch her back again.

Brach. No, I'll to bed:
Send Doctor Julio to me presently.—
Uncharitable woman! thy rash tongue
Hath raised a fearful and prodigious storm:
Be thou the cause of all ensuing harm.   [*Exit.*

Flam. Now, you that stand so much upon your honour,
Is this a fitting time o' night, think you,
To send a duke home without e'er a man?
I would fain know where lies the mass of wealth
Which you have hoarded for my maintenance,
That I may bear my beard out of the level
Of my lord's stirrup.

Cor. What! because we are poor
Shall we be vicious?

Flam. Pray, what means have you
To keep me from the galleys or the gallows?
My father proved himself a gentleman,
Sold all's land, and, like a fortunate fellow,
Died ere the money was spent. You brought me up
At Padua, I confess, where, I protest,
For want of means (the university judge me)
I have been fain to heel my tutor's stockings,
At least seven years: conspiring with a beard,
Made me a graduate; then to this duke's service.
I visited the court, whence I returned

More courteous, more lecherous by far,
But not a suit the richer: and shall I,
Having a path so open and so free
To my preferment, still retain your milk
In my pale forehead? no, this face of mine
I'll arm, and fortify with lusty wine,
'Gainst shame and blushing.
   Cor. O, that I ne'er had borne thee
   Flam. So would I;
I would the common'st courtezan in Rome
Had been my mother, rather than thyself.
Nature is very pitiful to whores,
To give them but few children, yet those children
Plurality of fathers: they are sure
They shall not want. Go, go,
Complain unto my great lord cardinal;
Yet may be he will justify the act.
Lycurgus wondered much men would provide
Good stallions for their mares, and yet would suffer
Their fair wives to be barren.
   Cor. Misery of miseries!   [*Exit.*
   Flam. The duchess come to court! I like not that.
We are engaged to mischief, and must on:
As rivers to find out the ocean
Flow with crook bendings beneath forcèd banks;
Or as we see, to aspire some mountain's top,
The way ascends not straight, but imitates
The subtle foldings of a winter snake;
So who knows policy and her true aspèct,
Shall find her ways winding and indirect.   [*Exit.*

ACT THE SECOND

SCENE I—*A Room in* FRANCISCO'S *Palace*

Enter FRANCISCO DE MEDICIS, Cardinal MONTICELSO, MAR-
CELLO, ISABELLA, GIOVANNI, *with* JAQUES *the Moor.*

FRAN. DE MED. Have you not seen your husband since you
     arrived?
   Isab. Not yet, sir.
   Fran. de Med. Surely he is wondrous kind

If I had such a dove-house as Camillo's,
I would set fire on't, were't but to destroy
The pole-cats that haunt to it.—My sweet cousin!

Giov. Lord uncle, you did promise me a horse
And armour.

Fran. de Med. That I did, my pretty cousin.—
Marcello, see it fitted.

Mar. My lord, the duke is here.

Fran. de Med. Sister, away! you must not yet be seen.

Isab. I do beseech you,
Entreat him mildly; let not your rough tongue
Set us at louder variance: all my wrongs
Are freely pardoned; and I do not doubt,
As men, to try the precious unicorn's horn,[21]
Make of the powder a preservative circle,
And in it put a spider, so these arms
Shall charm his poison, force it to obeying,
And keep him chaste from an infected straying.

Fran. de Med. I wish it may. Be gone, void the chamber.

[*Exeunt* ISABELLA, GIOVANNI, *and* JAQUES.

Enter BRACHIANO *and* FLAMINEO.

You are welcome: will you sit?—I pray, my lord,
Be you my orator, my heart's too full;
I'll second you anon.

Mont. Ere I begin,
Let me entreat your grace forego all passion,
Which may be raisèd by my free discourse.

Brach. As silent as i' the church: you may proceed.

Mont. It is a wonder to your noble friends,
That you, having, as 'twere, entered the world
With a free sceptre in your able hand,
And to the use of nature well applied
High gifts of learning, should in your prime age
Neglect your awful throne for the soft down
Of an insatiate bed. O, my lord,
The drunkard after all his lavish cups
Is dry, and then is sober; so at length,

---

[21] A prized antidote. "Andrea Racci, a physician of Florence, affirms the pound
of 16 ounces to have been sold in the apothecaries' shops for 1,536 crowns, when
the same weight of gold was only worth 148 crowns."—Chambers's *Dict.*, quoted
by Dyce.

When you awake from this lascivious dream,
Repentance then will follow, like the sting
Placed in the adder's tail. Wretched are princes
When fortune blasteth but a petty flower
Of their unwieldy crowns, or ravisheth
But one pearl from their sceptres: but, alas,
When they to wilful shipwreck lose good fame,
All princely titles perish with their name!

  Brach. You have said, my lord.

  Mont. Enough to give you taste
How far I am from flattering your greatness.

  Brach. Now you that are his second, what say you?
Do not like young hawks fetch a course about:
Your game flies fair and for you.

  Fran. de Med. Do not fear it:
I'll answer you in your own hawking phrase.
Some eagles that should gaze upon the sun
Seldom soar high, but take their lustful ease;
Since they from dunghill birds their prey can seize.
You know Vittoria!

  Brach. Yes.

  Fran. de Med. You shift your shirt there,
When you retire from tennis?

  Brach. Happily.[22]

  Fran. de Med. Her husband is lord of a poor fortune;
Yet she wears cloth of tissue.

  Brach. What of this?—
Will you urge that, my good lord cardinal,
As part of her confession at next shrift,
And know from whence it sails?

  Fran. de Med. She is your strumpet.

  Brach. Uncivil sir, there's hemlock in thy breath,
And that black slander. Were she a whore of mine,
All thy loud cannons, and thy borrowed Switzers,
Thy galleys, nor thy sworn confederates,
Durst not supplant her.

  Fran. de Med. Let's not talk on thunder.
Thou hast a wife, our sister: would I had given
Both her white hands to death, bound and locked fast
In her last winding-sheet, when I gave thee

---

[22] Haply, peradventure.

But one!

Brach. Thou hadst given a soul to God, then.

Fran. de Med. True:
Thy ghostly father, with all's absolution,
Shall ne'er do so by thee.

Brach. Spit thy poison.

Fran. de Med. I shall not need; lust carries her sharp whip
At her own girdle. Look to't, for our anger
Is making thunder-bolts.

Brach. Thunder! in faith,
They are but crackers.

Fran. de Med. We'll end this with the cannon.

Brach. Thou'lt get naught by it but iron in thy wounds,
And gunpowder in thy nostrils.

Fran. de Med. Better that,
Than change perfumes for plasters.

Brach. Pity on thee:
'Twere good you'd show your slaves or men condemned
Your new-ploughed forehead-defiance! and I'll meet thee,
Even in a thicket of thy ablest men.

Mont. My lords, you shall not word it any further
Without a milder limit.

Fran. de Med. Willingly.

Brach. Have you proclaimed a triumph, that you bait
A lion thus!

Mont. My lord!

Brach. I am tame, I am tame, sir.

Fran. de Med. We send unto the duke for conference
'Bout levies 'gainst the pirates; my lord duke
Is not at home: we come ourself in person;
Still my lord duke is busied. But we fear,
When Tiber to each prowling passenger
Discovers flocks of wild ducks; then, my lord,
'Bout moulting time I mean, we shall be certain
To find you sure enough, and speak with you.

Brach. Ha!

Fran. de Med. A mere tale of a tub, my words are idle;
But to express the sonnet by natural reason,—
When stags grow melancholic, you'll find the season.

Mont. No more, my lord: here comes a champion
Shall end the difference between you both,—

Re-enter GIOVANNI.

Your son, the Prince Giovanni. See, my lords,
What hopes you store in him: this is a casket
For both your crowns, and should be held like dear.
Now is he apt for knowledge; therefore know,
It is a more direct and even way
To train to virtue those of princely blood
By examples than by precepts: if by examples,
Whom should he rather strive to imitate
Than his own father? be his pattern, then;
Leave him a stock of virtue that may last,
Should fortune rend his sails and split his mast.

   Brach. Your hand, boy: growing to a soldier?
   Giov. Give me a pike.
   Fran. de Med. What, practising your pike so young, fair
     cuz?
   Giov. Suppose me one of Homer's frogs, my lord,
Tossing my bullrush thus. Pray, sir, tell me,
Might not a child of good discretion
Be leader to an army?
   Fran. de Med. Yes, cousin, a young prince
Of good discretion might.
   Giov. Say you so?
Indeed, I have heard, 'tis fit a general
Should not endanger his own person oft;
So that he make a noise when he's o' horseback,
Like a Dansk[23] drummer,—O, 'tis excellent!—
He need not fight:—methinks his horse as well
Might lead an army for him. If I live,
I'll charge the French foe in the very front
Of all my troops, the foremost man.
   Fran. de Med. What, what!
   Giov. And will not bid my soldiers up and follow,
But bid them follow me.
   Brach. Forward, lapwing!
He flies with the shell on's head.[24]
   Fran. de Med. Pretty cousin!
   Giov. The first year, uncle, that I go to war,

[23] Danish.
[24] See *Hamlet*, Act v. sc. 2. "This lapwing runs away with the shell on his head."

All prisoners that I take I will set free
Without their ransom.

Fran. de Med. Ha, without their ransom!
How, then, will you reward your soldiers
That took those prisoners for you?

Giov. Thus, my lord;
I'll marry them to all the wealthy widows
That fall that year.

Fran. de Med. Why, then, the next year following,
You'll have no men to go with you to war.

Giov. Why, then, I'll press the women to the war,
And then the men will follow.

Mont. Witty prince!

Fran. de Med. See, a good habit makes a child a man,
Whereas a bad one makes a man a beast.
Come, you and I are friends.

Brach. Most wishedly;
Like bones which, broke in sunder, and well set,
Knit the more strongly.

Fran. de Med. Call Camillo hither.   [*Exit* MARCELLO.
You have received the rumour, how Count Lodowick
Is turned a pirate?

Brach. Yes.

Fran. de Med. We are now preparing
Some ships to fetch him in. Behold your duchess.
We now will leave you, and expect from you
Nothing but kind entreaty.

Brach. You have charmed me.

[*Exeunt* FRANCISCO DE MEDICIS, MONTICELSO,
and GIOVANNI. FLAMINEO *retires*.

Re-enter ISABELLA.

You are in health, we see.

Isab. And above health,
To see my lord well.

Brach. So. I wonder much
What amorous whirlwind hurried you to Rome.

Isab. Devotion, my lord.

Brach. Devotion!
Is your soul charged with any grievous sin?

Isab. 'Tis burdened with too many; and I think,
The oftener that we cast our reckonings up,

Our sleeps will be the sounder.
    Brach. Take your chamber.
    Isab. Nay, my dear lord, I will not have you angry:
Doth not my absence from you, now two months,
Merit one kiss?
    Brach. I do not use to kiss:
If that will dispossess your jealousy,
I'll swear it to you.
    Isab. O my lovèd lord,
I do not come to chide: my jealousy!
I am to learn what that Italian means.
You are as welcome to these longing arms
As I to you a virgin.
    Brach. O, your breath!
Out upon sweet-meats and continued physic,—
The plague is in them!
    Isab. You have oft, for these two lips,
Neglected cassia or the natural sweets
Of the spring-violet: they are not yet much withered.
My lord, I should be merry: these your frowns
Show in a helmet lovely; but on me,
In such a peaceful interview, methinks
They are too-too roughly knit.
    Brach. O, dissemblance!
Do you bandy factions 'gainst me? have you learnt
The trick of impudent baseness, to complain
Unto your kindred?
    Isab. Never, my dear lord.
    Brach. Must I be hunted out? or was't your trick
To meet some amorous gallant here in Rome,
That must supply our discontinuance?
    Isab. I pray, sir, burst my heart; and in my death
Turn to your ancient pity, though not love.
    Brach. Because your brother is the corpulent duke,
That is, the great duke, 'sdeath, I shall not shortly
Racket away five hundred crowns at tennis,
But it shall rest upon record! I scorn him
Like a shaved Polack[25] all his reverend wit
Lies in his wardrobe; he's a discreet fellow
When he is made up in his robes of state.
Your brother, the great duke, because h'as galleys,

<hr>

[25] Polander.

And now and then ransacks a Turkish fly-boat,
(Now all the hellish Furies take his soul!)
First made this match: accursèd be the priest
That sang the wedding-mass, and even my issue!

Isab. O, too-too far you have cursed!

Brach. Your hand I'll kiss;
This is the latest ceremony of my love.
Henceforth I'll never lie with thee; by this,
This wedding-ring, I'll ne'er more lie with thee:
And this divorce shall be as truly kept
As if the judge had doomed it. Fare you well:
Our sleeps are severed.

Isab. Forbid it, the sweet union
Of all things blessèd! why, the saints in Heaven
Will knit their brows at that.

Brach. Let not thy love
Make thee an unbeliever; this my vow
Shall never, on my soul, be satisfied
With my repentance; let thy brother rage
Beyond a horrid tempest or sea-fight,
My vow is fixèd.

Isab. O my winding-sheet
Now shall I need thee shortly.—Dear my lord,
Let me hear once more what I would not hear:
Never?

Brach. Never.

Isab. O my unkind lord! may your sins find mercy,
As I upon a woful widowed bed
Shall pray for you, if not to turn your eyes
Upon your wretched wife and hopeful son,
Yet that in time you'll fix them upon Heaven!

Brach. No more: go, go complain to the great duke.

Isab. No, my dear lord; you shall have present witness
How I'll work peace between you. I will make
Myself the author of your cursèd vow;
I have some cause to do, you have none.
Conceal it, I beseech you, for the weal
Of both your dukedoms, that you wrought the means
Of such a separation: let the fault
Remain with my supposèd jealousy;
And think with what a piteous and rent heart
I shall perform this sad ensuing part.

Re-enter FRANCISCO DE MEDICIS *and* MONTICELSO.

Brach. Well, take your course.—My honourable brother!
Fran. de Med. Sister!—This is not well, my lord.—Why,
      sister!—
She merits not this welcome.
      Brach. Welcome, say!
She hath given a sharp welcome.
      Fran. de Med. Are you foolish?
Come, dry your tears: is this a modest course,
To better what is naught, to rail and weep?
Grow to a reconcilement, or, by Heaven,
I'll ne'er more deal between you.
      Isab. Sir, you shall not;
No, though Vittoria, upon that condition,
Would become honest.
      Fran. de Med. Was your husband loud
Since we departed?
      Isab. By my life, sir, no;
I swear by that I do not care to lose.
Are all these ruins of my former beauty
Laid out for a whore's triumph?
      Fran. de Med. Do you hear?
Look upon other women, with what patience
They suffer these slight wrongs, with what justice
They study to requite them: take that course.
      Isab. O, that I were a man, or that I had power
To execute my apprehended wishes!
I would whip some with scorpions.
      Fran. de Med. What! turned Fury!
      Isab. To dig the strumpet's eyes out; let her lie
Some twenty months a dying; to cut off
Her nose and lips, pull out her rotten teeth;
Preserve her flesh like mummia, for trophies
Of my just anger! Hell to my affliction
Is mere snow-water. By your favour, sir;—
Brother, draw near, and my lord cardinal;—
Sir, let me borrow of you but one kiss:
Henceforth I'll never lie with you, by this,
This wedding-ring.
      Fran. de Med. How, ne'er more lie with him!
      Isab. And this divorce shall be as truly kept

As if in throngèd court a thousand ears
Had heard it, and a thousand lawyers' hands
Sealed to the separation.

Brach. Ne'er lie with me!

Isab. Let not my former dotage
Make thee an unbeliever: this my vow
Shall never, on my soul, be satisfied
With my repentance; *manet alta mente repostum.*[26]

Fran. de Med. Now, by my birth, you are a foolish, mad,
And jealous woman.

Brach. You see 'tis not my seeking.

Fran. de Med. Was this your circle of pure unicorn's horn
You said should charm your lord? now, horns upon thee,
For jealousy deserves them! Keep your vow
And take your chamber.

Isab. No, sir, I'll presently to Padua;
I will not stay a minute.

Mont. O good madam!

Brach. 'Twere best to let her have her humour:
Some half day's journey will bring down her stomach,
And then she'll turn in post.

Fran. de Med. To see her come
To my lord cardinal for a dispensation
Of her rash vow, will beget excellent laughter.

Isab. Unkindness, do thy office; poor heart, break:
Those are the killing griefs which dare not speak.

[*Exit.*

Re-enter MARCELLO *with* CAMILLO.

Mar. Camillo's come, my lord.

Fran. de Med. Where's the commission?

Mar. 'Tis here.

Fran. de Med. Give me the signet.

[FRANCISCO DE MEDICIS, MONTICELSO, CAMILLO, *and* MAR-
CELLO *retire to the back of the stage.*

Flam. My lord, do you mark their whispering? I will
compound a medicine, out of their two heads, stronger
than garlic, deadlier than stibium:[27] the cantharides, which
are scarce seen to stick upon the flesh when they work to
the heart, shall not do it with more silence or invisible
cunning.

[26] Virgil, *Æn.* i. 26.
[27] Antimony.

Brach. About the murder?

Flam. They are sending him to Naples, but I'll send him to Candy.

Enter Doctor.

Here's another property too.

Brach. O, the doctor!

Flam. A poor quack-salving knave, my lord; one that should have been lashed for's lechery, but that he confessed a judgment, had an execution laid upon him, and so put the whip to a *non plus.*

Doc. And was cozened, my lord, by an arranter knave than myself, and made pay all the colourable execution.

Flam. He will shoot pills into a man's guts shall make them have more ventages than a cornet or a lamprey; he will poison a kiss; and was once minded, for his master-piece, because Ireland breeds no poison, to have prepared a deadly vapour in a Spaniard's fart, that should have poisoned all Dublin.

Brach. O, Saint Anthony's fire.

Doc. Your secretary is merry, my lord.

Flam. O thou cursed antipathy to nature!—Look, his eye's bloodshed, like a needle a surgeon stitcheth a wound with.—Let me embrace thee, toad, and love thee, O thou abominable loathsome[28] gargarism, that will fetch up lungs, lights, heart, and liver, by scruples!

Brach. No more.—I must employ thee, honest doctor: You must to Padua, and by the way, Use some of your skill for us.

Doc. Sir, I shall.

Brach. But, for Camillo?

Flam. He dies this night, by such a politic strain, Men shall suppose him by's own engine slain. But for your duchess' death—

Doc. I'll make her sure.

Brach. Small mischiefs are by greater made secure.

Flam. Remember this, you slave; when knaves come to preferment, they rise as gallowses are raised i' the Low Countries, one upon another's shoulders.

[*Exeunt* BRACHIANO, FLAMINEO, *and* Doctor.

---

[28] Read perhaps "lethal."

SCENE II—*The same*

FRANCISCO DE MEDICIS, MONTICELSO, CAMILLO *and*
MARCELLO.

Mont. Here is an emblem, nephew, pray peruse it:
'Twas thrown in at your window.
   Cam. At my window!
Here is a stag, my lord, hath shed his horns,
And, for the loss of them, the poor beast weeps:
The word,[29] *Inopem me copia fecit.*[30]
   Mont. That is,
Plenty of horns hath made him poor of horns.
   Cam. What should this mean?
   Mont. I'll tell you: 'tis given out
You are a cuckold.
   Cam. Is it given out so?
I had rather such report as that, my lord,
Should keep within doors.
   Fran. de Med. Have you any children?
   Cam. None, my lord.
   Fran. de Med. You are the happier:
I'll tell you a tale.
   Cam. Pray, my lord.
   Fran. de Med. An old tale.
Upon a time Phœbus, the god of light,
Or him we call the Sun, would needs be married:
The gods gave their consent, and Mercury
Was sent to voice it to the general world.
But what a piteous cry there straight arose
Amongst smiths and felt-makers, brewers and cooks,
Reapers and butterwomen, amongst fishmongers,
And thousand other trades, which are annoyed
By his excessive heat! 'twas lamentable.
They came to Jupiter all in a sweat,
And do forbid the bans. A great fat cook
Was made their speaker, who entreats of Jove
That Phœbus might be gelded; for, if now,

---

[29] *i.e.* The motto.
[30] Ovid, *Metam.* iii. 466.

When there was but one sun, so many men
Were like to perish by his violent heat,
What should they do if he were married,
And should beget more, and those children
Make fire-works like their father? So say I;
Only I will apply it to your wife:
Her issue, should not providence prevent it,
Would make both nature, time, and man repent it.

    Mont. Look you, cousin,
Go, change the air, for shame; see if your absence
Will blast your cornucopia. Marcello
Is chosen with you joint commissioner
For the relieving our Italian coast
From pirates.

    Mar. I am much honoured in't.

    Cam. But, sir,
Ere I return, the stag's horns may be sprouted
Greater than those are shed.

    Mont. Do not fear it:
I'll be your ranger.

    Cam. You must watch i' the nights;
Then's the most danger.

    Fran. de Med. Farewell, good Marcello:
All the best fortunes of a soldier's wish
Bring you a-ship-board!

    Cam. Were I not best, now I am turned soldier
Ere that I leave my wife, sell all she hath,
And then take leave of her?

    Mont. I expect good from you,
Your parting is so merry.

    Cam. Merry, my lord! o' the captain's humour right;
I am resolvèd to be drunk this night.

               [*Exeunt* CAMILLO *and* MARCELLO.

    Fran. de Med. So, 'twas well fitted: now shall we discern
How his wished absence will give violent way
To Duke Brachiano's lust.

    Mont. Why, that was it;
To what scorned purpose else should we make choice
Of him for a sea-captain? and, besides,
Count Lodowick, which was rumoured for a pirate,
Is now in Padua.

    Fran. de Med. Is't true?

Mont. Most certain.
I have letters from him, which are suppliant
To work his quick repeal from banishment:
He means to address himself for pension
Unto our sister duchess.

Fran. de Med. O, 'twas well:
We shall not want his absence past six days.
I fain would have the Duke Brachiano run
Into notorious scandal; for there's naught
In such cursed dotage to repair his name,
Only the deep sense of some deathless shame.

Mont. It may be objected, I am dishonourable
To play thus with my kinsman; but I answer,
For my revenge I'd stake a brother's life,
That, being wronged, durst not avenge himself.

Fran. de Med. Come, to observe this strumpet.

Mont. Curse of greatness!
Sure he'll not leave her?

Fran. de Med. There's small pity in't:
Like mistletoe on sear elms spent by weather,
Let him cleave to her, and both rot together.   [*Exeunt.*

SCENE III—*A Room in the House of* CAMILLO

Enter BRACHIANO, *with a* Conjurer.

Brach. Now, sir, I claim your promise: 'tis dead mid-
     night,
The time prefixed to show me, by your art,
How the intended murder of Camillo
And our loathed duchess grow to action.

Con. You have won me by your bounty to a deed
I do not often practise. Some there are
Which by sophistic tricks aspire that name,
Which I would gladly lose, of necromancer;
As some that use to juggle upon cards,
Seeming to conjure, when indeed they cheat;
Others that raise up their confederate spirits
'Bout wind-mills, and endanger their own necks
For making of a squib; and some there are

Will keep a curtal [31] to show juggling tricks,
And give out 'tis a spirit; besides these,
Such a whole realm of almanac-makers, figure-flingers,
Fellows, indeed, that only live by stealth,
Since they do merely lie about stol'n goods,
They'd make men think the devil were fast and loose,
With speaking fustian Latin. Pray, sit down:
Put on this night-cap, sir, 'tis charmed; and now
I'll show you, by my strong commanding art,
The circumstance that breaks your duchess' heart.

A DUMB SHOW.

Enter suspiciously JULIO *and* CHRISTOPHERO: *they draw a
curtain where* BRACHIANO'S *picture is, put on spectacles
of glass, which cover their eyes and noses, and then burn
perfumes before the picture, and wash the lips; that done,
quenching the fire, and putting off their spectacles, they
depart laughing.*

Enter ISABELLA *in her night-gown, as to bed-ward, with
lights after her,* COUNT LODOVICO, GIOVANNI, GUIDAN-
TONIO, *and others waiting on her: she kneels down as
to prayers, then draws the curtain of the picture, does
three reverences to it, and kisses it thrice; she faints,
and will not suffer them to come near it; dies: sorrow
expressed in* GIOVANNI *and* Count LODOVICO: *she is conveyed out solemnly.*

Brach. Excellent! then she's dead.
Con.   She's poisonèd
By the fumed picture. 'Twas her custom nightly,
Before she went to bed, to go and visit
Your picture, and to feed her eyes and lips
On the dead shadow. Doctor Julio,
Observing this, infects it with an oil
And other poisoned stuff, which presently
Did suffocate her spirits.
Brach.   Methought I saw
Count Lodowick there.
Con.   He was: and by my art
I find he did most passionately dote

31 Horse.

Upon your duchess. Now turn another way,
And view Camillo's far more politic fate.
Strike louder, music, from this charmèd ground,
To yield, as fits the act, a tragic sound

The second DUMB SHOW.

Enter FLAMINEO, MARCELLO, CAMILLO, *with four others, as*
  Captains; *they drink healths, and dance: a vaulting-horse*
  is brought into the room: MARCELLO *and two others*
  whispered out of the room, while FLAMINEO *and*
  CAMILLO *strip themselves to their shirts, to vault; they*
  compliment who shall begin: as CAMILLO *is about to*
  vault, FLAMINEO *pitcheth him upon his neck, and, with*
  help of the rest, writhes his neck about; seems to see if
  it be broke, and lays him folded double, as it were,
  under the horse; makes signs to call for help: MARCELLO
  comes in, laments; sends for the Cardinal *and* Duke,
  who come forth with armed men; wonder at the act;
  command the body to be carried home; apprehend
  FLAMINEO, MARCELLO, *and the rest, and go, as it were,*
  to apprehend VITTORIA.

  Brach. 'Twas quaintly done; but yet each circumstance
I taste not fully.
  Con. O, 'twas most apparent:
You saw them enter, charged with their deep healths
To their boon voyage; and, to second that,
Flamineo calls to have a vaulting-horse
Maintain their sport; the virtuous Marcello
Is innocently plotted forth the room;
Whilst your eye saw the rest, and can inform you
The engine of all.
  Brach. It seems Marcello and Flamineo
Are both committed.[32]
  Con. Yes, you saw them guarded;
And now they are come with purpose to apprehend
Your mistress, fair Vittoria. We are now
Beneath her roof: 'twere fit we instantly
Make out by some back-postern.
  Brach. Noble friend,
You bind me ever to you: this shall stand

[32] Given in charge.

As the firm seal annexèd to my hand;
It shall enforce a payment.

    Con. Sir, I thank you.   [*Exit* BRACHIANO.
Both flowers and weeds spring when the sun is warm,
And great men do great good or else great harm.   [*Exit.*

SCENE IV—*The Mansion of* MONTICELSO

Enter FRANCISCO DE MEDICIS *and* MONTICELSO, *their*
Chancellor *and* Register.

    Fran. de Med. You have dealt discreetly, to obtain the
        presence
Of all the grave lieger[33] ambassadors,
To hear Vittoria's trial.

    Mont. 'Twas not ill;
For, sir, you know we have naught but circumstances
To charge her with, about her husband's death:
Their approbation, therefore, to the proofs
Of her black lust shall make her infamous
To all our neighbouring kingdoms. I wonder
If Brachiano will be here.

    Fran. de Med. O fie.
'Twere impudence too palpable.   [*Exeunt.*

Enter FLAMINEO *and* MARCELLO *guarded, and a* Lawyer.

    Law. What, are you in by the week? so, I will try now
whether thy wit be close prisoner. Methinks none should
sit upon thy sister but old whore-masters.

    Flam. Or cuckolds; for your cuckold is your most terrible
tickler of lechery. Whore-masters would serve; for none
are judges at tilting but those that have been old tilters.

    Law. My lord duke and she have been very private.

    Flam. You are a dull ass; 'tis threatened they have been
very public.

    Law. If it can be proved they have but kissed one an-
other—

    Flam. What then?

    Law. My lord cardinal will ferret them.

    Flam. A cardinal, I hope, will not catch conies.

[33] Resident.

Law. For to sow kisses (mark what I say), to sow kisses
is to reap lechery; and, I am sure, a woman that will endure
kissing is half won.

Flam. True, her upper part, by that rule: if you will
win her nether part too, you know what follows.

Law. Hark; the ambassadors are lighted.

Flam. [*Aside*]. I do put on this feignèd garb of mirth
To gull suspicion.

Mar. O my unfortunate sister!
I would my dagger-point had cleft her heart
When she first saw Brachiano: you, 'tis said,
Were made his engine and his stalking-horse,
To undo my sister.

Flam. I am a kind of path
To her and mine own preferment.

Mar. Your ruin.

Flam. Hum! thou art a soldier,
Follow'st the great duke, feed'st his victories,
As witches do their serviceable spirits,
Even with thy prodigal blood: what hast got,
But, like the wealth of captains, a poor handful,
Which in thy palm thou bear'st as men hold water?
Seeking to gripe it fast, the frail reward
Steals through thy fingers.

Mar. Sir!

Flam. Thou hast scarce maintenance
To keep thee in fresh shamois.[34]

Mar. Brother!

Flam. Hear me:—
And thus, when we have even poured ourselves
Into great fights, for their ambition
Or idle spleen, how shall we find reward?
But as we seldom find the mistletoe
Sacred to physic, or the builder oak,
Without a mandrake by it; so in our quest of gain,
Alas, the poorest of their forced dislikes
At a limb proffers, but at heart it strikes!
This is lamented doctrine.

Mar. Come, come.

Flam. When age shall turn thee
White as a blooming hawthorn—

[34] Shoes of leather.

Mar. I'll interrupt you:—
For love of virtue bear an honest heart,
And stride o'er every politic respect,
Which, where they most advance, they most infect.
Were I your father, as I am your brother,
I should not be ambitious to leave you
A better patrimony.

Flam. I'll think on't.—
The lord ambassadors.

      [*The* Ambassadors *pass over the stage severally.*
Law. O my sprightly Frenchman!—Do you know him?
he's an admirable tilter.

Flam. I saw him at last tilting: he showed like a pewter
candlestick, fashioned like a man in armour, holding a
tilting-staff in his hand, little bigger than a candle of
twelve i' the pound.

Law. O, but he's an excellent horseman.

Flam. A lame one in his lofty tricks: he sleeps a-horseback, like a poulter.[35]

Law. Lo you, my Spaniard!

Flam. He carries his face in's ruff, as I have seen a
serving man carry glasses in a cypress hatband, monstrous
steady, for fear of breaking: he looks like the claw of a
blackbird, first salted, and then broiled in a candle.

                                    [*Exeunt.*

ACT THE THIRD

SCENE I—*A Hall in* MONTICELSO'S *Mansion*

Enter FRANCISCO DE MEDICIS, MONTICELSO, *the six lieger*
    Ambassadors, BRACHIANO, VITTORIA COROMBONA,
    FLAMINEO, MARCELLO, Lawyer, *and a* Guard.

MONT. Forbear, my lord, here is no place assigned you:
This business by his holiness is left
To our examination.   [*To* BRACH.

Brach. May it thrive with you!

                    [*Lays a rich gown under him.*
Fran. de Med. A chair there for his lordship!

35 Poulterer.

Brach. Forbear your kindness: an unbidden guest
Should travel as Dutchwomen go to church,
Bear their stools with them.

Mont. At your pleasure, sir.—
Stand to the table, gentlewoman [*To* VITTORIA].—Now, signior,
Fall to your plea.

Law. Domine judex, converte oculos in hanc pestem, mulierum corruptissimam.

Vit. Cor. What's he?

Fran. de Med. A lawyer that pleads against you.

Vit. Cor. Pray, my lord, let him speak his usual tongue:
I'll make no answer else.

Fran. de Med. Why, you understand Latin.

Vit. Cor. I do, sir; but amongst this auditory
Which come to hear my cause, the half or more
May be ignorant in't.

Mont. Go on, sir.

Vit. Cor. By your favour,
I will not have my accusation clouded
In a strange tongue; all this assembly
Shall hear what you can charge me with.

Fran. de Med. Signior,
You need not stand on't much; pray, change your language.

Mont. O, for God sake!—Gentlewoman, your credit
Shall be more famous by it.

Law. Well, then, have at you!

Vit. Cor. I am at the mark, sir: I'll give aim to you,
And tell you how near you shoot.

Law. Most literated judges, please your lordships
So to connive your judgments to the view
Of this debauched and diversivolent woman;
Who such a black concatenation
Of mischief hath effected, that to extirp
The memory of't, must be the consummation
Of her and her projections,—

Vit. Cor. What's all this?

Law. Hold your peace:
Exorbitant sins must have exulceration.

Vit. Cor. Surely, my lords, this lawyer here hath swallowed
Some pothecaries' bills, or proclamations;

And now the hard and undigestible words
Come up, like stones we use give hawks for physic:
Why, this is Welsh to Latin.

Law. My lords, the woman
Knows not her tropes nor figures, nor is perfect
In the academic derivation
Of grammatical elocution.

Fran. de Med. Sir, your pains
Shall be well spared, and your deep eloquence
Be worthily applauded amongst those
Which understand you.

Law. My good lord,—

Fran. de Med. Sir,
Put up your papers in your fustian bag,—

[FRANCISCO *speaks this as in scorn.*

Cry mercy, sir, 'tis buckram—and accept
My notion of your learned verbosity.

Law. I most graduatically thank your lordship:
I shall have use for them elsewhere.

Mont. I shall be plainer with you, and paint out
Your follies in more natural red and white
Than that upon your cheek.   [*To* VITTORIA.

Vit. Cor. O you mistake:
You raise a blood as noble in this cheek
As ever was your mother's.

Mont. I must spare you, till proof cry "whore" to that.—
Observe this creature here, my honoured lords,
A woman of a most prodigious spirit,
In her effected.

Vit. Cor. Honourable my lord,
It doth not suit a reverend cardinal
To play the lawyer thus.

Mont. O, your trade instructs your language.—
You see, my lords, what goodly fruit she seems;
Yet, like those apples[36] travellers report
To grow where Sodom and Gomorrah stood,
I will but touch her, and you straight shall see
She'll fall to soot and ashes.

Vit. Cor. Your envenomed
Pothecary should do't.

---

[36] "And there besyden growen trees, that beren fulle faire Apples, and faire of colour to beholde; but whoso brekethe hem, or cuttethe hem in two, he schalle fynde within hem Coles and Cyndres."—*Maundeville's Travels.*

Mont. I am resolved,[37]
Were there a second Paradise to lose,
This devil would betray it.

Vit. Cor. O poor charity!
Thou art seldom found in scarlet.

Mont. Who knows not how, when several night by night
Her gates were choked with coaches, and her rooms
Outbraved the stars with several kind of lights;
When she did counterfeit a prince's court
In music, banquets, and most riotous surfeits?
This whore, forsooth, was holy.

Vit. Cor. Ha! whore! what's that!

Mont. Shall I expound whore to you? sure, I shall;
I'll give their perfect character. They are first,
Sweetmeats which rot the eater; in man's nostrils
Poisoned perfumes: they are cozening alchemy;
Shipwrecks in calmest weather. What are whores!
Cold Russian winters, that appear so barren
As if that nature had forgot the spring:
They are the true material fire of hell:
Worse than those tributes i' the Low Countries paid,
Exactions upon meat, drink, garments, sleep,
Ay, even on man's perdition, his sin:
They are those brittle evidences of law
Which forfeit all a wretched man's estate
For leaving out one syllable. What are whores!
They are those flattering bells have all one tune,
At weddings and at funerals. Your rich whores
Are only treasuries by extortion filled,
And emptied by cursed riot. They are worse,
Worse than dead bodies which are begged at gallows,
And wrought upon by surgeons, to teach man
Wherein he is imperfect. What's a whore!
She's like the guilty counterfeited coin
Which, whosoe'er first stamps it, brings in trouble
All that receive it.

Vit. Cor. This character scapes me.

Mont. You, gentlewoman!
Take from all beasts and from all minerals
Their deadly poison—

Vit. Cor. Well, what then?

[37] *i.e.* Convinced.

Mont. I'll tell thee;
I'll find in thee a pothecary's shop,
To sample them all.

Fr. Am. She hath lived ill.

Eng. Am. True; but the cardinal's too bitter.

Mont. You know what whore is. Next the devil adultery,
Enters the devil murder.

Fran. de Med. Your unhappy
Husband is dead.

Vit. Cor. O, he's a happy husband:
Now he owes nature nothing.

Fran. de Med. And by a vaulting-engine.

Mont. An active plot; he jumped into his grave.

Fran. de Med. What a prodigy was't
That from some two yards' height a slender man
Should break his neck!

Mont. I' the rushes! [38]

Fran. de Med. And what's more,
Upon the instant lose all use of speech,
All vital motion, like a man had lain
Wound up three days. Now mark each circumstance.

Mont. And look upon this creature was his wife.
She comes not like a widow; she comes armed
With scorn and impudence: is this a mourning habit?

Vit. Cor. Had I foreknown his death, as you suggest,
I would have bespoke my mourning.

Mont. O, you are cunning.

Vit. Cor. You shame your wit and judgment,
To call it so. What! is my just defence
By him that is my judge called impudence?
Let me appeal, then, from this Christian court
To the uncivil Tartar.

Mont. See, my lords,
She scandals our proceedings.

Vit. Cor. Humbly thus,
Thus low, to the most worthy and respected
Lieger ambassadors, my modesty
And womanhood I tender; but withal,
So entangled in a cursèd accusation,
That my defence, of force, like Perseus,[39]

---

[38] With which floors were formerly strewed, before the introduction of carpets
[39] Corrupt text.

Must personate masculine virtue. To the point.
Find me but guilty, sever head from body,
We'll part good friends: I scorn to hold my life
At yours or any man's entreaty, sir.

Eng. Am. She hath a brave spirit.

Mont. Well, well, such counterfeit jewels
Make true ones oft suspected.

Vit. Cor. You are deceived:
For know, that all your strict-combinèd heads,
Which strike against this mine of diamonds,
Shall prove but glassen hammers,—they shall break.
These are but feignèd shadows of my evils:
Terrify babes, my lord, with painted devils;
I am past such needless palsy. For your names
Of whore and murderess, they proceed from you,
As if a man should spit against the wind;
The filth returns in's face.

Mont. Pray you, mistress, satisfy me one question:
Who lodged beneath your roof that fatal night
Your husband brake his neck?

Brach. That question
Enforceth me break silence: I was there.

Mont. Your business?

Brach. Why, I came to comfort her,
And take some course for settling her estate,
Because I heard her husband was in debt
To you, my lord.

Mont. He was.

Brach. And 'twas strangely feared
That you would cozen⁴⁰ her.

Mont. Who made you overseer?

Brach. Why, my charity, my charity, which should flow
From every generous and noble spirit
To orphans and to widows.

Mont. Your lust.

Brach. Cowardly dogs bark loudest: sirrah priest,
I'll talk with you hereafter. Do you hear?
The sword you frame of such an excellent temper
I'll sheathe in your own bowels.
There are a number of thy coat resemble
Your common post-boys.

⁴⁰ Cheat.

Mont. Ha!

Brach. Your mercenary post-boys:
Your letters carry truth, but 'tis your guise
To fill your mouths with gross and impudent lies.

Serv. My lord, your gown.

Brach. Thou liest, 'twas my stool:
Bestow't upon thy master, that will challenge
The rest o' the household-stuff; for Brachiano
Was ne'er so beggarly to take a stool
Out of another's lodging: let him make
Vallance for his bed on't, or a demi-foot-cloth
For his most reverent moil.[41] Monticelso,
Nemo me impune lacessit.   [*Exit.*

Mont. Your champion's gone.

Vit. Cor. The wolf may prey the better.

Fran. de Med. My lord, there's great suspicion of the
                murder,
But no sound proof who did it. For my part,
I do not think she hath a soul so black
To act a deed so bloody: if she have,
As in cold countries husbandmen plant vines,
And with warm blood manure them, even so
One summer she will bear unsavoury fruit,
And ere next spring wither both branch and root.
The act of blood let pass; only descend
To matter of incontinence.

Vit. Cor. I discern poison
Under your gilded pills.

Mont. Now the duke's gone, I will produce a letter,
Wherein 'twas plotted he and you should meet
At an apothecary's summer-house,
Down by the river Tiber,—view't, my lords,—
Where, after wanton bathing and the heat
Of a lascivious banquet,—I pray read it,
I shame to speak the rest.

Vit. Cor. Grant I was tempted;
Temptation to lust proves not the act:
Casta est quam nemo rogavit.[42]
You read his hot love to me, but you want
My frosty answer.

[41] Moile.
[42] Ovid, *Amor.* i. 8.

Mont. Frost i' the dog-days! strange!

Vit. Cor. Condemn you me for that the duke did love
    me!
So may you blame some fair and crystal river
For that some melancholic distracted man
Hath drowned himself in't.

Mont. Truly drowned, indeed.

Vit. Cor. Sum up my faults, I pray, and you shall find,
That beauty, and gay clothes, a merry heart,
And a good stomach to a feast, are all,
All the poor crimes that you can charge me with.
In faith, my lord, you might go pistol flies;
The sport would be more noble.

Mont. Very good.

Vit. Cor. But take you your course: it seems you have
    beggared me first,
And now would fain undo me. I have houses,
Jewels, and a poor remnant of crusadoes: [43]
Would those would make you charitable!

Mont. If the devil
Did ever take good shape, behold his picture.

Vit. Cor. You have one virtue left,—
You will not flatter me.

Fran. de Med. Who brought this letter?

Vit. Cor. I am not compelled to tell you.

Mont. My lord duke sent to you a thousand ducats
The twelfth of August.

Vit. Cor. 'Twas to keep your cousin
From prison: I paid use for't.

Mont. I rather think
'Twas interest for his lust.

Vit. Cor. Who says so
But yourself? if you be my accuser,
Pray, cease to be my judge: come from the bench;
Give in your evidence 'gainst me, and let these
Be moderators. My lord cardinal,
Were your intelligencing ears as loving
As to my thoughts, had you an honest tongue,
I would not care though you proclaimed them all.

Mont. Go to, go to.

[43] Portuguese coins, so called from the cross on one side.

After your goodly and vain-glorious banquet,
I'll give you a choke-pear.

Vit. Cor. O' your own grafting?

Mont. You were born in Venice, honourably descended
From the Vittelli: 'twas my cousin's fate,—
Ill may I name the hour,—to marry you:
He bought you of your father.

Vit. Cor. Ha!

Mont. He spent there in six months
Twelve thousand ducats, and (to my acquaintance
Received in dowry with you not one julio: [44]
'Twas a hard pennyworth, the ware being so light.
I yet but draw the curtain; now to your picture:
You came from thence a most notorious strumpet,
And so you have continued.

Vit. Cor. My lord,—

Mont. Nay, hear me;
You shall have time to prate. My Lord Brachiano—
Alas, I make but repetition
Of what is ordinary and Rialto talk,
And ballated, and would be played o' the stage,
But that vice many times finds such loud friends
That preachers are charmed silent.—
You gentlemen, Flamineo and Marcello,
The court hath nothing now to charge you with
Only you must remain upon your sureties
For your appearance.

Fran. de Med. I stand for Marcello.

Flam. And my lord duke for me.

Mont. For you, Vittoria, your public fault,
Joined to the condition of the present time,
Takes from you all the fruits of noble pity;
Such a corrupted trial have you made
Both of your life and beauty, and been styled
No less an ominous fate than blazing stars
To princes: here's your sentence; you are confined
Unto a house of convertites, and your bawd—

Flam. [*Aside*]. Who, I?

Mont. The Moor.

Flam. [*Aside*]. O, I am a sound man again.

44 Equal to sixpence.

Vit. Cor. A house of convertites! what's that?

Mont. A house
Of penitent whores.

Vit. Cor. Do the noblemen in Rome
Erect it for their wives, that I am sent
To lodge there?

Fran. de Med. You must have patience.

Vit. Cor. I must first have vengeance.
I fain would know if you have your salvation
By patent, that you proceed thus.

Mont. Away with her!
Take her hence.

Vit. Cor. A rape! a rape!

Mont. How!

Vit. Cor. Yes, you have ravished justice;
Forced her to do your pleasure.

Mont. Fie, she's mad!

Vit. Cor. Die with these pills in your most cursèd maw
Should bring you health! or while you sit o' the bench
Let your own spittle choke you!—

Mont. She's turned Fury.

Vit. Cor. That the last day of judgment may so find you,
And leave you the same devil you were before!
Instruct me, some good horse-leech, to speak treason;
For since you cannot take my life for deeds,
Take it for words: O woman's poor revenge,
Which dwells but in the tongue! I will not weep;
No, I do scorn to call up one poor tear
To fawn on your injustice; bear me hence
Unto this house of—what's your mitigating title?

Mont. Of convertites.

Vit. Cor. It shall not be a house of convertites;
My mind shall make it honester to me
Than the Pope's palace, and more peaceable
Than thy soul, though thou art a cardinal.
Know this, and let it somewhat raise your spite,
Through darkness diamonds spread their richest light.[45]

[*Exeunt* VITTORIA COROMBONA, Lawyer, *and* Guards.

[45] "This White Devil of Italy sets off a bad cause so speciously, and pleads with
such an innocence-resembling boldness, that we seem to see that matchless beauty
of her face which inspires such gay confidence into her; and are ready to expect,
when she has done her pleadings, that her very judges, her accusers, the grave
ambassadors who sit as spectators, and all the court, will rise and make proffer

Re-enter BRACHIANO.

Brach. Now you and I are friends, sir, we'll shake hands
In a friend's grave together; a fit place,
Being the emblem of soft peace, to atone our hatred.

Fran. de Med. Sir, what's the matter?

Brach. I will not chase more blood from that loved
    cheek;
You have lost too much already: fare you well. [*Exit.*

Fran. de Med. How strange these words sound! what's
    the interpretation?

Flam. [*Aside.*] Good; this is a preface to the discovery
of the duchess' death: he carries it well. Because now I
cannot counterfeit a whining passion for the death of my
lady, I will feign a mad humour for the disgrace of my
sister; and that will keep off idle questions. Treason's
tongue hath a villainous palsy in't: I will talk to any man,
hear no man, and for a time appear a politic madman.
    [*Exit.*

Enter GIOVANNI, *Count* LODOVICO, *and* Attendant.

Fran. de Med. How now, my noble cousin! what, in
    black!

Giov. Yes, uncle, I was taught to imitate you
In virtue, and you must imitate me
In colours of your garments. My sweet mother
Is—

Fran. de Med. How! where?

Giov. Is there; no, yonder: indeed, sir, I'll not tell you,
For I shall make you weep.

Fran. de Med. Is dead?

Giov. Do not blame me now,
I did not tell you so.

Lod. She's dead, my lord.

Fran. de Med. Dead!

Mont. Blessed lady, thou are now above thy woes!—

---

to defend her in spite of the utmost conviction of her guilt; as the shepherds
in Don Quixote make proffer to follow the beautiful shepherdess Marcela, 'without reaping any profit out of her manifest resolution made there in their
hearing.'

> 'So sweet and lovely does she make the shame,
> Which, like a canker in the fragrant rose,
> Does spot the beauty of her budding name.' "
> C. Lamb. (*Spec. of Eng. Dram. Poets.*)

Wilt please your lordships to withdraw a little?

                                  [Exeunt Ambassadors.

  Giov. What do the dead do, uncle? do they eat,
Hear music, go a hunting, and be merry,
As we that live?

  Fran. de Med. No, coz; they sleep.

  Giov. Lord, Lord, that I were dead!
I have not slept these six nights.—When do they wake?

  Fran. de Med. When God shall please.

  Giov. Good God, let her sleep ever!
For I have known her wake an hundred nights,
When all the pillow where she laid her head
Was brine-wet with her tears. I am to complain to you, sir;
I'll tell you how they have used her now she's dead:
They wrapped her in a cruel fold of lead,
And would not let me kiss her.

  Fran. de Med. Thou didst love her.

  Giov. I have often heard her say she gave me suck,
And it should seem by that she dearly loved me,
Since princes seldom do it.

  Fran. de Med. O, all of my poor sister that remains!—
Take him away, for God's sake!

                        [Exeunt GIOVANNI *and* Attendant.

  Mont. How now, my lord!

  Fran. de Med. Believe me, I am nothing but her grave;
And I shall keep her blessèd memory
Longer than thousand epitaphs.

      [Exeunt FRANCISCO DE MEDICIS *and* MONTICELSO.

      Re-enter FLAMINEO *as if distracted.*

  Flam. We endure the strokes like anvils or hard steel,
Till pain itself make us no pain to feel.
Who shall do me right now? is this the end of service?
I'd rather go weed garlic; travel through France, and be
mine own ostler; wear sheepskin linings, or shoes that
stink of blacking; be entered into the list of the forty
thousand pedlers in Poland.

              Re-enter Ambassadors.

Would I had rotted in some surgeon's house at Venice,
built upon the pox as well as on piles, ere I had served
Brachiano!

Savoy Am. You must have comfort.

Flam. Your comfortable words are like honey; they relish well in your mouth that's whole, but in mine that's wounded they go down as if the sting of the bee were in them. O, they have wrought their purpose cunningly, as if they would not seem to do it of malice! In this a politician imitates the devil, as the devil imitates a cannon; wheresoever he comes to do mischief, he comes with his backside towards you.

Fr. Am. The proofs are evident.

Flam. Proof! 'twas corruption. O gold, what a god art thou! and O man, what a devil art thou to be tempted by that cursed mineral! Your diversivolent lawyer, mark him: knaves turn informers, as maggots turn to flies; you may catch gudgeons with either. A cardinal! I would he would hear me: there's nothing so holy but money will corrupt and putrify it, like victual under the line. You are happy in England, my lord: here they sell justice with those weights they press men to death with. O horrible salary!

Eng. Am. Fie, fie, Flamineo!   [*Exeunt* Ambassadors.

Flam. Bells ne'er ring well, till they are at their full pitch; and I hope yon cardinal shall never have the grace to pray well till he come to the scaffold. If they were racked now to know the confederacy,——but your noblemen are privileged from the rack; and well may, for a little thing would pull some of them a-pieces afore they came to their arraignment. Religion, O, how it is commended [46] with policy! The first bloodshed in the world happened about religion. Would I were a Jew!

Mar. O, there are too many.

Flam. You are deceived: there are not Jews enough, priests enough, nor gentlemen enough.

Mar. How?

Flam. I'll prove it; for if there were Jews enough, so many Christians would not turn usurers; if priests enough, one should not have six benefices; and if gentlemen enough, so many early mushrooms, whose best growth sprang from a dunghill, should not aspire to gentility. Farewell: let others live by begging; be thou one of them practise the art of Wolner[47] in England, to swallow all's given thee;

---

[46] Muddled up.

[47] A man famous for his power of digesting all sorts of strange food.

and yet let one purgation make thee as hungry again as
fellows that work in a saw-pit. I'll go hear the screech-owl.
[*Exit.*

    Lod. [*Aside*]. This was Brachiano's pander and 'tis
      strange
That, in such open and apparent guilt
Of his adulterous sister, he dare utter
So scandalous a passion. I must wind him.

Re-enter FLAMINEO.

    Flam. [*Aside*]. How dares this banished count return
      to Rome,
His pardon not yet purchased! I have heard
The deceased duchess gave him pension,
And that he came along from Padua
I' the train of the young prince. There's somewhat in't:
Physicians, that cure poisons, still do work
With counter-poisons.
    Mar. Mark this strange encounter.
    Flam. The god of melancholy turn thy gall to poison,
And let the stigmatic[48] wrinkles in thy face,
Like to the boisterous waves in a rough tide,
One still overtake another.
    Lod. I do thank thee,
And I do wish ingeniously[49] for thy sake
The dog-days all year long.
    Flam. How croaks the raven?
Is our good duchess dead?
    Lod. Dead.
    Flam. O fate!
Misfortune comes, like the coroner's business,
Huddle upon huddle.
    Lod. Shalt thou and I join house-keeping?
    Flam. Yes, content:
Let's be unsociably sociable.
    Lod. Sit some three days together, and discourse.
    Flam. Only with making faces: lie in our clothes.
    Lod. With faggots for our pillows.
    Flam. And be lousy.

[48] Branded.
[49] Ingenuously.

Lod. In taffata linings; that's genteel melancholy:
Sleep all day.

Flam. Yes; and, like your melancholic hare,
Feed after midnight.—

We are observed: see how yon couple grieve!

Lod. What a strange creature is a laughing fool
As if man were created to no use
But only to show his teeth.

Flam. I'll tell thee what,—
It would do well, instead of looking-glasses,
To set one's face each morning by a saucer
Of a witch's congealèd blood.

Lod. Precious gue! [50]
We'll never part.

Flam. Never, till the beggary of courtiers,
The discontent of churchmen, want of soldiers,
And all the creatures that hang manacled,
Worse than strappadoed, on the lowest felly
Of Fortune's wheel, be taught, in our two lives,
To scorn that world which life of means deprives.

Enter ANTONELLI *and* GASPARO.

Anto. My lord, I bring good news. The Pope, on's death-
bed,
At the earnest suit of the Great Duke of Florence,
Hath signed your pardon, and restored unto you——

Lod. I thank you for your news.—Look up again,
    Flamineo; see my pardon.

Flam. Why do you laugh?
There was no such condition in our covenant.

Lod. Why!

Flam. You shall not seem a happier man than I:
You know our vow, sir; if you will be merry,
Do it i' the like posture as if some great man
Sate while his enemy were executed;
Though it be very lechery unto thee,
Do't with a crabbèd politician's face.

Lod. Your sister is a damnable whore.

Flam. Ha!

Lod. Look you, I spake that laughing.

Flam. Dost ever think to speak again?

[50] Rogue. Fr. *Gueux.*

Lod. Do you hear?
Wilt sell me forty ounces of her blood
To water a mandrake?
    Flam. Poor lord, you did vow
To live a lousy creature.
    Lod. Yes.
    Flam. Like one
That had for ever forfeited the daylight
By being in debt.
    Lod. Ha, ha!
    Flam. I do not greatly wonder you do break;
Your lordship learned 't long since. But I'll tell you,—
    Lod. What?
    Flam. And 't shall stick by you,—
    Lod. I long for it.
    Flam. This laughter scurvily becomes your face:
If you will not be melancholy, be angry. [*Strikes him.*
See, now I laugh too.
    Mar. You are to blame: I'll force you hence.
    Lod. Unhand me.   [*Exeunt* MARCELLO *and* FLAMINEO.
That e'er I should be forced to right myself
Upon a pander!
    Anto. My lord,—
    Lod. H'ad been as good met with his fist a thunderbolt.
    Gas. How this shows!
    Lod. Ud's death,[51] how did my sword miss him?
These rogues that are most weary of their lives
Still scape the greatest dangers.
A pox upon him! all his reputation,
Nay, all the goodness of his family,
Is not worth half this earthquake:
I learned it of no fencer to shake thus:
Come, I'll forget him, and go drink some wine.   [*Exeunt.*

SCENE II—*An Apartment in the Palace of* FRANCISCO

Enter FRANCISCO DE MEDICIS *and* MONTICELSO.

    Mont. Come, come, my lord, untie your folded thoughts,

[51] A corruption of God's death.

And let them dangle loose as a bride's hair.[52]
Your sister's poisoned.

Fran. de Med. Far be it from my thoughts
To seek revenge.

Mont. What, are you turned all marble?

Fran. de Med. Shall I defy him, and impose a war
Most burdensome on my poor subjects' necks,
Which at my will I have not power to end?
You know, for all the murders, rapes, and thefts,
Committed in the horrid lust of war,
He that unjustly caused it first proceed
Shall find it in his grave and in his seed.

Mont. That's not the course I'd wish you; pray, observe
me.
We see that undermining more prevails
Than doth the cannon. Bear your wrongs concealed,
And, patient as the tortoise, let this camel
Stalk o'er your back unbruised: sleep with the lion,
And let this brood of secure foolish mice
Play with your nostrils, till the time be ripe
For the bloody audit and the fatal gripe:
Aim like a cunning fowler, close one eye,
That you the better may your game espy.

Fran. de Med. Free me, my innocence, from treacherous
acts!
I know there's thunder yonder; and I'll stand
Like a safe valley, which low bends the knee
To some aspiring mountain; since I know
Treason, like spiders weaving nets for flies,
By her foul work is found, and in it dies.
To pass away these thoughts, my honoured lord,
It is reported you possess a book,
Wherein you have quoted,[53] by intelligence,
The names of all notorious offenders
Lurking about the city.

Mont. Sir, I do;
And some there are which call it my black book:
Well may the title hold; for though it teach not

---

[52] Brides formerly walked to church with their hair hanging loose behind. Anne Bullen's was thus dishevelled when she went to the altar with King Henry the Eighth.—*Steevens.*

[53] Registered.

The art of conjuring, yet in it lurk
The names of many devils.
    Fran. de Med. Pray, let's see it.
    Mont. I'll fetch it to your lordship.   [*Exit*.
    Fran. de Med. Monticelso,
I will not trust thee; but in all my plots
I'll rest as jealous as a town besieged.
Thou canst not reach what I intend to act:
Your flax soon kindles, soon is out again;
But gold slow heats, and long will hot remain.

    Re-enter MONTICELSO, *presents* FRANCISCO DE MEDICIS
        with a book.

    Mont. 'Tis here, my lord.
    Fran. de Med. First, your intelligencers, pray, let's see.
    Mont. Their number rises strangely; and some of them
You'd take for honest men. Next are panders,—
These are your pirates; and these following leaves
For base rogues that undo young gentlemen
By taking up commodities; [54] for politic bankrupts;
For fellows that are bawds to their own wives,
Only to put off horses, and slight jewels,
Clocks, defaced plate, and such commodities,
At birth of their first children.
    Fran. de Med. Are there such?
    Mont. These are for impudent bawds
That go in men's apparel; for usurers
That share with scriveners for their good reportage;
For lawyers that will antedate their writs:
And some divines you might find folded there,
But that I slip them o'er for conscience' sake.
Here is a general catalogue of knaves:
A man might study all the prisons o'er,
Yet never attain this knowledge.
    Fran. de Med. Murderers!
Fold down the leaf, I pray.
Good my lord, let me borrow this strange doctrine.
    Mont. Pray, use't, my lord.
    Fran. de Med. I do assure your lordship,
You are a worthy member of the state,
And have done infinite good in your discovery

---

[54] *i.e.* Supplying borrowers with goods to be debited to them as cash.

Of these offenders.

   Mont. Somewhat, sir.

   Fran. de Med. O God!
Better than tribute of wolves paid in England: [55]
'Twill hang their skins o' the hedge.

   Mont. I must make bold
To leave your lordship.

   Fran. de Med. Dearly, sir, I thank you:
If any ask for me at court, report
You have left me in the company of knaves.

                           [*Exit* MONTICELSO.

I gather now by this, some cunning fellow
That's my lord's officer, one that lately skipped
From a clerk's desk up to a justice' chair,
Hath made this knavish summons, and intends,
As the Irish rebels wont were to sell heads,
So to make prize of these. And thus it happens,
Your poor rogues pay for't which have not the means
To present bribe in fist: the rest o' the band
Are razed out of the knaves' record; or else
My lord he winks at them with easy will;
His man grows rich, the knaves are the knaves still.
But to the use I'll make of it; it shall serve
To point me out a list of murderers,
Agents for any villany. Did I want
Ten leash of courtezans, it would furnish me;
Nay, laundress three armies. That in so little paper
Should lie the undoing of so many men!
'Tis not so big as twenty declarations.
See the corrupted use some make of books:
Divinity, wrested by some factious blood,
Draws swords, swells battles, and o'erthrows all good.
To fashion my revenge more seriously,
Let me remember my dead sister's face:
Call for her picture? no, I'll close mine eyes,
And in a melancholic thought I'll frame

Enter ISABELLA's ghost.

Her figure 'fore me. Now I ha't:—how strong
Imagination works! how she can frame

[55] An allusion to the tribute imposed by Edgar which led to the extirpation of wolves in Britain.

Things which are not! Methinks she stands afore me,
And by the quick idea of my mind,
Were my skill pregnant, I could draw her picture.
Thought, as a subtle juggler, makes us deem
Things supernatural, which yet have cause
Common as sickness. 'Tis my melancholy.—
How cam'st thou by thy death?—How idle am I
To question mine own idleness!—Did ever
Man dream awake till now?—Remove this object;
Out of my brain with't: what have I to do
With tombs, or death-beds, funerals, or tears,
That have to meditate upon revenge?   [*Exit* Ghost.
So, now 'tis ended, like an old wife's story:
Statesmen think often they see stranger sights
Than madmen. Come, to this weighty business:
My tragedy must have some idle mirth in't,
Else it will never pass. I am in love,
In love with Corombona; and my suit
Thus halts to her in verse.—   [*Writes.*
I have done it rarely: O the fate of princes!
I am so used to frequent flattery,
That, being alone, I now flatter myself:
But it will serve; 'tis sealed.

Enter Servant.

                                 Bear this
To the house of convertites, and watch your leisure
To give it to the hands of Corombona,
Or to the matron, when some followers
Of Brachiano may be by. Away!   [*Exit* Servant
He that deals all by strength, his wit is shallow:
When a man's head goes through, each limb will follow.
The engine for my business, bold Count Lodowick:
'Tis gold must such an instrument procure;
With empty fist no man doth falcons lure.
Brachiano, I am now fit for thy encounter:
Like the wild Irish, I'll ne'er think thee dead
Till I can play at football with thy head.
Flectere si nequeo superos, Acheronta movebo.[56]   [*Exit.*

[56] Virgil, *Æn.* vii. 312.

ACT THE FOURTH

SCENE I—*A Room in the House of Convertites*

Enter the Matron *and* FLAMINEO.

MATRON. Should it be known the duke hath such recourse
To your imprisoned sister, I were like
To incur much damage by it.
  Flam. Not a scruple:
The Pope lies on his death-bed, and their heads
Are troubled now with other business
Than guarding of a lady.

Enter Servant.

Serv. Yonder's Flamineo in conference
With the matrona.—Let me speak with you;
I would entreat you to deliver for me
This letter to the fair Vittoria.
  Matron. I shall, sir.
  Serv. With all care and secrecy:
Hereafter you shall know me, and receive
Thanks for this courtesy.   [*Exit.*
  Flam. How now! what's that?
  Matron. A letter.
  Flam. To my sister? I'll see't delivered.

Enter BRACHIANO.

Brach. What's that you read, Flamineo?
  Flam. Look.
  Brach. Ha! [*Reads.*] "To the most unfortunate, his best
respected Vittoria."—
Who was the messenger?
  Flam. I know not.
  Brach. No! who sent it?
  Flam. Ud's foot, you speak as if a man
Should know what fowl is coffined in a baked meat
Afore you cut it up.
  Brach. I'll open't, were't her heart.—What's here sub-
      scribed!
"Florence!" this juggling is gross and palpable:

I have found out the conveyance.—Read it, read it.

Flam. [*Reads.*] "Your tears I'll turn to triumphs, be but
mine:

Your prop is fall'n: I pity, that a vine,

Which princes heretofore have longed to gather,

Wanting supporters, now should fade and wither."—

Wine, i' faith, my lord, with lees would serve his turn.—

"Your sad imprisonment I'll soon uncharm,

And with a princely uncontrollèd arm

Lead you to Florence, where my love and care

Shall hang your wishes in my silver hair."—

A halter on his strange equivocation!—

"Nor for my years return me the sad willow:

Who prefer blossoms before fruit that's mellow?"—

Rotten, on my knowledge, with lying too long i' the bed-
straw.—

"And all the lines of age this line convinces,

The gods never wax old, no more do princes."—

A pox on't, tear it; let's have no more atheists, for God's
sake.

Brach. Ud's death, I'll cut her into atomies,

And let the irregular north wind sweep her up,

And blow her into his nostrils! Where's this whore?

Flam. That what do you call her?

Brach. O, I could be mad,

Prevent[57] the cursed disease[58] she'll bring me to,

And tear my hair off! Where's this changeable stuff?

Flam. O'er head and ears in water, I assure you:
She is not for your wearing.

Brach. No, you pander?

Flam. What, me, my lord, am I your dog?

Brach. A blood-hound: do you brave, do you stand me?

Flam. Stand you! let those that have diseases run;
I need no plasters.

Brach. Would you be kicked?

Flam. Would you have your neck broke?
I tell you, duke, I am not in Russia;[59]
My shins must be kept whole.

---

[57] Anticipate.

[58] Syphilis.

[59] "Let him have Russian law for all his sins.

What's that? A hundred blows on his bare shins."—

Day's *Parliament of Bees*, 1641.

Brach. Do you know me?

Flam. O, my lord, methodically:
As in this world there are degrees of evils,
So in this world there are degrees of devils.
You're a great duke, I your poor secretary.
I do look now for a Spanish fig, or an Italian salad,[60] daily.

Brach. Pander, ply your convoy, and leave your prating.

Flam. All your kindness to me is like that miserable
courtesy of Polyphemus to Ulysses; you reserve me to be
devoured last: you would dig turfs out of my grave to feed
your larks; that would be music to you. Come, I'll lead
you to her.

Brach. Do you face me?

Flam. O, sir, I would not go before a politic enemy with
my back towards him, though there were behind me a
whirlpool.

Enter VITTORIA COROMBONA.

Brach. Can you read, mistress? look upon that letter:
There are no characters nor hieroglyphics;
You need no comment: I am grown your receiver.
God's precious! you shall be a brave great lady,
A stately and advancèd whore.

Vit. Cor. Say, sir?

Brach. Come, come, let's see your cabinet, discover
Your treasury of love-letters. Death and Furies!
I'll see them all.

Vit. Cor. Sir, upon my soul,
I have not any. Whence was this directed?

Brach. Confusion on your politic ignorance!
You are reclaimed,[61] are you? I'll give you the bells,
And let you fly to the devil.

Flam. Ware hawk, my lord.

Vit. Cor. "Florence!" this is some treacherous plot, my
        lord:
To me he ne'er was lovely, I protest,
So much as in my sleep.

Brach. Right! they are plots.
Your beauty! O, ten thousand curses on't!
How long have I beheld the devil in crystal![62]

---

[60] Two mediums for administering poison.
[61] A play upon terms of hawking.
[62] A magic glass.

Thou hast led me, like an heathen sacrifice,
With music and with fatal yokes of flowers,
To my eternal ruin. Woman to man
Is either a god or a wolf.

    Vit. Cor. My lord,—

    Brach. Away!
We'll be as differing as two adamants;
The one shall shun the other. What, dost weep?
Procure but ten of thy dissembling trade
Ye'd furnish all the Irish funerals
With howling past wild Irish.

    Flam. Fie, my lord!

    Brach. That hand, that cursèd hand, which I have wearied
With doting kisses!—O my sweetest duchess,
How lovely art thou now!—My loose thoughts
Scatter like quicksilver: I was bewitched;
For all the world speaks ill of thee.

    Vit. Cor. No matter:
I'll live so now, I'll make that world recant,
And change her speeches. You did name your duchess.

    Brach. Whose death God pardon!

    Vit. Cor. Whose death God revenge
On thee, most godless duke!

    Flam. Now for two whirlwinds.

    Vit. Cor. What have I gained by thee but infamy?
Thou hast stained the spotless honour of my house,
And frighted thence noble society:
Like those, which, sick o' the palsy, and retain
Ill-scenting foxes 'bout them, are still shunned
By those of choicer nostrils. What do you call this house?
Is this your palace? did not the judge style it
A house of penitent whores? who sent me to it!
Who hath the honour to advance Vittoria
To this incontinent college? is't not you?
Is't not your high preferment? Go, go, brag
How many ladies you have undone like me.
Fare you well, sir; let me hear no more of you:
I had a limb corrupted to an ulcer,
But I have cut it off; and now I'll go
Weeping to Heaven on crutches. For your gifts,
I will return them all; and I do wish
That I could make you full executor

To all my sins. O, that I could toss myself
Into a grave as quickly! for all thou art worth
I'll not shed one tear more,—I'll burst first.

       [*She throws herself upon a bed.*

 Brach. I have drunk Lethe.—Vittoria!
My dearest happiness! Vittoria!
What do you ail, my love? why do you weep?
 Vit. Cor. Yes, I now weep poniards, do you see?
 Brach. Are not those matchless eyes mine?
 Vit. Cor. I had rather
They were not matchless.
 Brach. Is not this lip mine?
 Vit. Cor. Yes; thus to bite it off, rather than give it thee.
 Flam. Turn to my lord, good sister.
 Vit. Cor. Hence, you pander!
 Flam. Pander! am I the author of your sin?
 Vit. Cor. Yes; he's a base thief that a thief lets in.
 Flam. We're blown up, my lord.
 Brach. Wilt thou hear me?
Once to be jealous of thee, is to express
That I will love thee everlastingly,
And never more be jealous.
 Vit. Cor. O thou fool,
Whose greatness hath by much o'ergrown thy wit!
What dar'st thou do that I not dare to suffer,
Excepting to be still thy whore? for that,
In the sea's bottom sooner thou shalt make
A bonfire.
 Flam. O, no oaths, for God's sake!
 Brach. Will you hear me?
 Vit. Cor. Never.
 Flam. What a damned imposthume is a woman's will!
Can nothing break it?—Fie, fie, my lord,
Women are caught as you take tortoises;
She must be turned on her back.—Sister, by this hand,
I am on your side.—Come, come, you have wronged her:
What a strange credulous man were you, my lord,
To think the Duke of Florence would love her!
Will any mercer take another's ware
When once 'tis toused and sullied?—And yet, sister,
How scurvily this frowardness becomes you!
Young leverets stand not long; and women's anger

Should, like their flight, procure a little sport;
A full cry for a quarter of an hour,
And then be put to the dead quat.[63]

Brach. Shall these eyes,
Which have so long time dwelt upon your face,
Be now put out?

Flam. No cruel landlady i' the world,
Which lends forth groats to broom-men, and takes use for
        them,
Would do't.—
Hand her, my lord, and kiss her: be not like
A ferret, to let go your hold with blowing.

Brach. Let us renew right hands.

Vit. Cor. Hence!

Brach. Never shall rage or the forgetful wine
Make me commit like fault.

Flam. Now you are i' the way on't, follow't hard.

Brach. Be thou at peace with me, let all the world
Threaten the cannon.

Flam. Mark his penitence:
Best natures do commit the grossest faults,
When they're given o'er to jealousy, as best wine,
Dying, makes strongest vinegar. I'll tell you,—
The sea's more rough and raging than calm rivers,
But not so sweet nor wholesome. A quiet woman
Is a still water under a great bridge;
A man may shoot her safely.

Vit. Cor. O ye dissembling men!—

Flam. We sucked that, sister,
From women's breasts, in our first infancy.

Vit. Cor. To add misery to misery!

Brach. Sweetest,—

Vit. Cor. Am I not low enough?
Ay, ay, your good heart gathers like a snow-ball,
Now your affection's cold.

Flam. Ud'sfoot, it shall melt
To a heart again, or all the wine in Rome
Shall run o' the lees for't.

Vit. Cor. Your dog or hawk should be rewarded better
Than I have been. I'll speak not one word more.

[63] Squat, *i.e.* the seat or form of a hare.

Flam. Stop her mouth with a sweet kiss, my lord. So,
Now the tide's turned, the vessel's come about.
He's a sweet armful. O, we curled-haired men
Are still most kind to women! This is well.

Brach. That you should chide thus!

Flam. O, sir, your little chimneys
Do ever cast most smoke! I sweat for you.
Couple together with as deep a silence
As did the Grecians in their wooden horse.
My lord, supply your promises with deeds;
You know that painted meat no hunger feeds.

Brach. Stay in ingrateful Rome—

Flam. Rome! it deserves to be called Barbary
For our villainous usage.

Brach. Soft! the same project which the Duke of Florence
(Whether in love or gullery I know not)
Laid down for her escape, will I pursue.

Flam. And no time fitter than this night, my lord:
The Pope being dead, and all the cardinals entered
The conclave for the electing a new Pope;
The city in a great confusion;
We may attire her in a page's suit,
Lay her post-horse, take shipping, and amain
For Padua.

Brach. I'll instantly steal forth the Prince Giovanni,
And make for Padua. You two with your old mother,
And young Marcello that attends on Florence,
If you can work him to it, follow me:
I will advance you all:—for you, Vittoria,
Think of a duchess' title.

Flam. Lo you, sister!—
Stay, my lord; I'll tell you a tale. The crocodile, which lives
in the river Nilus, hath a worm breeds i' the teeth of't,
which puts it to extreme anguish: a little bird, no bigger
than a wren, is barber-surgeon to this crocodile; flies into
the jaws of't, picks out the worm, and brings present
remedy. The fish, glad of ease, but ingrateful to her that
did it, that the bird may not talk largely of her abroad for
non-payment, closeth her chaps, intending to swallow her,
and so put her to perpetual silence. But nature, loathing
such ingratitude, hath armed this bird with a quill or prick

in the head, the top o' which wounds the crocodile i' the
mouth, forceth her to open her bloody prison, and away
flies the pretty tooth-picker from her cruel patient.[64]

Brach. Your application is, I have not rewarded
The service you have done me.

Flam. No, my lord.—
You, sister, are the crocodile: you are blemished in your
fame, my lord cures it; and though the comparison hold not
in every particle, yet observe, remember what good the bird
with the prick i' the head hath done you, and scorn ingratitude.—

It may appear to some ridiculous   [*Aside.*
Thus to talk knave and madman, and sometimes
Come in with a dried sentence, stuft with sage:
But this allows my varying of shapes;
Knaves do grow great by being great men's apes.

[*Exeunt.*

SCENE II—*Before a Church*

Enter FRANCISCO DE MEDICIS, LODOVICO, GASPARO,
and six Ambassadors.

Fran. de Med. So, my lord, I commend your diligence.
Guard well the conclave; and, as the order is,
Let none have conference with the cardinals.

Lod. I shall, my lord.—Room for the ambassadors!

Gasp. They're wondrous brave[65] to-day: why do they
wear
These several habits?

Lod. O, sir, they are knights
Of several orders:
That lord i' the black cloak, with the silver cross,
Is Knight of Rhodes; the next, Knight of St. Michael;
That, of the Golden Fleece; the Frenchman, there,
Knight of the Holy Ghost; my lord of Savoy,
Knight of the Annunciation; the Englishman
Is Knight of the honoured Garter, dedicated

---

[64] See *Herodotus*, lib. ii. c. 68, on the trochilus.
[65] *i.e.* Fine.

Unto their saint, St. George. I could describe to you
Their several institutions, with the laws
Annexèd to their orders; but that time
Permits not such discovery.

Fran. de Med. Where's Count Lodowick?

Lod. Here, my lord.

Fran. de Med. 'Tis o' the point of dinner time:
Marshal the cardinals' service.

Lod. Sir, I shall.

Enter Servants, *with several dishes covered.*

Stand, let me search your dish: who's this for?

Serv. For my Lord Cardinal Monticelso.

Lod. Whose this?

Serv. For my Lord Cardinal of Bourbon.

Fr. Am. Why doth he search the dishes? to observe
What meat is drest?

Eng. Am. No, sir, but to prevent
Lest any letters should be conveyed in,
To bribe or to solicit the advancement
Of any cardinal. When first they enter,
'Tis lawful for the ambassadors of princes
To enter with them, and to make their suit
For any man their prince affecteth best;
But after, till a general election,
No man may speak with them.

Lod. You that attend on the lord cardinals,
Open the window, and receive their viands!

A Cardinal. [*At the window.*] You must return the
          service: the lord cardinals
Are busied 'bout electing of the Pope;
They have given over scrutiny, and are fall'n
To admiration.

Lod. Away, away!

Fran. de Med. I'll lay a thousand ducats you hear news.
Of a Pope presently. Hark! sure, he's elected:
Behold, my Lord of Arragon appears
On the church-battlements.

Arragon. [*On the church battlements.*] *Denuntio vobis*[66]

---

[66] This was nearly the form in which the election of a Pope was declared to the people.

*gaudium magnum. Reverendissimus cardinalis Lorenzo de
Monticelso electus est in sedem apostolicam, et elegit sibi
nomen Paulum Quartum.*

  Omnes. Vivat sanctus pater Paulus Quartus!

Enter Servant.

  Serv. Vittoria, my lord,—

  Fran. de Med. Well, what of her?

  Serv. Is fled the city,—

  Fran. de Med. Ha!

  Serv. With Duke Brachiano.

  Fran. de Med. Fled! Where's the Prince Giovanni?

  Serv. Gone with his father.

  Fran. de Med. Let the matrona of the convertites
Be apprehended.—Fled! O, damnable!   [*Exit* Servant.
How fortunate are my wishes! why, 'twas this
I only laboured: I did send the letter
To instruct him what to do. Thy fame, fond [67] duke
I first have poisoned; directed thee the way
To marry a whore: what can be worse? This follows,—
The hand must act to drown the passionate tongue:
I scorn to wear a sword and prate of wrong.

Enter Monticelso in state.

  *Mont. Concedimus vobis apostolicam benedictionem et
remissionem peccatorum.*
My lord reports Vittoria Corombona
Is stol'n from forth the house of convertites
By Brachiano, and they're fled the city.
Now, though this be the first day of our state,
We cannot better please the divine power
Than to sequester from the holy church
These cursèd persons. Make it therefore known,
We do denounce excommunication
Against them both: all that are theirs in Rome
We likewise banish. Set on.

   [*Exeunt* Monticelso, *his train,* Ambassadors, *&c.*
  Fran. de Med. Come, dear Lodovico;
You have ta'en the sacrament to prosecute
The intended murder.

  Lod. With all constancy.

[67] Foolish.

But, sir, I wonder you'll engage yourself
In person, being a great prince.
　　Fran. de Med. Divert me not.
Most of his court are of my faction,
And some are of my council. Noble friend,
Our danger shall be like in this design:
Give leave, part of the glory may be mine.

　　　　　　　[*Exeunt* FRAN. DE MED. *and* GASPARO.

Re-enter MONTICELSO.

　　Mont. Why did the duke of Florence with such care
Labour your pardon? say.
　　Lod. Italian beggars will resolve you that,
Who, begging of an alms, bid those they beg of,
Do good for their own sakes; or it may be,
He spreads his bounty with a sowing hand,
Like kings, who many times give out of measure,
Not for desert so much, as for their pleasure.
　　Mont. I know you're cunning. Come, what devil was
　　　　that
That you were raising?
　　Lod. Devil, my lord!
　　Mont. I ask you
How doth the duke employ you, that his bonnet
Fell with such compliment unto his knee,
When he departed from you?
　　Lod. Why, my lord,
He told me of a resty Barbary horse
Which he would fain have brought to the career,
The sault, and the ring-galliard;[68] now, my lord,
I have a rare French rider.
　　Mont. Take you heed
Lest the jade break your neck. Do you put me off
With your wild horse-tricks? Sirrah, you do lie.
O, thou'rt a foul black cloud, and thou dost threat
A violent storm!
　　Lod. Storms are i' the air, my lord:
I am too low to storm.
　　Mont. Wretched creature!
I know that thou art fashioned for all ill,
Like dogs that once get blood, they'll ever kill.

---

68 Terms of the *manège*.

About some murder? was't not?

Lod. I'll not tell you:
And yet I care not greatly if I do,
Marry, with this preparation. Holy father,
I come not to you as an intelligencer,
But as a penitent sinner: what I utter
Is in confession merely; which you know
Must never be revealed.

Mont. You have o'erta'en me.

Lod. Sir, I did love Brachiano's duchess dearly,
Or rather I pursued her with hot lust,
Though she ne'er knew on't. She was poisoned;
Upon my soul, she was; for which I have sworn
To avenge her murder.

Mont. To the Duke of Florence?

Lod. To him I have.

Mont. Miserable creature!
If thou persist in this, 'tis damnable.
Dost thou imagine thou canst slide on blood,
And not be tainted with a shameful fall?
Or, like the black and melancholic yew-tree,
Dost think to root thyself in dead men's graves,
And yet to prosper? Instruction to thee
Comes like sweet showers to over-hardened ground;
They wet, but pierce not deep. And so I leave thee,
With all the Furies hanging 'bout thy neck,
Till by thy penitence thou remove this evil,
In conjuring from thy breast that cruel devil.   [*Exit.*

Lod. I'll give it o'er; he says 'tis damnable,
Besides I did expect his suffrage,
By reason of Camillo's death.

Re-enter FRANCISCO DE MEDICIS *with a* Servant.

Fran. de Med. Do you know that count?

Serv. Yes, my lord.

Fran. de Med. Bear him these thousand ducats to his
    lodging;
Tell him the Pope hath sent them.—[*Aside.*] Happily
That will confirm him more than all the rest.   [*Exit.*

Serv. Sir,—

Lod. To me, sir?

Serv. His Holiness hath sent you a thousand crowns,

And wills you, if you travel, to make him
Your patron for intelligence.
 Lod. His creature ever to be commanded.
             [Exit Servant.
Why, now 'tis come about. He railed upon me;
And yet these crowns were told out and laid ready
Before he knew my voyage. O the art,
The modest form of greatness! that do sit,
Like brides at wedding-dinners, with their looks turned
From the least wanton jest, their puling stomach
Sick of the modesty, when their thoughts are loose,
Even acting of those hot and lustful sports
Are to ensue about midnight: such his cunning:
He sounds my depth thus with a golden plummet.
I am doubly armed now. Now to the act of blood.
There's but three Furies found in spacious hell,
But in a great man's breast three thousand dwell. *[Exit.*

ACT THE FIFTH

SCENE I—*An Apartment in a Palace at Padua*

A passage over the stage of BRACHIANO, FLAMINEO, MAR-
 CELLO, HORTENSIO, VITTORIA COROMBONA, CORNELIA,
 ZANCHE, *and others.*

    [Exeunt omnes except FLAMINEO *and* HORTENSIO.

FLAM. In all the weary minutes of my life,
Day ne'er broke up till now. This marriage
Confirms me happy.
 Hort. 'Tis a good assurance.
Saw you not yet the Moor that's come to court?
 Flam. Yes, and conferred with him i' the duke's closet:
I have not seen a goodlier personage,
Nor ever talked with man better experienced
In state affairs or rudiments of war:
He hath, by report, served the Venetian
In Candy these twice seven years, and been chief
In many a bold design.
 Hort. What are those two
That bear him company?

Flam. Two noblemen of Hungary, that, living in the
emperor's service as commanders, eight years since, contrary to the expectation of all the court, entered into religion, into the strict order of Capuchins: but, being not
well settled in their undertaking, they left their order, and
returned to court; for which, being after troubled in conscience, they vowed their service against the enemies of
Christ, went to Malta, were there knighted, and in their
return back, at this great solemnity, they are resolved for
ever to forsake the world, and settle themselves here in a
house of Capuchins in Padua.

Hort. 'Tis strange.

Flam. One thing makes it so: they have vowed for ever
to wear, next their bare bodies, those coats of mail they
served in.

Hort. Hard penance! Is the Moor a Christian?

Flam. He is.

Hort. Why proffers he his service to our duke?

Flam. Because he understands there's like to grow
Some wars between us and the Duke of Florence,
In which he hopes employment.
I never saw one in a stern bold look
Wear more command, nor in a lofty phrase
Express more knowing or more deep contempt
Of our slight airy courtiers. He talks
As if he had travelled all the princes' courts
Of Christendom: in all things strives to express,
That all that should dispute with him may know,
Glories, like glow-worms, afar off shine bright,
But looked to near, have neither heat nor light.—
The duke!

Re-enter BRACHIANO; *with* FRANCISCO DE MEDICIS *disguised
  like* MULINASSAR, LODOVICO, ANTONELLI, GASPARO,
  FARNESE, CARLO, *and* PEDRO, *bearing their swords
  and helmets; and* MARCELLO.

Brach. You are nobly welcome. We have heard at full
Your honourable service 'gainst the Turk.
To you, brave Mulinassar, we assign
A competent pension: and are inly sorry,
The vows of those two worthy gentlemen
Make them incapable of our proffered bounty.

Your wish is, you may leave your warlike swords
For monuments in our chapel: I accept it
As a great honour done me, and must crave
Your leave to furnish out our duchess' revels.
Only one thing, as the last vanity
You e'er shall view, deny me not to stay
To see a barriers prepared to-night:
You shall have private standings. It hath pleased
The great ambassadors of several princes,
In their return from Rome to their own countries,
To grace our marriage, and to honour me
With such a kind of sport.

    Fran. de Med. I shall persuade them
To stay, my lord.

    Brach. Set on there to the presence!

              [*Exeunt* BRACHIANO, FLAMINEO, MARCELLO,
                and HORTENSIO.

    Car. Noble my lord, most fortunately welcome:

              [*The* Conspirators *here embrace.*
You have our vows, sealed with the sacrament,
To second your attempts.

    Ped. And all things ready:
He could not have invented his own ruin
(Had he despaired) with more propriety.

    Lod. You would not take my way.

    Fran. de Med. 'Tis better ordered.

    Lod. To have poisoned his prayer-book, or a pair of
        beads,
The pummel of his saddle,[69] his looking-glass,
Or the handle of his racket,—O, that, that!
That while he had been bandying at tennis,
He might have sworn himself to hell, and strook
His soul into the hazard! O, my lord,
I would have our plot be ingenious,
And have it hereafter recorded for example,
Rather than borrow example.

    Fran. de Med. There's no way
More speeding than this thought on.

    Lod. On, then.

    Fran. de Med. And yet methinks that this revenge is poor,

<hr>

[69] In the year 1598 Edward Squire was convicted of anointing the pummel of
the Queen's saddle with poison, for which he was afterwards executed.—*Reed.*

Because it steals upon him like a thief.
To have ta'en him by the casque in a pitched field,
Led him to Florence!—

Lod. It had been rare: and there
Have crowned him with a wreath of stinking garlic,
To have shown the sharpness of his government
And rankness of his lust.—Flamineo comes.

[*Exeunt* LODOVICO, ANTONELLI, GASPARO,
FARNESE, CARLO, *and* PEDRO.

Re-enter FLAMINEO, MARCELLO, *and* ZANCHE.

Mar. Why doth this devil haunt you, say?
Flam. I know not;
For, by this light, I do not conjure for her.
'Tis not so great a cunning as men think,
To raise the devil; for here's one up already:
The greatest cunning were to lay him down.

Mar. She is your shame.
Flam. I prithee, pardon her.
In faith, you see, women are like to burs,
Where their affection throws them, there they'll stick.

Zan. That is my countryman, a goodly person:
When he's at leisure, I'll discourse with him
In our own language.

Flam. I beseech you do.   [*Exit* ZANCHE.
How is't, brave soldier? O, that I had seen
Some of your iron days! I pray, relate
Some of your service to us.

Fran. de Med. 'Tis a ridiculous thing for a man to be
his own chronicle: I did never wash my mouth with mine
own praise for fear of getting a stinking breath.

Mar. You're too stoical. The duke will expect other discourse from you.

Fran. de Med. I shall never flatter him: I have studied
man too much to do that. What difference is between the
duke and I? no more than between two bricks, all made
of one clay: only 't may be one is placed on the top of a
turret, the other in the bottom of a well, by mere chance.
If I were placed as high as the duke, I should stick as fast,
make as fair a show, and bear out weather equally.

Flam. [*Aside.*] If this soldier had a patent to beg in
churches, then he would tell them stories.

Mar. I have been a soldier too.

Fran. de Med. How have you thrived?

Mar. Faith, poorly.

Fran. de Med. That's the misery of peace: only outsides are then respected. As ships seem very great upon the river, which show very little upon the seas, so some men i' the court seem colossuses in a chamber, who, if they came into the field, would appear pitiful pigmies.

Flam. Give me a fair room yet hung with arras, and some great cardinal to lug me by the ears as his endeared minion.

Fran. de Med. And thou mayst do the devil knows what villany.

Flam. And safely.

Fran. de Med. Right: you shall see in the country, in harvest-time, pigeons, though they destroy never so much corn, the farmer dare not present the fowling-piece to them: why? because they belong to the lord of the manor; whilst your poor sparrows, that belong to the Lord of Heaven, they go to the pot for't.

Flam. I will now give you some politic instructions. The duke says he will give you a pension: that's but bare promise; get it under his hand. For I have known men that have come from serving against the Turk, for three or four months they have had pension to buy them new wooden legs and fresh plasters; but, after, 'twas not to be had. And this miserable courtesy shows as if a tormentor should give hot cordial drinks to one three quarters dead o' the rack, only to fetch the miserable soul again to endure more dog-days.   [*Exit* FRANCISCO DE MEDICIS.

Re-enter HORTENSIO *and* ZANCHE, *with a* Young Lord *and two others.*

How now, gallants! what, are they ready for the barriers?

Young Lord. Yes; the lords are putting on their armour.

Hort. What's he?

Flam. A new up-start; one that swears like a falconer, and will lie in the duke's ear day by day, like a maker of almanacs: and yet I knew him, since he came to the court, smell worse of sweat than an under-tennis-court-keeper.

Hort. Look you, yonder's your sweet mistress.

Flam. Thou art my sworn brother: I'll tell thee, I do

love that Moor, that witch, very constrainedly. She knows some of my villany. I do love her just as a man holds a wolf by the ears: but for fear of turning upon me and pulling out my throat, I would let her go to the devil.

Hort. I hear she claims marriage of thee.

Flam. Faith, I made to her some such dark promise; and, in seeking to fly from't, I run on, like a frighted dog with a bottle at's tail, that fain would bite it off, and yet dares not look behind him.—Now, my precious gipsey.

Zanche. Ay, your love to me rather cools than heats.

Flam. Marry, I am the sounder lover: we have many wenches about the town heat too fast.

Hort. What do you think of these perfumed gallants, then?

Flam. Their satin cannot save them: I am confident
They have a certain spice of the disease;
For they that sleep with dogs shall rise with fleas.

Zanche. Believe it, a little painting and gay clothes make you love me.

Flam. How! love a lady for painting or gay apparel? I'll unkennel one example more for thee. Æsop had a foolish dog that let go the flesh to catch the shadow: I would have courtiers be better divers.

Zanche. You remember your oaths?

Flam. Lovers' oaths are like mariners' prayers, uttered in extremity; but when the tempest is o'er, and that the vessel leaves tumbling, they fall from protesting to drinking. And yet, amongst gentlemen, protesting and drinking go together, and agree as well as shoemakers and West-phalia bacon: they are both drawers on; for drink draws on protestation, and protestation draws on more drink. Is not this discourse better now than the morality of your sunburnt gentleman?

Re-enter CORNELIA.

Cor. Is this your perch, you haggard? fly to the stews.
[*Striking* ZANCHE.

Flam. You should be clapt by the heels now: strike i'
the court! [*Exit* CORNELIA.

Zanche. She's good for nothing, but to make her maids
Catch cold a-nights: they dare not use a bed-staff
For fear of her light fingers.

Mar. You're a strumpet,
An impudent one.   [*Kicking* ZANCHE.

Flam. Why do you kick her, say?
Do you think that she is like a walnut tree?
Must she be cudgelled ere she bear good fruit?

Mar. She brags that you shall marry her.

Flam. What then?

Mar. I had rather she were pitched upon a stake
In some new-seeded garden, to affright
Her fellow crows thence.

Flam. You're a boy, a fool:
Be guardian to your hound; I am of age.

Mar. If I take her near you, I'll cut her throat.

Flam. With a fan of feathers?

Mar. And, for you, I'll whip
This folly from you.

Flam. Are you choleric?
I'll purge't with rhubarb.

Hort. O, your brother!

Flam. Hang him,
He wrongs me most that ought to offend me least.—
I do suspect my mother played foul play
When she conceived thee.

Mar. Now, by all my hopes,
Like the two slaughtered sons of Œdipus,
The very flames of our affection,
Shall turn two ways. Those words I'll make thee answer
With thy heart-blood.

Flam. Do, like the geese in the progress:
You know where you shall find me.

Mar. Very good.   [*Exit* FLAMINEO.
An thou be'st a noble friend, bear him my sword,
And bid him fit the length on't.

Young Lord. Sir, I shall.

          [*Exeunt* Young Lord, MARCELLO, HORTENSIO, *and
          the two others.*

Zanche. He comes. Hence petty thought of my disgrace!

Re-enter FRANCISCO DE MEDICIS.

I ne'er loved my complexion till now,
'Cause I may boldly say, without a blush,
I love you.

Fran. de Med. Your love is untimely sown; there's a
spring at Michaelmas, but 'tis but a faint one: I am sunk
in years, and I have vowed never to marry.

Zanche. Alas! poor maids get more lovers than husbands:
yet you may mistake my wealth. For, as when ambassadors
are sent to congratulate princes, there's commonly sent
along with them a rich present, so that, though the prince
like not the ambassador's person nor words, yet he likes
well of the presentment; so I may come to you in the
same manner, and be better loved for my dowry than my
virtue.

Fran. de Med. I'll think on the motion.

Zanche. Do: I'll now
Detain you no longer. At your better leisure
I'll tell you things shall startle your blood:
Nor blame me that this passion I reveal;
Lovers die inward that their flames conceal.   [*Exit.*

Fran. de Med. Of all intelligence this may prove the best:
Sure, I shall draw strange fowl from this foul nest.   [*Exit.*

SCENE II—*Another Apartment in the same*

Enter MARCELLO *and* CORNELIA.

Cor. I hear a whispering all about the court
You are to fight: who is your opposite?
What is the quarrel?

Mar. 'Tis an idle rumour.

Cor. Will you dissemble? sure, you do not well
To fright me thus: you never look thus pale,
But when you are most angry. I do charge you
Upon my blessing,—nay, I'll call the duke,
And he shall school you.

Mar. Publish not a fear
Which would convert to laughter: 'tis not so.
Was not this crucifix my father's?

Cor. Yes.

Mar. I have heard you say, giving my brother suck,
He took the crucifix between his hands,
And broke a limb off.

Cor. Yes; but 'tis mended.

Enter FLAMINEO.

Flam. I have brought your weapon back.

                         [*Runs* MARCELLO *through.*

Cor. Ha! O my horror!

Mar. You have brought it home, indeed.

Cor. Help! O, he's murdered!

Flam. Do you turn your gall up? I'll to sanctuary,
And send a surgeon to you.   [*Exit.*

Enter CARLO, HORTENSIO, *and* PEDRO.

Hort. How! o' the ground!

Mar. O mother, now remember what I told
Of breaking of the crucifix! Farewell.
There are some sins which Heaven doth duly punish
In a whole family. This it is to rise
By all dishonest means! Let all men know,
That tree shall long time keep a steady foot
Whose branches spread no wider than the root.   [*Dies.*

Cor. O my perpetual sorrow!

Hort. Virtuous Marcello!
He's dead.—Pray, leave him, lady: come, you shall.

Cor. Alas, he is not dead; he's in a trance. Why, here's
nobody shall get any thing by his death. Let me call him
again, for God's sake!

Car. I would you were deceived.

Cor. O, you abuse me, you abuse me, you abuse me!
How many have gone away thus, for lack of tendance!
Rear up's head, rear up's head: his bleeding inward will
kill him.

Hort. You see he is departed.

Cor. Let me come to him; give me him as he is: if
he be turned to earth, let me but give him one hearty kiss,
and you shall put us both into one coffin. Fetch a looking
glass; see if his breath will not stain it: or pull out some
feathers from my pillow, and lay them to his lips. Will
you lose him for a little pains-taking?

Hort. Your kindest office is to pray for him.

Cor. Alas, I would not pray for him yet. He may live
to lay me i' the ground, and pray for me, if you'll let me
come to him.

Enter BRACHIANO *all armed save the beaver, with* FLAMINEO,
FRANCISCO DE MEDICIS, LODOVICO, *and* Page.

Brach. Was this your handiwork?

Flam. It was my misfortune.

Cor. He lies, he lies; he did not kill him: these have
killed him that would not let him be better looked to.

Brach. Have comfort, my grieved mother.

Cor. O you screech-owl!

Hort. Forbear, good madam.

Cor. Let me go, let me go.

[*She runs to* FLAMINEO *with her knife drawn, and,
    coming to him, lets it fall.*

The God of Heaven forgive thee! Dost not wonder
I pray for thee? I'll tell thee what's the reason;
I have scarce breath to number twenty minutes;
I'd not spend that in cursing. Fare thee well:
Half of thyself lies there; and mayst thou live
To fill an hour-glass with his mouldered ashes,
To tell how thou shouldst spend the time to come
In blest repentance!

Brach.   Mother, pray tell me
How came he by his death? what was the quarrel?

Cor. Indeed, my younger boy presumed too much
Upon his manhood, gave him bitter words,
Drew his sword first; and so, I know not how,
For I was out of my wits, he fell with's head
Just in my bosom.

Page. This is not true, madam.

Cor. I pray thee, peace.
One arrow's grazed already: it were vain
To lose this for that will ne'er be found again.

Brach. Go bear the body to Cornelia's lodging:
And we command that none acquaint our duchess
With this sad accident. For you, Flamineo,
Hark you, I will not grant your pardon.

Flam. No?

Brach. Only a lease of your life; and that shall last
But for one day: thou shalt be forced each evening
To renew it, or be hanged.

Flam. At your pleasure.

[Lodovico *sprinkles* Brachiano's *beaver with a poison.*

Your will is law now, I'll not meddle with it.

Brach. You once did brave me in your sister's lodging;
I'll now keep you in awe for't.—Where's our beaver?

Fran. de Med. [*Aside*]. He calls for his destruction. No-
ble youth,
I pity thy sad fate! Now to the barriers.
This shall his passage to the black lake further;
The last good deed he did, he pardoned murther.

[*Exeunt.*

SCENE III—*The Lists at Padua*

*Charges and shouts. They fight at barriers; first single
pairs, then three to three.*

Enter Brachiano, Vittoria Corombona, Giovanni,
Francisco de Medicis, Flamineo, *with others.*

Brach. An armorer! ud's death, an armorer!

Flam. Armorer! where's the armorer?

Brach. Tear off my beaver.

Flam. Are you hurt, my lord?

Brach. O, my brain's on fire!

Enter Armorer.

The helmet is poisoned.

Armorer. My lord, upon my soul,—

Brach. Away with him to torture!
There are some great ones that have hand in this,
And near about me.

Vit. Cor. O my loved lord! poisoned!

Flam. Remove the bar. Here's unfortunate revels!
Call the physicians.

Enter two Physicians.

A plague upon you!
We have too much of your cunning here already:
I fear the ambassadors are likewise poisoned.

Brach. O, I am gone already! the infection
Flies to the brain and heart. O thou strong heart!
There's such a covenant 'tween the world and it,
They're loth to break.

Giov. O my most lovèd father!

Brach. Remove the boy away.—
Where's this good woman?—Had I infinite worlds,
They were too little for thee: must I leave thee?—
What say you, screech-owls, is the venom mortal?

1st Phys. Most deadly.

Brach. Most corrupted politic hangman,
You kill without book; but your art to save
Fails you as oft as great men's needy friends.
I that have given life to offending slaves
And wretched murderers, have I not power
To lengthen mine own a twelvemonth?—
Do not kiss me, for I shall poison thee.
This unction's sent from the great Duke of Florence.

Fran. de Med. Sir, be of comfort.

Brach. O thou soft natural death, that art joint-twin
To sweetest slumber! no rough-bearded comet
Stares on thy mild departure; the dull owl
Beats not against thy casement; the hoarse wolf
Scents not thy carrion: pity winds thy corse,
Whilst horror waits on princes.

Vit. Cor. I am lost for ever.

Brach. How miserable a thing it is to die
'Mongst women howling!

Enter LODOVICO *and* GASPARO, *in the habit of* Capuchins.

What are those?

Flam. Franciscans:
They have brought the extreme unction.

Brach. On pain of death, let no man name death to me:
It is a word infinitely terrible.
Withdraw into our cabinet.

[*Exeunt all except* FRANCISCO DE MEDICIS *and* FLAMINEO.

Flam. To see what solitariness is about dying princes! as heretofore they have unpeopled towns, divorced friends, and made great houses unhospitable, so now, O justice! where are their flatterers now? Flatterers are but the shadows of princes' bodies; the least thick cloud makes them invisible.

Fran. de Med. There's great moan made for him.

Flam. Faith, for some few hours salt-water will run most plentifully in every office o' the court: but, believe it, most of them do but weep over their stepmothers' graves.

Fran. de Med. How mean you?

Flam. Why, they dissemble; as some men do that live within compass o' the verge.

Fran. de Med. Come, you have thrived well under him.

Flam. Faith, like a wolf in a woman's breast; [70] I have been fed with poultry: but, for money, understand me, I had as good a will to cozen him as e'er an officer of them all; but I had not cunning enough to do it.

Fran. de Med. What didst thou think of him? faith, speak freely.

Flam. He was a kind of statesman that would sooner have reckoned how many cannon-bullets he had discharged against a town, to count his expence that way, than how many of his valiant and deserving subjects he lost before it.

Fran. de Med. O, speak well of the duke.

Flam. I have done. Wilt hear some of my court-wisdom? To reprehend princes is dangerous; and to over-commend some of them is palpable lying.

Re-enter LODOVICO.

Fran. de Med. How is it with the duke?

Lod. Most deadly ill.
He's fall'n into a strange distraction:
He talks of battles and monopolies,
Levying of taxes; and from that descends
To the most brain-sick language. His mind fastens
On twenty several objects, which confound
Deep sense with folly. Such a fearful end
May teach some men that bear too lofty crest,
Though they live happiest, yet they die not best.
He hath conferred the whole state of the dukedom
Upon your sister, till the prince arrive
At mature age.

Flam. There's some good luck in that yet.

[70] Alluding to a woman's longing during pregnancy.

Fran. de Med. See, here he comes.

Enter BRACHIANO, *presented in a bed,*[71] VITTORIA
COROMBONA, GASPARO, *and* Attendants.

There's death in's face already.

Vit. Cor. O my good lord!

Brach. Away! you have abused me:

[*These speeches are several kinds of distractions,*
and in the action should appear so.

You have conveyed coin forth our territories,
Bought and sold offices, oppressed the poor,
And I ne'er dreamt on't. Make up your accounts:
I'll now be mine own steward.

Flam. Sir, have patience.

Brach. Indeed, I am to blame:
For did you ever hear the dusky raven
Chide blackness? or was't ever known the devil
Railed against cloven creatures?

Vit. Cor. O my lord!

Brach. Let me have some quails to supper.

Flam. Sir, you shall.

Brach. No, some fried dog-fish; your quails feed on
    poison.
That old dog-fox, that politician, Florence!
I'll forswear hunting, and turn dog-killer:
Rare! I'll be friends with him; for, mark you, sir, one dog
Still sets another a-barking. Peace, peace!
Yonder's a fine slave come in now.

Flam. Where?

Brach. Why, there,
In a blue bonnet, and a pair of breeches
With a great cod-piece: ha, ha, ha!
Look you, his cod-piece is stuck full of pins,
With pearls o' the head of them. Do not you know him?

Flam. No, my lord.

Brach. Why, 'tis the devil;
I know him by a great rose[72] he wears on's shoe,
To hide his cloven foot. I'll dispute with him;

---

[71] Here the audience were to suppose that a change of scene had taken place—
that the stage now represented Brachiano's chamber: later on Gasparo says, "For
Christian charity, avoid the chamber."
[72] Rosette.

He's a rare linguist.

Vit. Cor. My lord, here's nothing.

Brach. Nothing! rare! nothing! when I want money,
Our treasury is empty, there is nothing:
I'll not be used thus.

Vit. Cor. O, lie still, my lord!

Brach. See, see Flamineo, that killed his brother,
Is dancing on the ropes there, and he carries
A money-bag in each hand, to keep him even,
For fear of breaking's neck: and there's a lawyer,
In a gown whipt with velvet, stares and gapes
When the money will fall. How the rogue cuts capers!
It should have been in a halter. 'Tis there: what's she?

Flam. Vittoria, my lord.

Brach. Ha, ha, ha! her hair is sprinkled with arras-
powder,[73]
That makes her look as if she had sinned in the pastry,—
What's he?

Flam. A divine, my lord,

> [BRACHIANO *seems here near his end:* LODOVICO *and*
> GASPARO, *in the habit of* Capuchins, *present him
> in his bed with a crucifix and hallowed candle.*

Brach. He will be drunk; avoid him: the argument
Is fearful, when churchmen stagger in't.
Look you, six grey rats, that have lost their tails,
Crawl up the pillow: send for a rat-catcher:
I'll do a miracle, I'll free the court
From all foul vermin. Where's Flamineo?

Flam. I do not like that he names me so often,
Especially on's death-bed: 'tis a sign   [*Aside.*
I shall not live long.—See, he's near his end.

Lod. Pray, give us leave.—*Attende, domine Brachiane.*

Flam. See, see how firmly he doth fix his eye
Upon the crucifix.

Vit. Cor. O, hold it constant!
'It settles his wild spirits; and so his eyes
Melt into tears.

*Lod. Domine Brachiane, solebas in bello tutus esse tuo
clypeo; nunc hunc clypeum hosti tuo opponas infernali.*
[*By the crucifix.*

73 Orris powder.

Gas. Olim hastâ valuisti in bello; nunc hanc sacram hastam vibrabis contra hostem animarum.

[*By the hallowed taper.*

Lod. Attende, domine Brachiane; si nunc quoque probas ea quæ acta sunt inter nos, flecte caput in dextrum.

Gas. Esto securus, domine Brachiane; cogita quantum habeas meritorum; denique memineris meam animam pro tuâ oppignoratam si quid esset periculi.

Lod. Si nunc quoque probas ea quæ acta sunt inter nos, flecte caput in lævum.—

He is departing: pray, stand all apart,
And let us only whisper in his ears
Some private meditations, which our order
Permits you not to hear.

[*Here, the rest being departed,* Lodovico *and* Gasparo *discover themselves.*

Gas. Brachiano,—

Lod. Devil Brachiano, thou art damned.

Gas. Perpetually.

Lod. A slave condemned and given up to the gallows
Is thy great lord and master.

Gas. True; for thou
Art given up to the devil.

Lod. O you slave!
You that were held the famous politician,
Whose art was poison!

Gas. And whose conscience, murder!

Lod. That would have broke your wife's neck down the
      stairs,
Ere she was poisoned!

Gas. That had your villanous salads!

Lod. And fine embroidered bottles and perfumes,
Equally mortal with a winter-plague!

Gas. Now there's mercury—

Lod. And copperas—

Gas. And quicksilver—

Lod. With other devilish pothecary stuff,
A-melting in your politic brains: dost hear?

Gas. This is Count Lodovico.

Lod. This, Gasparo:
And thou shalt die like a poor rogue.

Gas. And stink

Like a dead fly-blown dog.
   Lod. And be forgotten
Before thy funeral sermon.
   Brach. Vittoria!
Vittoria!
   Lod. O, the cursèd devil
Comes to himself again! we are undone.
   Gas. Strangle him in private.

     Enter Vittoria Corombona, Francisco de Medicis,
       Flamineo, *and* Attendants.

                What, will you call him again
To live in treble torments? for charity,
For Christian charity, avoid the chamber.

     [*Exeunt* Vittoria Corombona, Francisco de Medicis,
       Flamineo, *and* Attendants.

   Lod. You would prate, sir? This is a true-love knot
Sent from the Duke of Florence.

                [*He strangles* Brachiano.

   Gas. What, is it done?
   Lod. The snuff is out. No woman-keeper i' the world,
Though she had practised seven year at the pest-house,
Could have done't quaintlier.

     Re-enter Vittoria Corombona, Francisco de Medicis,
       Flamineo, *and* Attendants.

                 My lords, he's dead.
   Omnes. Rest to his soul!
   Vit. Cor. O me! this place is hell.   [*Exit.*
   Fran. de Med. How heavily she takes it!
   Flam. O, yes, yes;
Had women navigable rivers in their eyes,
They would dispend them all: surely, I wonder
Why we should wish more rivers to the city,
When they sell water so good cheap. I'll tell thee,
These are but moonish shades of griefs or fears;
There's nothing sooner dry than women's tears.
Why, here's an end of all my harvest; he has given me
     nothing.
Court promises! let wise men count them cursed,
For while you live, he that scores best pays worst.
   Fran. de Med. Sure, this was Florence' doing.

Flam. Very likely.
Those are found weighty strokes which come from the
hand,
But those are killing strokes which come from the head.
O, the rare tricks of a Machiavelian!
He doth not come, like a gross plodding slave,
And buffet you to death: no, my quaint knave,
He tickles you to death, makes you die laughing,
As if you had swallowed down a pound of saffron.
You see the feat, 'tis practised in a trice;
To teach court honesty, it jumps on ice.

Fran. de Med. Now have the people liberty to talk,
And descant on his vices.

Flam. Misery of princes,
That must of force be censured by their slaves!
Not only blamed for doing things are ill,
But for not doing all that all men will:
One were better be a thresher.
Ud's death, I would fain speak with this duke yet.

Fran. de Med. Now he's dead?

Flam. I cannot conjure; but if prayers or oaths
Will get to the speech of him, though forty devils
Wait on him in his livery of flames,
I'll speak to him, and shake him by the hand,
Though I be blasted.   [*Exit.*

Fran. de Med. Excellent Lodovico!
What, did you terrify him at the last gasp?

Lod. Yes, and so idly, that the duke had like
To have terrified us.

Fran. de Med. How?

Lod. You shall hear that hereafter.

Enter ZANCHE.

See, yon's the infernal that would make up sport.
Now to the revelation of that secret
She promised when she fell in love with you.

Fran. de Med. You're passionately met in this sad world.

Zanche. I would have you look up, sir; these court-tears
Claim not your tribute to them: let those weep
That guiltily partake in the sad cause.
I knew last night, by a sad dream I had,
Some mischief would ensue; yet, to say truth,

My dream most concerned you.

 Lod. Shall's fall a-dreaming?

 Fran. de Med. Yes; and for fashion sake I'll dream with
her.

 Zanche. Methought, sir, you came stealing to my bed.

 Fran. de Med. Wilt thou believe me, sweeting? by this
light,

I was a-dreamt on thee too; for methought

I saw thee naked.

 Zanche. Fie, sir! As I told you,

Methought you lay down by me.

 Fran. de Med. So dreamt I;

And lest thou shouldst take cold, I covered thee

With this Irish mantle.

 Zanche. Verily, I did dream

You were somewhat bold with me: but to come to't—

 Lod. How, how! I hope you will not go to't here.

 Fran. de Med. Nay, you must hear my dream out.

 Zanche. Well, sir, forth.

 Fran. de Med. When I threw the mantle o'er thee, thou
didst laugh

Exceedingly, methought.

 Zanche. Laugh!

 Fran. de Med. And cried'st out,

The hair did tickle thee.

 Zanche. There was a dream indeed!

 Lod. Mark her, I prithee; she simpers like the suds

A collier hath been washed in.

 Zanche. Come, sir, good fortune tends you. I did tell you

I would reveal a secret: Isabella,

The Duke of Florence' sister, was impoisoned

By a fumed picture; and Camillo's neck

Was broke by damned Flamineo, the mischance

Laid on a vaulting-horse.

 Fran. de Med. Most strange!

 Zanche. Most true.

 Lod. The bed of snakes is broke.

 Zanche. I sadly do confess I had a hand

In the black deed.

 Fran. de Med. Thou kept'st their counsel?

 Zanche. Right;

For which, urged with contrition, I intend

This night to rob Vittoria.

Lod. Excellent penitence!
Usurers dream on't while they sleep out sermons.

Zanche. To further our escape, I have entreated
Leave to retire me, till the funeral,
Unto a friend i' the country: that excuse
Will further our escape. In coin and jewels
I shall at least make good unto your use
An hundred thousand crowns.

Fran. de Med. O noble wench!

Lod. Those crowns we'll share.

Zanche. It is a dowry,
Methinks, should make that sun-burnt proverb false,
And wash the Æthiop white.

Fran. de Med. It shall. Away!

Zanche. Be ready for our flight.

Fran. de Med. An hour 'fore day.   [*Exit* ZANCHE.
O strange discovery! why, till now we knew not
The circumstance of either of their deaths.

Re-enter ZANCHE.

Zanche. You'll wait about midnight in the chapel?

Fran. de Med. There.   [*Exit* ZANCHE.

Lod. Why, now our action's justified.

Fran. de Med. Tush for justice!
What harms it justice? we now, like the partridge,
Purge the disease with laurel; [74] for the fame
Shall crown the enterprize, and quit the shame.   [*Exeunt.*

SCENE IV—*An Apartment in a Palace at Padua*

Enter FLAMINEO *and* GASPARO, *at one door; another way,*
GIOVANNI, *attended.*

Gas. The young duke: did you e'er see a sweeter prince?

Flam. I have known a poor woman's bastard better
favoured; this is behind him; now, to his face, all com-
parisons were hateful. Wise was the courtly peacock that,
being a great minion, and being compared for beauty by

74 See Pliny, Nat. Hist., viii. 27.

some dottrels,[75] that stood by to the kingly eagle, said the
eagle was a far fairer bird than herself, not in respect of
her feathers, but in respect of her long talons: his will
grow out in time.—My gracious lord!

Gio. I pray, leave me, sir.

Flam. Your grace must be merry: 'tis I have cause to
mourn; for, wot you, what said the little boy that rode
behind his father on horseback?

Gio. Why, what said he?

Flam. "When you are dead, father," said he, "I hope
that I shall ride in the saddle." O, 'tis a brave thing for
a man to sit by himself! he may stretch himself in the
stirrups, look about, and see the whole compass of the
hemisphere. You're now, my lord, i' the saddle.

Gio. Study your prayers, sir, and be penitent:
'Twere fit you'd think on what hath former bin;
I have heard grief named the eldest child of sin.   [*Exit.*

Flam. Study my prayers! he threatens me divinely:
I am falling to pieces already. I care not though, like
Anacharsis, I were pounded to death in a mortar: and yet
that death were fitter for usurers, gold and themselves to
be beaten together, to make a most cordial cullis[76] for the
devil.
He hath his uncle's villainous look already,
In decimo sexto.

Enter Courtier.

Now, sir, what are you?

Cour. It is the pleasure, sir, of the young duke,
That you forbear the presence, and all rooms
That owe him reverence.

Flam. So, the wolf and the raven
Are very pretty fools when they are young.
Is it your office, sir, to keep me out?

Cour. So the duke wills.

Flam. Verily, master courtier, extremity is not to be used
in all offices: say that a gentlewoman were taken out of
her bed about midnight, and committed to Castle Angelo,
or to the tower yonder, with nothing about her but her
smock, would it not show a cruel part in the gentleman-

---

[75] A species of plover.
[76] Strong broth.

porter to lay claim to her upper garment, pull it o'er her
head and ears, and put her in naked?

Cour. Very good: you are merry.   [*Exit.*

Flam. Doth he make a court-ejectment of me? a flaming
fire-brand casts more smoke without a chimney than
within't. I'll smoor[77] some of them.

Enter FRANCISCO DE MEDICIS.

How now! thou art sad.

Fran. de Med. I met even now with the most piteous
        sight.

Flam. Thou meet'st another here, a pitiful
Degraded courtier.

Fran. de Med. Your reverend mother
Is grown a very old woman in two hours.
I found them winding of Marcello's corse;
And there is such a solemn melody,
'Tween doleful songs, tears, and sad elegies,—
Such as old grandams watching by the dead
Were wont to outwear the nights with,—that, believe me,
I had no eyes to guide me forth the room,
They were so o'ercharged with water.

Flam. I will see them.

Fran. de Med. 'Twere much uncharity in you; for your
        sight
Will add unto their tears.

Flam. I will see them:
They are behind the traverse;[78] I'll discover
Their superstitious howling.   [*Draws the curtain.*

CORNELIA, ZANCHE, *and three other* Ladies *discovered
winding* MARCELLO'S *corse. A Song.*

Cor. This rosemary is withered; pray, get fresh.
I would have these herbs grow up in his grave,
When I am dead and rotten. Reach the bays,
I'll tie a garland here about his head;
'Twill keep my boy from lightning. This sheet
I have kept this twenty year, and every day
Hallowed it with my prayers: I did not think
He should have wore it.

Zanche. Look you who are yonder.

[77] Smother.
[78] A curtain on the stage.

Cor. O, reach me the flowers.

Zanche. Her ladyship's foolish.

Lady. Alas, her grief
Hath turned her child again!

Cor. You're very welcome:
There's rosemary for you;—and rue for you;—

[*To* FLAMINEO.

Heart's-ease for you; I pray make much of it:
I have left more for myself.

Fran. de Med. Lady, who's this?

Cor. You are, I take it, the grave-maker.

Flam. So.

Zanche. 'Tis Flamineo.

Cor. Will you make me such a fool? here's a white hand:
Can blood so soon be washed out? let me see;
When screech-owls croak upon the chimney-tops,
And the strange cricket i' the oven sings and hops,
When yellow spots do on your hands appear,
Be certain then you of a corse shall hear.
Out upon't, how 'tis speckled! h'as handled a toad, sure.
Cowslip-water is good for the memory:
Pray, buy me three ounces of't.

Flam. I would I were from hence.

Cor. Do you hear, sir?
I'll give you a saying which my grandmother
Was wont, when she heard the bell toll, to sing o'er
Unto her lute.

Flam. Do, an you will, do.

Cor. "Call for the robin-red-breast and the wren,

[CORNELIA *doth this in several forms of distraction.*

Since o'er shady groves they hover,
And with leaves and flowers do cover
The friendless bodies of unburied men.
Call unto his funeral dole
The ant, the field-mouse, and the mole,
To rear him hillocks that shall keep him warm,
And (when gay tombs are robbed) sustain no harm:
But keep the wolf far thence, that's foe to men,
For with his nails he'll dig them up again." [79]

---

[79] "I never saw anything like this dirge, except the ditty which reminds Ferdinand of his drowned father in the Tempest. As that is of the water, watery; so this is of the earth, earthy. Both have that intenseness of feeling, which seems to resolve itself into the elements which it contemplates."—C. LAMB. *Spec. of Eng. Dram. Poets.*

They would not bury him 'cause he died in a quarrel;
But I have an answer for them:
    "Let holy church receive him duly,
    Since he paid the church-tithes truly."
His wealth is summed, and this is all his store,
This poor men get, and great men get no more.
Now the wares are gone, we may shut up shop.
Bless you all, good people.

                    [*Exeunt* CORNELIA, ZANCHE, *and* Ladies.

Flam. I have a strange thing in me, to the which
I cannot give a name, without it be
Compassion. I pray, leave me.

                    [*Exit* FRANCISCO DE MEDICIS.

This night I'll know the utmost of my fate;
I'll be resolved [80] what my rich sister means
To assign me for my service. I have lived
Riotously ill, like some that live in court,
And sometimes when my face was full of smiles,
Have felt the maze of conscience in my breast.
Oft gay and honoured robes those tortures try:
We think caged birds sing, when indeed they cry.

Enter BRACHIANO's *ghost, in his leather cassock and breeches,
    boots and cowl; in his hand a pot of lily-flowers, with
    a skull in it.*

Ha! I can stand thee: nearer, nearer yet.
What a mockery hath death made thee! thou look'st sad.
In what place art thou? in yon starry gallery?
Or in the cursèd dungeon?—No? not speak?
Pray, sir, resolve me, what religion's best
For a man to die in? or is it in your knowledge
To answer me how long I have to live?
That's the most necessary question.
Not answer? are you still like some great men
That only walk like shadows up and down,
And to no purpose? say:—

                    [*The* Ghost *throws earth upon him, and shows
                        him the skull.*

What's that? O, fatal! he throws earth upon me!
A dead man's skull beneath the roots of flowers!—
I pray, speak, sir: our Italian churchmen
Make us believe dead men hold conference

[80] Assured.

With their familiars, and many times
Will come to bed to them, and eat with them.

            [*Exit* Ghost.

He's gone; and see, the skull and earth are vanished.
This is beyond melancholy. I do dare my fate
To do its worst. Now to my sister's lodging,
And sum up all these horrors: the disgrace
The prince threw on me; next the piteous sight
Of my dead brother; and my mother's dotage;
And last this terrible vision: all these
Shall with Vittoria's bounty turn to good,
Or I will drown this weapon in her blood.   [*Exit.*

SCENE V—*A Street in Padua*

Enter Francisco de Medicis, Lodovico, *and* Hortensio.

 Lod. My lord, upon my soul, you shall no further;
You have most ridiculously engaged yourself
Too far already. For my part, I have paid
All my debts; so, if I should chance to fall,
My creditors fall not with me; and I vow
To quit all in this bold assembly
To the meanest follower. My lord, leave the city,
Or I'll forswear the murder.   [*Exit.*

 Fran. de Med. Farewell, Lodovico:
If thou dost perish in this glorious act,
I'll rear unto thy memory that fame
Shall in the ashes keep alive thy name.   [*Exit.*

 Hor. There's some black deed on foot. I'll presently
Down to the citadel, and raise some force.
These strong court-factions, that do brook no checks,
In the career oft break the riders' necks.   [*Exit.*

SCENE VI—*An Apartment in* Vittoria's *House*

Enter Vittoria Corombona *with a book in her hand, and*
Zanche; Flamineo *following them.*

 Flam. What, are you at your prayers? give o'er.
 Vit. Cor. How, ruffian!

Flam. I come to you 'bout worldly business:
Sit down, sit down:—nay, stay, blouze,[81] you may hear
it:—
The doors are fast enough.

Vit. Cor. Ha, are you drunk?

Flam. Yes, yes, with wormwood-water: you shall taste
Some of it presently.

Vit. Cor. What intends the Fury?

Flam. You are my lord's executrix; and I claim
Reward for my long service.

Vit. Cor. For your service!

Flam. Come, therefore, here is pen and ink; set down
What you will give me.

Vit. Cor. There.   [*Writes.*

Flam. Ha! have you done already?
'Tis a most short conveyance.

Vit. Cor. I will read it: [*Reads.*
"I give that portion to thee, and no other,
Which Cain groaned under, having slain his brother."

Flam. A most courtly patent to beg by!

Vit. Cor. You are a villain.

Flam. Is't come to this? They say, affrights cure agues:
Thou hast a devil in thee; I will try
If I can scare him from thee. Nay, sit still:
My lord hath left me yet two case[82] of jewels
Shall make me scorn your bounty; you shall see them.

                                                      [*Exit.*

Vit. Cor. Sure, he's distracted.

Zanche. O, he's desperate:
For your own safety give him gentle language.

Re-enter FLAMINEO *with two case of pistols.*

Flam. Look, these are better far at a dead lift
Than all your jewel-house.

Vit. Cor. And yet, methinks,
These stones have no air lustre, they are ill set.

Flam. I'll turn the right side towards you: you shall see
How they will sparkle.

Vit. Cor. Turn this horror from me!
What do you want? what would you have me do?

[81] A low term for women.
[82] Pir.

Is not all mine yours? have I any children?

Flam. Pray thee, good woman, do not trouble me
With this vain worldly business; say your prayers:
I made a vow to my deceasèd lord,
Neither yourself nor I should outlive him
The numbering of four hours.

Vit. Cor. Did he enjoin it?

Flam. He did; and 'twas a deadly jealousy,
Lest any should enjoy thee after him,
That urged him vow me to it. For my death,
I did propound it voluntarily, knowing,
If he could not be safe in his own court,
Being a great duke, what hope, then, for us?

Vit. Cor. This is your melancholy and despair.

Flam. Away!
Fool thou art to think that politicians
Do use to kill the effects of injuries
And let the cause live. Shall we groan in irons,
Or be a shameful and a weighty burden
To a public scaffold? This is my resolve;
I would not live at any man's entreaty,
Nor die at any's bidding.

Vit. Cor. Will you hear me?

Flam. My life hath done service to other men;
My death shall serve mine own turn. Make you ready.

Vit. Cor. Do you mean to die indeed?

Flam. With as much pleasure
As e'er my father gat me.

Vit. Cor. Are the doors locked?

Zanche. Yes, madam.

Vit. Cor. Are you grown an atheist? will you turn your
        body,
Which is the goodly palace of the soul,
To the soul's slaughter-house? O, the cursèd devil,
Which doth present us with all other sins
Thrice-candied o'er; despair with gall and stibium;
Yet we carouse it off;—Cry out for help!—
                                    [*Aside to* ZANCHE.
Makes us forsake that which was made for man,
The world, to sink to that was made for devils,
Eternal darkness!

Zanche. Help, help!

Flam. I'll stop your throat
With winter-plums.

Vit. Cor. I prithee, yet remember,
Millions are now in graves, which at last day
Like mandrakes shall rise shrieking.[83]

Flam. Leave your prating,
For these are but grammatical laments,
Feminine arguments: and they move me,
As some in pulpits move their auditory,
More with their exclamation than sense
Of reason or sound doctrine.

Zanche [*Aside to* VIT.]. Gentle madam,
Seem to consent, only persuade him teach
The way to death; let him die first.

Vit. Cor. 'Tis good. I apprehend it,
To kill one's self is meat that we must take
Like pills, not chew't, but quickly swallow it;
The smart o' the wound, or weakness of the hand,
May else bring treble torments.

Flam. I have held it
A wretched and most miserable life
Which is not able to die.

Vit. Cor. O, but frailty!
Yet I am now resolved: farewell, affliction!
Behold, Brachiano, I that while you lived
Did make a flaming altar of my heart
To sacrifice unto you, now am ready
To sacrifice heart and all.—Farewell, Zanche!

Zanche. How, madam! do you think that I'll outlive you;
Especially when my best self, Flamineo,
Goes the same voyage?

Flam. O, most lovèd Moor!

Zanche. Only by all my love let me entreat you,—
Since it is most necessary one of us
Do violence on ourselves,—let you or I
Be her sad taster, teach her how to die.

Flam. Thou dost instruct me nobly: take these pistols,
Because my hand is stained with blood already:
Two of these you shall level at my breast,
The other 'gainst your own, and so we'll die

---

[83] This plant, respecting which many superstitions prevailed, was said to give a loud shriek when it was torn up.

Most equally contented: but first swear
Not to outlive me.

Vit. Cor. and Zanche. Most religiously.

Flam. Then here's an end of me; farewell, daylight!
And, O contemptible physic, that dost take
So long a study, only to preserve
So short a life, I take my leave of thee!—
These are two cupping-glasses that shall draw

                               [Showing the pistols.

All my infected blood out. Are you ready?

Vit. Cor. and Zanche. Ready.

Flam. Whither shall I go now? O Lucian, thy ridiculous
purgatory! to find Alexander the Great cobbling shoes,
Pompey tagging points, and Julius Cæsar making hair-
buttons! Hannibal selling blacking, and Augustus crying
garlic! Charlemagne selling lists by the dozen, and King
Pepin crying apples in a cart drawn with one horse!
Whether I resolve to fire, earth, water, air,
Or all the elements by scruples, I know not,
Nor greatly care.—Shoot, shoot:
Of all deaths the violent death is best;
For from ourselves it steals ourselves so fast,
The pain, once apprehended, is quite past.

    *[They shoot: he falls; and they run to him, and tread
        upon him.*

Vit. Cor. What, are you dropt?

Flam. I am mixed with earth already: as you are noble,
Perform your vows, and bravely follow me.

Vit. Cor. Whither? to hell?

Zanche. To most assured damnation?

Vit. Cor. O thou most cursèd devil!

Zanche. Thou art caught—

Vit. Cor. In thine own engine. I tread the fire out
That would have been my ruin.

Flam. Will you be perjured? what a religious oath was
Styx, that the gods never durst swear by, and violate! O,
that we had such an oath to minister, and to be so well
kept in our courts of justice!

Vit. Cor. Think whither thou art going.

Zanche. And remember
What villanies thou hast acted.

Vit. Cor. This thy death

Shall make me like a blazing ominous star:
Look up and tremble.

 Flam. O, I am caught with a springe!

 Vit. Cor. You see the fox comes many times short home;
'Tis here proved true.

 Flam. Killed with a couple of braches! [84]

 Vit. Cor. No fitter offering for the infernal Furies
Than one in whom they reigned while he was living.

 Flam. O, the way's dark and horrid! I cannot. see:
Shall I have no company?

 Vit. Cor. O, yes, thy sins
Do run before thee to fetch fire from hell,
To light thee thither.

 Flam. O, I smell soot,
Most stinking soot! the chimney is a-fire:
My liver's parboiled, like Scotch holly-bread;
There's a plumber laying pipes in my guts, it scalds.—
Wilt thou outlive me?

 Zanche. Yes, and drive a stake
Through thy body; for we'll give it out
Thou didst this violence upon thyself.

 Flam. O cunning devils! now I have tried your love,
And doubled all your reaches.—I am not wounded;

             [Rises.
The pistols held no bullets: 'twas a plot
To prove your kindness to me; and I live
To punish your ingratitude. I knew,
One time or other, you would find a way
To give me a strong potion.—O men
That lie upon your death-beds, and are haunted
With howling wives, ne'er trust them! they'll re-marry
Ere the worm pierce your winding-sheet, ere the spider
Make a thin curtain for your epitaphs.—
How cunning you were to discharge! do you practise at
the Artillery-yard?—Trust a woman! never, never! Brachi-
ano be my precedent. We lay our souls to pawn to the
devil for a little pleasure, and a woman makes the bill of
sale. That ever man should marry! For one Hypermnestra[85]
that saved her lord and husband, forty-nine of her sisters

---

[84] Bitch-hounds.
[85] One of the fifty daughters of Danaus, the son of Belus, brother of Ægyptus.
She preserved her husband Lynceus, who afterwards slew Danaus.

cut their husbands' throats all in one night: there was a
shoal of virtuous horse-leeches!—Here are two other instruments.

Vit. Cor. Help, help!

Enter LODOVICO, GASPARO, PEDRO, *and* CARLO.

Flam. What noise is that? ha! false keys i' the court!
Lod. We have brought you a mask.
Flam. A matachin,[86] it seems by your drawn swords.
Churchmen turned revellers!

Carlo. Isabella! Isabella!
Lod. Do you know us now?
Flam. Lodovico! and Gasparo!
Lod. Yes; and that Moor the duke gave pension to
Was the great Duke of Florence.

Vit. Cor. O, we are lost!
Flam. You shall not take justice from forth my hands,—
O, let me kill her!—I'll cut my safety
Through your coats of steel. Fate's a spaniel,
We cannot beat it from us. What remains now?
Let all that do ill, take this precedent,—
Man may his fate foresee, but not prevent:
And of all axioms this shall win the prize,—
'Tis better to be fortunate than wise.

Gas. Bind him to the pillar.
Vit. Cor. O, your gentle pity!
I have seen a blackbird that would sooner fly
To a man's bosom, than to stay the gripe
Of the fierce sparrowhawk.

Gas. Your hope deceives you.
Vit. Cor. If Florence be i' the court, would he would kill
me!

Gas. Fool! princes give rewards with their own hands,
But death or punishment by the hands of others.

Lod. Sirrah, you once did strike me: I'll strike you
Into the centre.

Flam. Thou'lt do it like a hangman, a base hangman,
Not like a noble fellow; for thou see'st
I cannot strike again.

Lod. Dost laugh?

---

[86] A French and Italian sword dance of fools.

Flam. Would'st have me die, as I was born, in whining?

Gas. Recommend yourself to Heaven.

Flam. No, I will carry mine own commendations thither.

Lod. O, could I kill you forty times a day,
And use't four year together, 'twere too little!
Naught grieves but that you are too few to feed
The famine of our vengeance. What dost think on?

Flam. Nothing; of nothing: leave thy idle questions.
I am i' the way to study a long silence:
To prate were idle. I remember nothing.
There's nothing of so infinite vexation
As man's own thoughts.

Lod. O thou glorious strumpet!
Could I divide thy breath from this pure air
When't leaves thy body, I would suck it up,
And breathe't upon some dunghill.

Vit. Cor. You, my death's-man!
Methinks thou dost not look horrid enough,
Thou hast too good a face to be a hangman:
If thou be, do thy office in right form;
Fall down upon thy knees, and ask forgiveness.

Lod. O, thou hast been a most prodigious comet
But I'll cut off your train,—kill the Moor first.

Vit. Cor. You shall not kill her first; behold my breast:
I will be waited on in death; my servant
Shall never go before me.

Gas. Are you so brave?

Vit. Cor. Yes, I shall welcome death
As princes do some great ambassadors;
I'll meet thy weapon half way.

Lod. Thou dost tremble:
Methinks fear should dissolve thee into air.

Vit. Cor. O, thou art deceived, I am too true a woman:
Conceit can never kill me. I'll tell thee what,
I will not in my death shed one base tear;
Or if look pale, for want of blood, not fear.

Carlo. Thou art my task, black Fury.

Zanche. I have blood
As red as either of theirs: wilt drink some?
'Tis good for the falling-sickness. I am proud
Death cannot alter my complexion,
For I shall ne'er look pale.

Lod. Strike, strike,
With a joint motion.

[*They stab* VITTORIA, ZANCHE, *and* FLAMINEO.

Vit. Cor. 'Twas a manly blow:
The next thou giv'st, murder some sucking infant;
And then thou wilt be famous.

Flam. O, what blade is't?
A Toledo, or an English fox? [87]
I ever thought a cutler should distinguish
The cause of my death, rather than a doctor.
Search my wound deeper; tent it with the steel
That made it.

Vit. Cor. O, my greatest sin lay in my blood!
Now my blood pays for't.

Flam. Thou'rt a noble sister!
I love thee now: if woman do breed man,
She ought to teach him manhood: fare thee well.
Know, many glorious women that are famed
For masculine virtue have been vicious,
Only a happier silence did betide them:
She hath no faults who hath the art to hide them.

Vit. Cor. My soul, like to a ship in a black storm,
Is driven, I know not whither.

Flam. Then cast anchor.
Prosperity doth bewitch men, seeming clear;
But seas do laugh, show white, when rocks are near.
We cease to grieve, cease to be fortune's slaves,
Nay, cease to die, by dying. Art thou gone?
And thou so near the bottom? false report,
Which says that women vie with the nine Muses
For nine tough durable lives! I do not look
Who went before, nor who shall follow me;
No, at myself I will begin and end.
While we look up to Heaven, we confound
Knowledge with knowledge. O, I am in a mist!

Vit. Cor. O, happy they that never saw the court,
Nor ever knew great men but by report!   [*Dies.*

Flam. I recover like a spent taper, for a flash,
And instantly go out.
Let all that belong to great men remember the old wives'
tradition, to be like the lions i' the Tower on Candlemas-

[87] Slang for "sword."

day: to mourn if the sun shine, for fear of the pitiful re-
mainder of winter to come.
'Tis well yet there's some goodness in my death;
My life was a black charnel. I have caught
An everlasting cold; I have lost my voice
Most irrecoverably. Farewell, glorious villains!
This busy trade of life appears most vain,
Since rest breeds rest, where all seek pain by pain.
Let no harsh flattering bells resound my knell;
Strike, thunder, and strike loud, to my farewell!   [Dies.
    Eng. Am. [*Within*]. This way, this way! break ope the
        doors! this way!
    Lod. Ha! are we betrayed?
Why, then let's constantly die all together;
And having finished this most noble deed,
Defy the worst of fate, not fear to bleed.

        Enter Ambassadors *and* GIOVANNI.

    Eng. Am. Keep back the prince: shoot, shoot.
        [*They shoot, and* LODOVICO *falls.*
    Lod. O, I am wounded!
I fear I shall be ta'en.
    Gio. You bloody villains,
By what authority have you committed
This massacre?
    Lod. By thine.
    Gio. Mine?
    Lod. Yes; thy uncle,
Which is a part of thee, enjoined us to't:
Thou know'st me, I am sure; I am Count Lodowick;
And thy most noble uncle in disguise
Was last night in thy court.
    Gio. Ha!
    Carlo. Yes, that Moor
Thy father chose his pensioner.
    Gio. He turned murderer!—
Away with them to prison and to torture!
All that have hands in this shall taste our justice,
As I hope Heaven.
    Lod. I do glory yet
That I can call this act mine own. For my part,
The rack, the gallows, and the torturing wheel,

Shall be but sound sleeps to me: here's my rest;
I limned this night-piece, and it was my best.

Gio. Remove the bodies.—See, my honoured lords,
What use you ought make of their punishment:
Let guilty men remember, their black deeds
Do lean on crutches made of slender reeds. [*Exeunt.*

Instead of an EPILOGUE, only this of Martial
supplies me:

Hæc fuerint nobis præmia, si placui.[88]

FOR the action of the play, 'twas generally well, and I dare
affirm, with the joint-testimony of some of their own quality,
for the true imitation of life, without striving to make
nature a monster, the best that ever became them: whereof
as I make a general acknowledgment, so in particular I
must remember the well-approved industry of my friend
Master Perkins,[89] and confess the worth of his action did
crown both the beginning and end.

[88] Martial ii. 91.
[89] An actor of considerable eminence, who is supposed to have originally played
the part of Brachiano. He is known to have been the original performer of
Captain Goodlack in Heywood's *Fair Maid of the West*, of Sir John Belfare in
Shirley's *Wedding*, and of Hanno in Nabbes's *Hannibal and Scipio*. When
Marlowe's *Jew of Malta* was revived about 1633 Perkins acted Barabas.

THE DUCHESS OF MALFI

WEBSTER's tragedy of *The Duchess of Malfi*—"the perfect and exact Copy, with diverse things printed, that the length of the Play would not bear in the Presentment"—was printed in 1623, having been acted by the King's servants at Blackfriars and the Globe, Burbadge playing the part of Ferdinand. It was printed again in 1640 and in 1678. Theobald published an adaptation of it, called *The Fatal Secret,* in 1735. *The Duchess of Malfi* was revived at the Haymarket in 1707, and again at Sadler's Wells in 1850. Concerning its performance at the latter theatre Professor Ward remarks, "I remember, not many years ago, seeing *The Duchess of Malfi* well acted by Miss Glyn; the impression which the tragedy produces on the stage is indescribable."

The story of this play is in the *Novelle* of Bendello, Part I., N. 26. Through Belleforest's French version it found its way into Paynter's *Palace of Pleasure*. Lope de Vega in 1618 wrote *El Mayordomo de la Duquesa de Amalfi.*

To the Rt. Hon. GEORGE HARDING, Baron Berkeley,[1]
Of Berkeley Castle, and Knight of the Order of the Bath to the
illustrious Prince Charles.

My Noble Lord,

THAT I may present my excuse why, being a stranger to your
lordship, I offer this poem to your patronage, I plead this warrant:—men who never saw the sea yet desire to behold that regi-
ment of waters, choose some eminent river to guide them thither,
and make that, as it were, their conduct or postilion: by the like
ingenious means has your fame arrived at my knowledge, receiving it from some of worth, who both in contemplation and
practice owe to your honour their clearest service. I do not altogether look up at your title; the ancientest nobility being but
a relic of time past, and the truest honour indeed being for a
man to confer honour on himself, which your learning strives
to propagate, and shall make you arrive at the dignity of a
great example. I am confident this work is not unworthy your
honour's perusal; for by such poems as this poets have kissed the
hands of great princes, and drawn their gentle eyes to look down
upon their sheets of paper when the poets themselves were bound
up in their winding-sheets. The like courtesy from your lordship
shall make you live in your grave, and laurel spring out of it,
when the ignorant scorners of the Muses, that like worms in
libraries seem to live only to destroy learning, shall wither
neglected and forgotten. This work and myself I humbly present to your approved censure, it being the utmost of my wishes
to have your honourable self my weighty and perspicuous comment; which grace so done me shall ever be acknowledged

By your lordship's in all duty and observance,

JOHN WEBSTER.

COMMENDATORY VERSES

IN THE JUST WORTH OF THAT WELL-DESERVER, MR. JOHN
WEBSTER, AND UPON THIS MASTER-PIECE OF TRAGEDY.

In this thou imitat'st one rich and wise,
That sees his good deeds done before he dies:
As he by works, thou by this work of fame
Hath well provided for thy living name.

[1] The twelfth Lord Berkeley. "My good lord," says Massinger, inscribing *The
Renegado* to him, "to be honoured for old nobility or hereditary titles, is not
alone proper to yourself, but to some few of your rank, who may challenge
the like privilege with you: but in our age to vouchsafe (as you have often
done) a ready hand to raise the dejected spirits of the contemned sons of the
Muses, such as would not suffer the glorious fire of poesy to be wholly extinguished, is so remarkable and peculiar to your lordship, that, with a full
vote and suffrage, it is acknowledged that the patronage and protection of the
dramatic poem is yours and almost without a rival."

To trust to others' honourings is worth's crime,
Thy monument is raised in thy life-time;
And 'tis most just; for every worthy man
Is his own marble, and his merit can
Cut him to any figure, and express
More art than death's cathedral palaces
Where royal ashes keep their court. Thy note
Be ever plainness; 'tis the richest coat:
Thy epitaph only the title be,
Write DUCHESS, that will fetch a tear for thee;
For who e'er saw this Duchess live and die,
That could get off under a bleeding eye?
   In Tragœdiam.
Ut lux ex tenebris ictu percussa tonantis,
Illa, ruina malis, claris fit vita poetis.
     THOMAS MIDDLETONUS,
     Poeta et Chron. Londinensis.

TO HIS FRIEND MR. JOHN WEBSTER, UPON HIS "DUCHESS OF MALFI."

I never saw thy Duchess till the day
That she was lively bodied in thy play:
Howe'er she answered her low-rated love
Her brothers' anger did so fatal prove,
Yet my opinion is, she might speak more,
But never in her life so well before.
     WIL. ROWLEY.

TO THE READER OF THE AUTHOR, AND HIS "DUCHESS OF MALFI."

Crown him a poet, whom nor Rome nor Greece
Transcend in all their's for a masterpiece;
In which, whiles words and matter change, and men
Act one another, he, from whose clear pen
They all took life, to memory hath lent
A lasting fame to raise his monument.
     JOHN FORD.

DRAMATIS PERSONÆ

FERDINAND, Duke of Calabria.
The CARDINAL, his Brother.
ANTONIO BOLOGNA, Steward of the household to the DUCHESS.
DELIO, his Friend.
DANIEL DE BOSOLA, Gentleman of the horse to the DUCHESS.
CASTRUCCIO.
MARQUIS OF PESCARA.
COUNT MALATESTI.
RODERIGO.
SILVIO.
GRISOLAN.
Doctor.
Several Madmen, Pilgrims, Executioners, Officers, Attendants,
&c.

DUCHESS OF MALFI.
CARIOLA, her Woman.
JULIA, Castruccio's Wife, and the Cardinal's Mistress.
Old Lady, Ladies and Children.

SCENE—MALFI, ROME, and MILAN.

THE DUCHESS OF MALFI

ACT THE FIRST

SCENE I—*The Presence-chamber in the* DUCHESS' *Palace at Malfi*

Enter ANTONIO *and* DELIO.

DELIO. You are welcome to your country, dear Antonio;
You have been long in France, and you return
A very formal Frenchman in your habit:
How do you like the French court?
  Ant. I admire it:
In seeking to reduce both state and people
To a fixed order, their judicious king
Begins at home; quits first his royal palace
Of flattering sycophants, of dissolute
And infamous persons,—which he sweetly terms
His master's master-piece, the work of Heaven;
Considering duly that a prince's court
Is like a common fountain, whence should flow
Pure silver drops in general, but if't chance
Some cursed example poison't near the head,
Death and diseases through the whole land spread.
And what is't makes this blessèd government
But a most provident council, who dare freely
Inform him the corruption of the times?
Though some o' the court hold it presumption
To instruct princes what they ought to do,
It is a noble duty to inform them
What they ought to foresee.—Here comes Bosola,
The only court-gall; yet I observe his railing
Is not for simple love of piety:
Indeed, he rails at those things which he wants;
Would be as lecherous, covetous, or proud,
Bloody, or envious, as any man,
If he had means to be so.—Here's the cardinal.

Enter the Cardinal *and* BOSOLA.

Bos. I do haunt you still.

Card. So.

Bos. I have done you better service than to be slighted thus. Miserable age, where only the reward of doing well is the doing of it!

Card. You enforce your merit too much.

Bos. I fell into the galleys in your service; where, for two years together, I wore two towels instead of a shirt, with a knot on the shoulder, after the fashion of a Roman mantle. Slighted thus! I will thrive some way: blackbirds fatten best in hard weather; why not I in these dog-days?

Card. Would you could become honest!

Bos. With all your divinity do but direct me the way to it. I have known many travel far for it, and yet return as arrant knaves as they went forth, because they carried themselves always along with them. [*Exit* Cardinal.] Are you gone? Some fellows, they say, are possessed with the devil, but this great fellow were able to possess the greatest devil, and make him worse.

Ant. He hath denied thee some suit?

Bos. He and his brother are like plum-trees that grow crooked over standing-pools; they are rich and o'er-laden with fruit, but none but crows, pies, and caterpillars feed on them. Could I be one of their flattering panders, I would hang on their ears like a horseleech, till I were full, and then drop off. I pray, leave me. Who would rely upon these miserable dependancies, in expectation to be advanced to-morrow? what creature ever fed worse than hoping Tantalus? nor ever died any man more fearfully than he that hoped for a pardon. There are rewards for hawks and dogs when they have done us service; but for a soldier that hazards his limbs in a battle, nothing but a kind of geometry is his last supportation.

Delio. Geometry!

Bos. Ay, to hang in a fair pair of slings, take his latter swing in the world upon an honourable pair of crutches, from hospital to hospital. Fare ye well, sir: and yet do not you scorn us; for places in the court are but like beds in the hospital, where this man's head lies at that man's foot, and so lower and lower. [*Exit.*

Delio. I knew this fellow seven years in the galleys
For a notorious murder; and 'twas thought
The cardinal suborned it: he was released
By the French general, Gaston de Foix,
When he recovered Naples.

Ant. 'Tis great pity,
He should be thus neglected: I have heard
He's very valiant. This foul melancholy
Will poison all his goodness; for, I'll tell you,
If too immoderate sleep be truly said
To be an inward rust unto the soul,
It then doth follow want of action
Breeds all black malcontents; and their close rearing,
Like moths in cloth, do hurt for want of wearing.

Delio. The presence 'gins to fill: you promised me
To make me the partaker of the natures
Of some of your great courtiers.

Ant. The lord cardinal's,
And other strangers' that are now in court?
I shall.—Here comes the great Calabrian duke.

Enter FERDINAND, CASTRUCCIO, SILVIO, RODERIGO,
GRISOLAN, *and* Attendants.

Ferd. Who took the ring oftenest? [1]

Sil. Antonio Bologna, my lord.

Ferd. Our sister duchess' great-master of her household?
give him the jewel.—When shall we leave this sportive
action, and fall to action indeed?

Cast. Methinks, my lord, you should not desire to go to
war in person.

Ferd. Now for some gravity:—why, my lord?

Cast. It is fitting a soldier arise to be a prince, but not
necessary a prince descend to be a captain.

Ferd. No?

Cast. No, my lord; he were far better do it by a deputy.

Ferd. Why should he not as well sleep or eat by a deputy?
this might take idle, offensive, and base office from him,
whereas the other deprives him of honour.

Cast. Believe my experience, that realm is never long in
quiet where the ruler is a soldier.

[1] An allusion to the sport called "Running at the Ring," at which the tilter,
while riding at full speed, endeavoured to thrust the point of his lance through,
and to bear away, the ring, which was suspended in the air.—*Dyce.*

Ferd. Thou toldest me thy wife could not endure fighting.

Cast. True, my lord.

Ferd. And of a jest she broke of a captain she met full of wounds: I have forgot it.

Cast. She told him, my lord, he was a pitiful fellow, to lie, like the children of Ismael, all in tents.[2]

Ferd. Why, there's a wit were able to undo all the surgeons o' the city; for although gallants should quarrel, and had drawn their weapons, and were ready to go to it, yet her persuasions would make them put up.

Cast. That she would, my lord.—How do you like my Spanish gennet?

Rod. He is all fire.

Ferd. I am of Pliny's opinion, I think he was begot by the wind; he runs as if he were ballassed with quicksilver.

Silvio. True, my lord, he reels from the tilt often.

Rod. Gris. Ha, ha, ha!

Ferd. Why do you laugh? methinks you that are courtiers should be my touchwood, take fire when I give fire; that is, laugh but when I laugh, were the subject never so witty.

Cast. True, my lord: I myself have heard a very good jest, and have scorned to seem to have so silly a wit as to understand it.

Ferd. But I can laugh at your fool, my lord.

Cast. He cannot speak, you know, but he makes faces: my lady cannot abide him.

Ferd. No?

Cast. Nor endure to be in merry company; for she says too much laughing, and too much company, fills her too full of the wrinkle.

Ferd. I would, then, have a mathematical instrument made for her face, that she might not laugh out of compass.—I shall shortly visit you at Milan, Lord Silvio.

Silvio. Your grace shall arrive most welcome.

Ferd. You are a good horseman, Antonio: you have excellent riders in France: what do you think of good horsemanship?

Ant. Nobly, my lord: as out of the Grecian horse issued many famous princes, so out of brave horsemanship arise the first sparks of growing resolution that raise the mind to noble action.

[2] A play upon the word, "tent" meaning also a roll of lint or other bandage.

Ferd. You have bespoke it worthily.

Silvio. Your brother, the lord cardinal, and sister duchess.

Re-enter Cardinal, *with* DUCHESS, CARIOLA, *and* JULIA.

Card. Are the galleys come about?

Gris. They are, my lord.

Ferd. Here's the Lord Silvio is come to take his leave.

Delio. Now, sir, your promise; what's that cardinal?
I mean his temper? they say he's a brave fellow,
Will play his five thousand crowns at tennis, dance,
Court ladies, and one that hath fought single combats.

Ant. Some such flashes superficially hang on him for
form; but observe his inward character: he is a melancholy
churchman; the spring in his face is nothing but the engendering of toads; where he is jealous of any man, he lays
worse plots for them than ever was imposed on Hercules,
for he strews in his way flatterers, panders, intelligencers,
atheists, and a thousand such political monsters. He should
have been Pope; but instead of coming to it by the primitive
decency of the church, he did bestow bribes so largely and
so impudently as if he would have carried it away without
Heaven's knowledge. Some good he hath done—

Delio. You have given too much of him. What's his
    brother?

Ant. The duke there? a most perverse and turbulent
    nature:
What appears in him mirth is merely outside;
If he laugh heartily, it is to laugh
All honesty out of fashion.

Delio. Twins?

Ant. In quality.
He speaks with others' tongues, and hears men's suits
With others' ears; will seem to sleep o' the bench
Only to entrap offenders in their answers;
Dooms men to death by information;
Rewards by hearsay.

Delio. Then the law to him
Is like a foul black cobweb to a spider,—
He makes it his dwelling and a prison
To entangle those shall feed him.

Ant. Most true:
He never pays debts unless they be shrewd turns,

And those he will confess that he doth owe.
Last, for his brother there, the cardinal,
They that do flatter him most say oracles
Hang at his lips; and verily I believe them,
For the devil speaks in them.
But for their sister, the right noble duchess,
You never fixed your eye on three fair medals
Cast in one figure, of so different temper.
For her discourse, it is so full of rapture,
You only will begin then to be sorry
When she doth end her speech, and wish, in wonder,
She held it less vain-glory to talk much,
Than your penance to hear her: whilst she speaks,
She throws upon a man so sweet a look,
That it were able to raise one to a galliard [3]
That lay in a dead palsy, and to dote
On that sweet countenance; but in that look
There speaketh so divine a continence
As cuts off all lascivious and vain hope.
Her days are practised in such noble virtue,
That sure her nights, nay, more, her very sleeps,
Are more in Heaven than other ladies' shrifts.
Let all sweet ladies break their flattering glasses,
And dress themselves in her.
    Delio. Fie, Antonio,
You play the wire-drawer with her commendations.
    Ant. I'll case the picture up: only thus much;
All her particular worth grows to this sum,—
She stains the time past, lights the time to come.
    Cari. You must attend my lady in the gallery,
Some half an hour hence.
    Ant. I shall.   [*Exeunt* Antonio *and* Delio.
    Ferd. Sister, I have a suit to you.
    Duch. To me, sir?
    Ferd. A gentleman here, Daniel de Bosola,
One that was in the galleys—
    Duch. Yes, I know him.
    Ferd. A worthy fellow he is: pray, let me entreat for
The provisorship of your horse.
    Duch. Your knowledge of him
Commends him and prefers him.

---

[3] A lively dance.

Ferd. Call him hither.   [*Exit* Attendant.
We are now upon parting. Good Lord Silvio,
Do us commend to all our noble friends
At the leaguer.

Silvio. Sir, I shall.

Ferd. You are for Milan?

Silvio. I am.

Duch. Bring the caroches.[4] We'll bring you down to the
haven.

[*Exeunt* DUCHESS, SILVIO, CASTRUCCIO, RODERIGO,
GRISOLAN, CARIOLA, JULIA, *and* Attendants.

Card. Be sure you entertain that Bosola
For your intelligence: I would not be seen in't;
And therefore many times I have slighted him
When he did court our furtherance, as this morning.

Ferd. Antonio, the great-master of her household,
Had been far fitter.

Card. You are deceived in him:
His nature is too honest for such business.—
He comes: I'll leave you.   [*Exit.*

Re-enter BOSOLA.

Bos. I was lured to you.

Ferd. My brother, here, the cardinal could never
Abide you.

Bos. Never since he was in my debt.

Ferd. May be some oblique character in your face
Made him suspect you.

Bos. Doth he study physiognomy?
There's no more credit to be given to the face
Than to a sick man's urine, which some call
The physician's whore because she cozens him.
He did suspect me wrongfully.

Ferd. For that
You must give great men leave to take their times.
Distrust doth cause us seldom be deceived:
You see the oft shaking of the cedar-tree
Fastens it more at root.

Bos. Yet, take heed;
For to suspect a friend unworthily

---

⁴ Coaches.

Instructs him the next way to suspect you,
And prompts him to deceive you.

Ferd. There's gold.

Bos. So:
What follows? never rained such showers as these
Without thunderbolts i' the tail of them: whose throat
    must I cut?

Ferd. Your inclination to shed blood rides post
Before my occasion to use you. I give you that
To live i' the court here, and observe the duchess;
To note all the particulars of her haviour,[5]
What suitors do solicit her for marriage,
And whom she best affects. She's a young widow:
I would not have her marry again.

Bos. No, sir?

Ferd. Do not you ask the reason; but be satisfied
I say I would not.

Bos. It seems you would create me
One of your familiars.

Ferd. Familiar! what's that?

Bos. Why, a very quaint invisible devil in flesh,
An intelligencer.

Ferd. Such a kind of thriving thing
I would wish thee; and ere long thou mayest arrive
At a higher place by't.

Bos. Take your devils,
Which hell calls angels; these cursed gifts would make
You a corrupter, me an impudent traitor;
And should I take these, they'd take me to hell.

Ferd. Sir, I'll take nothing from you that I have given:
There is a place that I procured for you
This morning, the provisorship o' the horse;
Have you heard on't?

Bos. No.

Ferd. 'Tis yours: is't not worth thanks?

Bos. I would have you curse yourself now, that your
    bounty
(Which makes men truly noble) e'er should make me
A villain. O, that to avoid ingratitude
For the good deed you have done me, I must do
All the ill man can invent! Thus the devil

[5] Behaviour.

Candies all sins o'er; and what Heaven terms vile,
That names he complimental.[6]

Ferd. Be yourself;
Keep your old garb of melancholy; 'twill express
You envy those that stand above your reach,
Yet strive not to come near 'em: this will gain
Access to private lodgings, where yourself
May, like a politic dormouse—

Bos. As I have seen some
Feed in a lord's dish, half asleep, not seeming
To listen to any talk; and yet these rogues
Have cut his throat in a dream. What's my place?
The provisorship o' the horse? say, then, my corruption
Grew out of horse-dung: I am your creature.

Ferd. Away!

Bos. Let good men, for good deeds, covet good fame,
Since place and riches oft are bribes of shame:
Sometimes the devil doth preach.   [*Exit.*

Re-enter DUCHESS, Cardinal, *and* CARIOLA.

Card. We are to part from you; and your own discretion
Must now be your director.

Ferd. You are a widow:
You know already what man is; and therefore
Let not youth, high promotion, eloquence—

Card. No,
Nor any thing without the addition, honour,
Sway your high blood.

Ferd. Marry! they are most luxurious[7]
Will wed twice.

Card. O, fie!

Ferd. Their livers are more spotted
Than Laban's sheep.

Duch. Diamonds are of most value,
They say, that have passed through most jewellers' hands.

Ferd. Whores by that rule are precious.

Duch. Will you hear me?
I'll never marry.

Card. So most widows say;
But commonly that motion lasts no longer

---

[6] *i.e.* Ornamental, belonging to accomplishments.—*Dyce.*
[7] Incontinent.

Than the turning of an hour-glass: the funeral sermon
And it end both together.

Ferd. Now hear me:
You live in a rank pasture, here, i' the court;
There is a kind of honey-dew that's deadly;
'Twill poison your fame; look to't: be not cunning;
For they whose faces do belie their hearts
Are witches ere they arrive at twenty years,
Ay, and give the devil suck.

Duch. This is terrible good counsel.

Ferd. Hypocrisy is woven of a fine small thread,
Subtler than Vulcan's engine:[8] yet, believe't,
Your darkest actions, nay, your privat'st thoughts,
Will come to light.

Card. You may flatter yourself,
And take your own choice; privately be married
Under the eyes of night—

Ferd. Think't the best voyage
That e'er you made; like the irregular crab,
Which, though't goes backward, thinks that it goes right
Because it goes its own way; but observe,
Such weddings may more properly be said
To be executed than celebrated.

Card. The marriage night
Is the entrance into some prison.

Ferd. And those joys,
Those lustful pleasures, are like heavy sleeps
Which do fore-run man's mischief.

Card. Fare you well.
Wisdom begins at the end: remember it.   [*Exit.*

Duch. I think this speech between you both was studied,
It came so roundly off.

Ferd. You are my sister;
This was my father's poniard, do you see?
I'd be loth to see't look rusty, 'cause 'twas his.
I would have you give o'er these chargeable revels:
A visor and a mask are whispering-rooms
That were never built for goodness;—fare ye well;—
And women like that part which, like the lamprey,
Hath never a bone in't.

Duch. Fie, sir!

---

[8] The net in which he caught Mars and Venus.

Ferd. Nay,
I mean the tongue; variety of courtship:
What cannot a neat knave with a smooth tale
Make a woman believe? Farewell, lusty widow.   [*Exit.*
   Duch. Shall this move me? If all my royal kindred
Lay in my way unto this marriage,
I'd make them my low footsteps: and even now,
Even in this hate, as men in some great battles,
By apprehending danger, have achieved
Almost impossible actions (I have heard soldiers say so),
So I through frights and threatenings will assay
This dangerous venture. Let old wives report
I winked and chose a husband.—Cariola,
To thy known secrecy I have given up
More than my life—my fame.
   Cari. Both shall be safe;
For I'll conceal this secret from the world
As warily as those that trade in poison
Keep poison from their children.
   Duch. Thy protestation
Is ingenious[9] and hearty: I believe it.
Is Antonio come?
   Cari. He attends you.
   Duch. Good, dear soul,
Leave me; but place thyself behind the arras,
Where thou mayst overhear us. Wish me good speed;
For I am going into a wilderness
Where I shall find nor path nor friendly clue
To be my guide.   [CARIOLA *goes behind the arras.*

Enter ANTONIO.[10]

          I sent for you: sit down;
Take pen and ink, and write: are you ready?
   Ant. Yes.
   Duch. What did I say?
   Ant. That I should write somewhat.
   Duch. O, I remember.
After these triumphs and this large expense,

---

[9] *i.e.* Ingenuous.
[10] As previously Antonio has been told that he must attend the Duchess "in the gallery," it would seem that the audience were to imagine a change of scene had taken place (*i.e.*, at the exit of Ferdinand).—*Dyce.*

It's fit, like thrifty husbands, we inquire
What's laid up for to-morrow.

Ant. So please your beauteous excellence.

Duch. Beauteous!
Indeed, I thank you: I look young for your sake;
You have ta'en my cares upon you.

Ant. I'll fetch your grace
The particulars of your revenue and expense.

Duch. O, you are
An upright treasurer: but you mistook;
For when I said I meant to make inquiry
What's laid up for to-morrow, I did mean
What's laid up yonder for me.

Ant. Where?

Duch. In Heaven.
I am making my will (as 'tis fit princes should,
In perfect memory), and, I pray, sir, tell me,
Were not one better make it smiling, thus,
Than in deep groans and terrible ghastly looks,
As if the gifts we parted with procured
That violent distraction?

Ant. O, much better.

Duch. If I had a husband now, this care were quit:
But I intend to make you overseer.
What good deed shall we first remember? say.

Ant. Begin with that first good deed began i' the world
After man's creation, the sacrament of marriage:
I'd have you first provide for a good husband;
Give him all.

Duch. All!

Ant. Yes, your excellent self.

Duch. In a winding-sheet?

Ant. In a couple.

Duch. Saint Winifred, that were a strange will!

Ant. 'Twere stranger if there were no will in you
To marry again.

Duch. What do you think of marriage?

Ant. I take't, as those that deny purgatory,
It locally contains or Heaven or hell;
There's no third place in't.

Duch. How do you affect it?

Ant. My banishment, feeding my melancholy,
Would often reason thus.

Duch. Pray, let's hear it.

Ant. Say a man never marry, nor have children,
What takes that from him? only the bare name
Of being a father, or the weak delight
To see the little wanton ride a-cock-horse
Upon a painted stick, or hear him chatter
Like a taught starling.

Duch. Fie, fie, what's all this?
One of your eyes is blood-shot; use my ring to't,
They say 'tis very sovereign: 'twas my wedding-ring,
And I did vow never to part with it
But to my second husband.

Ant. You have parted with it now.

Duch. Yes, to help your eye-sight.

Ant. You have made me stark blind.

Duch. How?

Ant. There is a saucy and ambitious devil
Is dancing in this circle.

Duch. Remove him.

Ant. How?

Duch. There needs small conjuration, when your finger
May do it: thus; is it fit?

       [*She puts the ring upon his finger: he kneels.*

Ant. What said you?

Duch. Sir,
This goodly roof of yours is too low built;
I cannot stand upright in't nor discourse,
Without I raise it higher: raise yourself;
Or, if you please, my hand to help you: so.   [*Raises him.*

Ant. Ambition, madam, is a great man's madness,
That is not kept in chains and close-pent rooms,
But in fair lightsome lodgings, and is girt
With the wild noise of prattling visitants,
Which makes it lunatic beyond all cure.
Conceive not I am so stupid but I aim
Whereto your favours tend: but he's a fool
That, being a-cold, would thrust his hands i' the fire
To warm them.

Duch. So, now the ground's broke,

You may discover what a wealthy mine
I make you lord of.

 Ant. O my unworthiness!

 Duch. You were ill to sell yourself:
This darkening of your worth is not like that
Which tradesmen use i' the city; their false lights
Are to rid bad wares off: and I must tell you,
If you will know where breathes a complete man
(I speak it without flattery), turn your eyes,
And progress through yourself.

 Ant. Were there nor Heaven nor hell,
I should be honest: I have long served virtue,
And ne'er ta'en wages of her.

 Duch. Now she pays it.
The misery of us that are born great!
We are forced to woo, because none dare woo us;
And as a tyrant doubles with his words,
And fearfully equivocates, so we
Are forced to express our violent passions
In riddles and in dreams, and leave the path
Of simple virtue, which was never made
To seem the thing it is not. Go, go brag
You have left me heartless; mine is in your bosom:
I hope 'twill multiply love there. You do tremble:
Make not your heart so dead a piece of flesh,
To fear more than to love me. Sir, be confident:
What is't distracts you? This is flesh and blood, sir;
'Tis not the figure cut in alabaster
Kneels at my husband's tomb. Awake, awake, man!
I do here put off all vain ceremony,
And only do appear to you a young widow
That claims you for her husband, and, like a widow,
I use but half a blush in't.

 Ant. Truth speak for me;
I will remain the constant sanctuary
Of your good name.

 Duch. I thank you, gentle love:
And 'cause you shall not come to me in debt,
Being now my steward, here upon your lips
I sign your *Quietus est.* This you should have begged now:
I have seen children oft eat sweetmeats thus,
As fearful to devour them too soon.

Ant. But for your brothers?

Duch. Do not think of them:
All discord without this circumference
Is only to be pitied, and not feared:
Yet, should they know it, time will easily
Scatter the tempest.

Ant. These words should be mine,
And all the parts you have spoke, if some part of it
Would not have savoured flattery.

Duch. Kneel.

[CARIOLA *comes from behind the arras.*

Ant. Ha!

Duch. Be not amazed; this woman's of my counsel:
I have heard lawyers say, a contract in a chamber
Per verba presenti is absolute marriage.

[*She and* ANTONIO *kneel.*

Bless, Heaven, this sacred gordian, which let violence
Never untwine!

Ant. And may our sweet affections, like the spheres,
Be still in motion!

Duch. Quickening, and make
The like soft music!

Ant. That we may imitate the loving palms,
Best emblem of a peaceful marriage,
That never bore fruit, divided!

Duch. What can the church force more?

Ant. That fortune may not know an accident,
Either of joy or sorrow, to divide
Our fixèd wishes!

Duch. How can the church build faster?
We now are man and wife, and 'tis the church
That must but echo this.—Maid, stand apart:
I now am blind.

Ant. What's your conceit in this?

Duch. I would have you lead your fortune by the hand
Unto your marriage bed:
(You speak in me this, for we now are one:)
We'll only lie, and talk together, and plot
To appease my humorous kindred; and if you please,
Like the old tale in Alexander and Lodowick,[11]

11 *The Two Faithful Friends, the pleasant History of Alexander and Lodowicke,
who were so like one another, that none could know them asunder; wherein is*

Lay a naked sword between us, keep us chaste.
O, let me shrowd my blushes in your bosom,
Since 'tis the treasury of all my secrets!

[*Exeunt* DUCHESS *and* ANTONIO.

Cari. Whether the spirit of greatness or of woman
Reign most in her, I know not; but it shows
A fearful madness: I owe her much of pity. [*Exit.*

ACT THE SECOND

SCENE I—*An Apartment in the Palace of the* DUCHESS

Enter BOSOLA *and* CASTRUCCIO.

Bos. You say you would fain be taken for an eminent courtier?

Cast. 'Tis the very main of my ambition.

Bos. Let me see: you have a reasonable good face for't already, and your night-cap expresses your ears sufficient largely. I would have you learn to twirl the strings of your band with a good grace, and in a set speech, at the end of every sentence, to hum three or four times, or blow your nose till it smart again, to recover your memory. When you come to be a president in criminal causes, if you smile upon a prisoner, hang him; but if you frown upon him and threaten him, let him be sure to scape the gallows.

Cast. I would be a very merry president.

Bos. Do not sup o' nights; 'twill beget you an admirable wit.

Cast. Rather it would make me have a good stomach to quarrel; for they say, your roaring boys[12] eat meat seldom, and that makes them so valiant. But how shall I know whether the people take me for an eminent fellow?

Bos. I will teach a trick to know it: give out you lie a-dying, and if you hear the common people curse you, be sure you are taken for one of the prime night-caps.[13]

---

declared *how Lodwicke married the Princesse of Hungaria, in Alexander's name, and how each night he layd a naked sword betweene him and the Princesse, because he would not wrong his friend,* is reprinted from the Pepys collection in Evans's *Old Ballads.* There was also a play written by Martin Slaughter, called *Alexander and Lodowick.—Dyce.*

[12] A cant term for the insolent bloods and vapourers of the time.—*Dyce.*

[13] Another cant term.

Enter an Old Lady.

You come from painting now.

Old Lady. From what?

Bos. Why, from your scurvy face-physic. To behold thee
not painted inclines somewhat near a miracle; these in thy
face here were deep ruts and foul sloughs the last progress.[14]
There was a lady in France that, having had the small-pox,
flayed the skin off her face to make it more level; and
whereas before she looked like a nutmeg-grater, after she
resembled an abortive hedgehog.

Old Lady. Do you call this painting?

Bos. No, no, but you call it careening of an old mor-
phewed[15] lady, to make her disembogue again; there's
rough-cast phrase to your plastic.

Old Lady. It seems you are well acquainted with my
closet.

Bos. One would suspect it for a shop of witchcraft, to
find in it the fat of serpents, spawn of snakes, Jews' spittle,
and their young children's ordure; and all these for the
face. I would sooner eat a dead pigeon taken from the soles
of the feet of one sick of the plague than kiss one of you
fasting. Here are two of you, whose sin of your youth is
the very patrimony of the physician; makes him renew his
foot-cloth[16] with the spring, and change his high-priced
courtezan with the fall of the leaf. I do wonder you do
not loathe yourselves. Observe my meditation now.
What thing is in this outward form of man
To be beloved? We account it ominous,
If nature do produce a colt, or lamb,
A fawn, or goat, in any limb resembling
A man, and fly from't as a prodigy:
Man stands amazed to see his deformity
In any other creature but himself.
But in our own flesh, though we bear diseases
Which have their true names only ta'en from beasts,—
As the most ulcerous wolf and swinish measle,—
Though we are eaten up of lice and worms,
And though continually we bear about us
A rotten and dead body, we delight

---

[14] State journey.
[15] A leperous eruption.
[16] Buy new housings for his beast.

To hide it in rich tissue: all our fear,
Nay, all our terror, is lest our physician
Should put us in the ground to be made sweet.—
Your wife's gone to Rome: you two couple, and get you
to the wells at Lucca to recover your aches. I have other
work on foot.   [*Exeunt* CASTRUCCIO *and* Old Lady.
I observe our duchess
Is sick a-days, she pukes, her stomach seethes,
The fins of her eye-lids looks most teeming blue,
She wanes i' the cheek, and waxes fat i' the flank,
And, contrary to our Italian fashion,
Wears a loose-bodied gown: there's somewhat in't.
I have a trick may chance discover it,
A pretty one; I have bought some apricocks,
The first our spring yields.

Enter ANTONIO and DELIO.

Delio. And so long since married!
You amaze me.

Ant. Let me seal your lips for ever:
For, did I think that any thing but the air
Could carry these words from you, I should wish
You had no breath at all.—Now, sir, in your contemplation?
You are studying to become a great wise fellow.

Bos. O, sir, the opinion of wisdom is a foul tether that
runs all over a man's body: if simplicity direct us to have
no evil, it directs us to a happy being; for the subtlest folly
proceeds from the subtlest wisdom: let me be simply honest.

Ant. I do understand your inside.

Bos. Do you so?

Ant. Because you would not seem to appear to the world
Puffed up with your preferment, you continue
This out-of-fashion melancholy: leave it, leave it.

Bos. Give me leave to be honest in any phrase, in any
compliment whatsoever. Shall I confess myself to you? I
look no higher than I can reach: they are the gods that
must ride on winged horses. A lawyer's mule of a slow
pace will both suit my disposition and business; for, mark
me, when a man's mind rides faster than his horse can
gallop, they quickly both tire.

Ant. You would look up to Heaven, but I think
The devil, that rules i' the air, stands in your light.

Bos. O, sir, you are lord of the ascendant, chief man with
the duchess; a duke was your cousin-german removed. Say
you are lineally descended from King Pepin, or he himself,
what of this? search the heads of the greatest rivers in the
world, you shall find them but bubbles of water. Some
would think the souls of princes were brought forth by
some more weighty cause than those of meaner persons:
they are deceived, there's the same hand to them; the like
passions sway them; the same reason that makes a vicar
to go to law for a tithe-pig, and undo his neighbours, makes
them spoil a whole province, and batter down goodly cities
with the cannon.

Enter DUCHESS *and* Ladies.

Duch. Your arm, Antonio; do I not grow fat?
I am exceeding short-winded.—Bosola,
I would have you, sir, provide for me a litter;
Such a one as the Duchess of Florence rode in.

Bos. The duchess used one when she was great with
　　child.

Duch. I think she did.—Come hither, mend my ruff;
Here, when? thou art such a tedious lady; and
Thy breath smells of lemon-pills; would thou hadst done!
Shall I swoon under thy fingers! I am
So troubled with the mother! [17]

Bos. [*Aside.*] I fear too much.

Duch. I have heard you say that the French courtiers
Wear their hats on 'fore the king.

Ant. I have seen it.

Duch. In the presence?

Ant. Yes.

Duch. Why should not we bring up that fashion?
'Tis ceremony more than duty that consists
In the removing of a piece of felt:
Be you the example to the rest o' the court;
Put on your hat first.

Ant. You must pardon me:
I have seen, in colder countries than in France,
Nobles stand bare to the prince; and the distinction
Methought showed reverently.

Bos. I have a present for your grace.

[17] Hysterics.

Duch. For me, sir?

Bos. Apricocks, madam.

Duch. O, sir, where are they?
I have heard of none to-year.

Bos. [*Aside.*] Good; her colour rises.

Duch. Indeed, I thank you: they are wondrous fair ones.
What an unskilful fellow is our gardener!
We shall have none this month.

Bos. Will not your grace pare them?

Duch. No: they taste of musk, methinks; indeed they do.

Bos. I know not: yet I wish your grace had pared 'em.

Duch. Why?

Bos. I forgot to tell you, the knave gardener,
Only to raise his profit by them the sooner,
Did ripen them in horse-dung.

Duch. O, you jest—
You shall judge: pray taste one.

Ant. Indeed, madam,
I do not love the fruit.

Duch. Sir, you are loth
To rob us of our dainties: 'tis a delicate fruit;
They say they are restorative.

Bos. 'Tis a pretty art,
This grafting.

Duch. 'Tis so; bettering of nature.

Bos. To make a pippin grow upon a crab,
A damson on a blackthorn.—[*Aside.*] How greedily she
        eats them!
A whirlwind strike off these bawd farthingales!
For, but for that and the loose-bodied gown,
I should have discovered apparently
The young springal [18] cutting a caper in her belly.

Duch. I thank you, Bosola: they are right good ones,
If they do not make me sick.

Ant. How now, madam!

Duch. This green fruit and my stomach are not friends:
How they swell me!

Bos. [*Aside.*] Nay, you are too much swelled already.

Duch. O, I am in an extreme cold sweat!

Bos. I am very sorry.

[18] Rascal.

Duch. Lights to my chamber!—O good Antonio,
I fear I am undone!

Delio. Lights there, lights!

[*Exeunt* DUCHESS *and* Ladies.—*Exit, on the other
side,* BOSOLA.]

Ant. O my most trusty Delio, we are lost!
I fear she's fall'n in labour; and there's left
No time for her remove.

Delio.	Have you prepared
Those ladies to attend her? and procured
That politic safe conveyance for the midwife
Your duchess plotted?

Ant. I have.

Delio. Make use, then, of this forced occasion:
Give out that Bosola hath poisoned her
With these apricocks; that will give some colour
For her keeping close.

Ant.	Fie, fie, the physicians
Will then flock to her.

Delio.	For that you may pretend
She'll use some prepared antidote of her own,
Lest the physicians should re-poison her.

Ant. I am lost in amazement: I know not what to think
on't.	[*Exeunt.*

SCENE II—*A Hall in the same Palace*

Enter BOSOLA.

Bos. So, so, there's no question but her techiness and
most vulturous eating of the apricocks are apparent signs
of breeding.

Enter an Old Lady.

Now?

Old Lady. I am in haste, sir.

Bos. There was a young waiting-woman had a monstrous
desire to see the glass-house—

Old Lady. Nay, pray let me go.

Bos. And it was only to know what strange instrument

it was should swell up a glass to the fashion of a woman's
belly.

Old Lady. I will hear no more of the glass-house. You
are still abusing women?

Bos. Who, I? no; only, by the way now and then, men-
tion your frailties. The orange-tree bears ripe and green
fruit and blossoms all together; and some of you give
entertainment for pure love, but more for more precious
reward. The lusty spring smells well; but drooping autumn
tastes well. If we have the same golden showers that
rained in the time of Jupiter the thunderer, you have the
same Danäes still, to hold up their laps to receive them.
Didst thou never study the mathematics?

Old Lady. What's that, sir?

Bos. Why to know the trick how to make a many lines
meet in one centre. Go, go, give your foster-daughters good
counsel: tell them, that the devil takes delight to hang at
a woman's girdle, like a false rusty watch, that she cannot discern how the time passes.   [*Exit* Old Lady.

Enter ANTONIO, RODERIGO, *and* GRISOLAN.

Ant. Shut up the court-gates.

Rod. Why, sir? what's the danger?

Ant. Shut up the posterns presently, and call
All the officers o' the court.

Gris. I shall instantly.   [*Exit.*

Ant. Who keeps the key o' the park-gate?

Rod. Forobosco.

Ant. Let him bring't presently.

Re-enter GRISOLAN *with* Servants.

1st Serv. O, gentlemen o' the court, the foule treason!

Bos. [*Aside.*] If that these apricocks should be poisoned
now,
Without my knowledge!

1st Serv. There was taken even now a Switzer in the
duchess' bed-chamber—

2nd Serv. A Switzer!

1st Serv. With a pistol in his great cod-piece.

Bos. Ha, ha, ha!

1st Serv. The cod-piece was the case for't.

2nd Serv. There was a cunning traitor: who would have searched his cod-piece?

1st Serv. True, if he had kept out of the ladies' chambers: and all the moulds of his buttons were leaden bullets.

2nd Serv. O wicked cannibal! a fire-lock in's cod-piece!

1st Serv. 'Twas a French plot, upon my life.

2nd Serv. To see what the devil can do!

Ant. Are all the officers here?

Servants. We are.

Ant. Gentlemen,
We have lost much plate you know; and but this evening
Jewels, to the value of four thousand ducats,
Are missing in the duchess' cabinet.
Are the gates shut?

Serv. Yes.

Ant. 'Tis the duchess' pleasure
Each officer be locked into his chamber
Till the sun-rising; and to send the keys
Of all their chests and of their outward doors
Into her bed-chamber. She is very sick.

Rod. At her pleasure.

Ant. She entreats you take't not ill: the innocent
Shall be the more approved by it.

Bos. Gentleman o' the wood-yard, where's your Switzer now?

1st Serv. By this hand, 'twas credibly reported by one o' the black guard.[19]

[*Exeunt all except* ANTONIO *and* DELIO.

Delio. How fares it with the duchess?

Ant. She's exposed
Unto the worst of torture, pain and fear.

Delio. Speak to her all happy comfort.

Ant. How I do play the fool with mine own danger!
You are this night, dear friend, to post to Rome:
My life lies in your service.

Delio. Do not doubt me.

Ant. O, 'tis far from me: and yet fear presents me
Somewhat that looks like danger.

Delio. Believe it,
'Tis but the shadow of your fear, no more:

19 The lowest class of menials.

How superstitiously we mind our evils!
The throwing down salt, or crossing of a hare,
Bleeding at nose, the stumbling of a horse,
Or singing of a cricket, are of power
To daunt whole man in us. Sir, fare you well:
I wish you all the joys of a blessed father:
And, for my faith, lay this unto your breast,—
Old friends, like old swords, still are trusted best.   [*Exit.*

Enter CARIOLA.

Cari. Sir, you are the happy father of a son:
Your wife commends him to you.
    Ant. Blessèd comfort!—
For Heaven' sake tend her well: I'll presently
Go set a figure for's nativity.   [*Exeunt.*

SCENE III—*The Court of the same Palace*

Enter BOSOLA, *with a dark lantern.*

Bos. Sure I did hear a woman shriek: list, ha!
And the sound came, if I received it right,
From the duchess' lodgings. There's some stratagem
In the confining all our courtiers
To their several wards: I must have part of it;
My intelligence will freeze else. List, again!
It may be 'twas the melancholy bird,
Best friend of silence and of solitariness,
The owl, that screamed so.—Ha! Antonio!

Enter ANTONIO.

Ant. I heard some noise.—Who's there? what art thou?
    speak.
Bos. Antonio, put not your face nor body
To such a forced expression of fear:
I am Bosola, your friend.
    Ant. Bosola!—
[*Aside.*] This mole does undermine me.—Heard you not
A noise even now?
    Bos. From whence?
    Ant. From the duchess' lodging.

Bos. Not I: did you?

Ant. I did, or else I dreamed.

Bos. Let's walk towards it.

Ant. No: it may be 'twas
But the rising of the wind.

Bos. Very likely.
Methinks 'tis very cold, and yet you sweat:
You look wildly.

Ant. I have been setting a figure
For the duchess' jewels.

Bos. Ah, and how falls your question?
Do you find it radical?

Ant. What's that to you?
'Tis rather to be questioned what design,
When all men were commanded to their lodgings,
Makes you a night-walker.

Bos. In sooth, I'll tell you:
Now all the court's asleep, I thought the devil
Had least to do here; I came to say my prayers;
And if it do offend you I do so,
You are a fine courtier.

Ant. [*Aside.*] This fellow will undo me.—
You gave the duchess apricocks to-day:
Pray Heaven they were not poisoned!

Bos. Poisoned! A Spanish fig
For the imputation.

Ant. Traitors are ever confident
Till they are discovered. There were jewels stol'n too:
In my conceit, none are to be suspected
More than yourself.

Bos. You are a false steward.

Ant. Saucy slave, I'll pull thee up by the roots.

Bos. May be the ruin will crush you to pieces.

Ant. You are an impudent snake indeed, sir:
Are you scarce warm, and do you show your sting?
You libel well, sir.

Bos. No, sir: copy it out,
And I will set my hand to't.

Ant. [*Aside.*] My nose bleeds.
One that were superstitious would count
This ominous, when it merely comes by chance:
Two letters, that are wrote here for my name,

Are drowned in blood!
Mere accident.—For you, sir, I'll take order
I' the morn you shall be safe:—[*Aside*.] 'tis that must
　　colour
Her lying-in:—sir, this door you pass not:
I do not hold it fit that you come near
The duchess' lodgings, till you have quit yourself.—
[*Aside*.] The great are like the base, nay, they are the same,
When they seek shameful ways to avoid shame.   [*Exit*.

　　Bos. Antonio hereabout did drop a paper:—
Some of your help, false friend:—O, here it is.
What's here? a child's nativity calculated!   [*Reads*.
　　"The duchess was delivered of a son, 'tween the hours
twelve and one in the night, *Anno Dom.* 1504,"—that's
this year—"*decimo nono Decembris*,"—that's this night,—
"taken according to the meridian of Malfi,"—that's our
duchess: happy discovery!—"The lord of the first house
being combust in the ascendant, signifies short life; and
Mars being in a human sign, joined to the tail of the
Dragon, in the eighth house, doth threaten a violent death.
Cætera non scrutantur."
Why, now 'tis most apparent: this precise fellow
Is the duchess' bawd:—I have it to my wish!
This is a parcel of intelligency
Our courtiers were cased up for: it needs must follow
That I must be committed on pretence
Of poisoning her; which I'll endure, and laugh at.
If one could find the father now! but that
Time will discover. Old Castruccio
I' the morning posts to Rome: by him I'll send
A letter that shall make her brothers' galls
O'erflow their livers. This was a thrifty way.
Though lust do mask in ne'er so strange disguise,
She's oft found witty, but is never wise.   [*Exit*.

SCENE IV—*An Apartment in the Palace of the* Cardinal
at Rome

Enter Cardinal *and* JULIA.

Card. Sit: thou art my best of wishes. Prithee, tell me
What trick didst thou invent to come to Rome
Without thy husband.
    Julia. Why, my lord, I told him
I came to visit an old anchorite
Here for devotion.
    Card. Thou art a witty false one,—
I mean, to him.
    Julia. You have prevailed with me
Beyond my strongest thoughts: I would not now
Find you inconstant.
    Card. Do not put thyself
To such a voluntary torture, which proceeds
Out of your own guilt.
    Julia. How, my lord!
    Card. You fear
My constancy, because you have approved
Those giddy and wild turnings in yourself.
    Julia. Did you e'er find them?
    Card. Sooth, generally for women,
A man might strive to make glass malleable,
Ere he should make them fixèd.
    Julia. So, my lord.
    Card. We had need go borrow that fantastic glass
Invented by Galileo the Florentine
To view another spacious world i' the moon,
And look to find a constant woman there.
    Julia. This is very well, my lord.
    Card. Why do you weep?
Are tears your justification? the self-same tears
Will fall into your husband's bosom, lady,
With a loud protestation that you love him
Above the world. Come, I'll love you wisely,
That's jealously; since I am very certain
You cannot make me cuckold.

Julia. I'll go home
To my husband.

Card. You may thank me, lady,
I have taken you off your melancholy perch,
Bore you upon my fist, and showed you game,
And let you fly at it.—I pray thee, kiss me.—
When thou wast with thy husband, thou wast watched
Like a tame elephant:—still you are to thank me:—
Thou hadst only kisses from him and high feeding;
But what delight was that? 'twas just like one
That hath a little fingering on the lute,
Yet cannot tune it:—still you are to thank me.

Julia. You told me of a piteous wound i' the heart
And a sick liver, when you wooed me first,
And spake like one in physic.

Card. Who's that?—

Enter Servant.

Rest firm, for my affection to thee,
Lightning moves slow to't.

Serv. Madam, a gentleman,
That come post from Malfi, desires to see you.

Card. Let him enter: I'll withdraw.   [*Exit.*

Serv. He says
Your husband, old Castruccio, is come to Rome,
Most pitifully tired with riding post.   [*Exit.*

Enter Delio.

Julia. [*Aside.*] Signior Delio! 'tis one of my old suitors.

Delio. I was bold to come and see you.

Julia. Sir, you are welcome.

Delio. Do you lie here?

Julia. Sure, your own experience
Will satisfy you no: our Roman prelates
Do not keep lodging for ladies.

Delio. Very well:
I have brought you no commendations from your husband,
For I know none by him.

Julia. I hear he's come to Rome.

Delio. I never knew man and beast, of a horse and a
                knight,
So weary of each other: if he had had a good back,

He would have undertook to have borne his horse,
His breech was so pitifully sore.
  Julia. Your laughter
Is my pity.
  Delio. Lady, I know not whether
You want money, but I have brought you some.
  Julia. From my husband?
  Delio. No, from mine own allowance.
  Julia. I must hear the condition, ere I be bound to take
    it.
  Delio. Look on't, 'tis gold: hath it not a fine colour?
  Julia. I have a bird more beautiful.
  Delio. Try the sound on't.
  Julia. A lute-string far exceeds it:
It hath no smell, like cassia or civet;
Nor is it physical, though some fond doctors
Persuade us seethe't in cullises.[20] I'll tell you,
This is a creature bred by—

                Re-enter Servant.

  Serv. Your husband's come,
Hath delivered a letter to the Duke of Calabria
That, to my thinking, hath put him out of his wits.
                                              [*Exit.*

  Julia. Sir, you hear:
Pray, let me know your business and your suit
As briefly as can be.
  Delio. With good speed: I would wish you,
At such time as you are non-resident
With your husband, my mistress.
  Julia. Sir, I'll go ask my husband if I shall,
And straight return your answer.   [*Exit.*
  Delio. Very fine!
Is this her wit, or honesty, that speaks thus?
I heard one say the duke was highly moved
With a letter sent from Malfi. I do fear
Antonio is betrayed: how fearfully
Shows his ambition now! unfortunate fortune!
They pass through whirlpools, and deep woes do shun,
Who the event weigh ere the action's done.   [*Exit.*

---

[20] Strong broths. The old receipt-books recommend "pieces of gold" among the
ingredients.—*Dyce.*

SCENE V—*Another Apartment in the same Palace*

Enter Cardinal, *and* FERDINAND *with a letter.*

Ferd. I have this night digged up a mandrake.
Card. Say you?
Ferd. And I am grown mad with't.[21]
Card. What's the prodigy?
Ferd. Read there,—a sister damned: she's loose i' the hilts;
Grown a notorious strumpet.
Card. Speak lower.
Ferd. Lower!
Rogues do not whisper't now, but seek to publish't
(As servants do the bounty of their lords)
Aloud; and with a covetous searching eye,
To mark who note them. O, confusion seize her!
She hath had most cunning bawds to serve her turn,
And more secure conveyances for lust
Than towns of garrison for service.
Card. Is't possible?
Can this be certain?
Ferd. Rhubarb, O, for rhubarb
To purge this choler! here's the cursèd day
To prompt my memory; and here't shall stick
Till her bleeding heart I make a sponge
To wipe it out.
Card. Why do you make yourself
So wild a tempest?
Ferd. Would I could be one,
That I might toss her palace 'bout her ears,
Root up her goodly forests, blast her meads,
And lay her general territory as waste
As she hath done her honours.
Card. Shall our blood,
The royal blood of Arragon and Castile,
Be thus attainted?

---

[21] Compare Shakespeare:

> "And shrieks, like mandrakes torn out of the earth,
> That living mortals hearing them run mad."

Romeo and Juliet, A. IV. s. 3.

Ferd. Apply desperate physic:
We must not now use balsamum, but fire,
The smarting cupping-glass, for that's the mean
To purge infected blood, such blood as hers.
There is a kind of pity in mine eye,—
I'll give it to my handkercher; and now 'tis here,
I'll bequeath this to her bastard.

Card. What to do?

Ferd. Why, to make soft lint for his mother's wounds,
When I have hewed her to pieces.

Card. Cursèd creature!
Unequal nature, to place women's hearts
So far upon the left side!

Ferd. Foolish men,
That e'er will trust their honour in a bark
Made of so slight weak bulrush as is woman,
Apt every minute to sink it!

Card. Thus
Ignorance, when it hath purchased honour,
It cannot wield it.

Ferd. Methinks I see her laughing—
Excellent hyena! Talk to me somewhat quickly,
Or my imagination will carry me
To see her in the shameful act of sin.

Card. With whom?

Ferd. Happily with some strong-thighed bargeman.
Or one o' the woodyard that can quoit the sledge
Or toss the bar, or else some lovely squire
That carries coals up to her privy lodgings.

Card. You fly beyond your reason.

Ferd. Go to, mistress!
'Tis not your whore's milk that shall quench my wild fire,
But your whore's blood.

Card. How idly shows this rage, which carries you,
As men conveyed by witches through the air,
On violent whirlwinds! this intemperate noise
Fitly resembles deaf men's shrill discourse,
Who talk aloud, thinking all other men
To have their imperfection.

Ferd. Have not you
My palsy?

Card. Yes, but I can be angry

Without this rupture: [22] there is not in nature
A thing that makes man so deformed, so beastly,
As doth intemperate anger. Chide yourself.
You have divers men who never yet expressed
Their strong desire of rest but by unrest,
By vexing of themselves. Come, put yourself
In tune.

Ferd. So I will only study to seem
The thing I am not. I could kill her now,
In you, or in myself; for I do think
It is some sin in us Heaven doth revenge
By her.

Card. Are you stark mad?

Ferd. I would have their bodies
Burnt in a coal-pit with the ventage stopped,
That their cursed smoke might not ascend to Heaven
Or dip the sheets they lie in in pitch or sulphur,
Wrap them in't, and then light them like a match;
Or else to boil their bastard to a cullis,
And give't his lecherous father to renew
The sin of his back.

Card. I'll leave you.

Ferd. Nay, I have done.
I am confident, had I been damned in hell,
And should have heard of this, it would have put me
Into a cold sweat. In, in; I'll go sleep.
Till I know who leaps my sister, I'll not stir:
That known, I'll find scorpions to string my whips,
And fix her in a general eclipse.   [*Exeunt.*

ACT THE THIRD

SCENE I—*An Apartment in the Palace of the* DUCHESS

Enter ANTONIO *and* DELIO.

ANT. Our noble friend, my most belovèd Delio!
O, you have been a stranger long at court;
Came you along with the Lord Ferdinand?

Delio. I did, sir: and how fares your noble duchess?

[22] Query "rapture."

Ant. Right fortunately well: she's an excellent
Feeder of pedigrees; since you last saw her,
She hath had two children more, a son and daughter.

Delio. Methinks 'twas yesterday: let me but wink,
And not behold your face, which to mine eye
Is somewhat leaner, verily I should dream
It were within this half hour.

Ant. You have not been in law, friend Delio,
Nor in prison, nor a suitor at the court,
Nor begged the reversion of some great man's place,
Nor troubled with an old wife, which doth make
Your time so insensibly hasten.

Delio. Pray, sir, tell me,
Hath not this news arrived yet to the ear
Of the lord cardinal?

Ant. I fear it hath:
The Lord Ferdinand, that's newly come to court,
Doth bear himself right dangerously.

Delio. Pray, why?

Ant. He is so quiet that he seems to sleep
The tempest out, as dormice do in winter:
Those houses that are haunted are most still
Till the devil be up.

Delio. What say the common people?

Ant. The common rabble do directly say
She is a strumpet.

Delio. And your graver heads
Which would be politic, what censure they?

Ant. They do observe I grow to infinite purchase,[23]
The left hand way, and all suppose the duchess
Would amend it, if she could; for, say they,
Great princes, though they grudge their officers
Should have such large and unconfinèd means
To get wealth under them, will not complain,
Lest thereby they should make them odious
Unto the people; for other obligation
Of love or marriage between her and me
They never dream of.

Delio. The Lord Ferdinand
Is going to bed.

---

[23] Substance or property.

Enter DUCHESS, FERDINAND, *and* Attendants.

Ferd. I'll instantly to bed,
For I am weary.—I am to bespeak
A husband for you.

   Duch. For me, sir! pray, who is't?

   Ferd. The great Count Malatesti.

   Duch. Fie upon him!
A count! he's a mere stick of sugar-candy;
You may look quite through him. When I choose
A husband, I will marry for your honour.

   Ferd. You shall do well in't.—How is't, worthy Antonio?

   Duch. But, sir, I am to have private conference with you
About a scandalous report is spread
Touching mine honour.

   Ferd. Let me be ever deaf to't:
One of Pasquil's paper bullets, court-calumny,
A pestilent air, which princes' palaces
Are seldom purged of. Yet say that it were true,
I pour it in your bosom, my fixed love
Would strongly excuse, extenuate, nay, deny
Faults, were they apparent in you. Go, be safe
In your own innocency.

   Duch. [*Aside.*] O blessed comfort!
This deadly air is purged.

       [*Exeunt* DUCHESS, ANTONIO, DELIO, *and* Attendants.

   Ferd. Her guilt treads on
Hot-burning coulters.

Enter BOSOLA.

       Now, Bosola,
How thrives our intelligence?

   Bos. Sir, uncertainly:
'Tis rumoured she hath had three bastards, but
By whom we may go read i' the stars.

   Ferd. Why, some
Hold opinion all things are written there.

   Bos. Yes, if we could find spectacles to read them.
I do suspect there hath been some sorcery
Used on the duchess.

   Ferd. Sorcery! to what purpose?

   Bos. To make her dote on some desertless fellow

She shames to acknowledge.

  Ferd. Can your faith give way
To think there's power in potions or in charms,
To make us love whether we will or no?

  Bos. Most certainly.

  Ferd. Away! these are mere gulleries, horrid things,
Invented by some cheating mountebanks
To abuse us. Do you think that herbs or charms
Can force the will? Some trials have been made
In this foolish practice, but the ingredients
Were lenitive poisons, such as are of force
To make the patient mad; and straight the witch
Swears by equivocation they are in love.
The witchcraft lies in her rank blood. This night
I will force confession from her. You told me
You had got, within these two days, a false key
Into her bed-chamber.

  Bos. I have.

  Ferd. As I would wish.

  Bos. What do you intend to do?

  Ferd. Can you guess?

  Bos. No.

  Ferd. Do not ask, then:
He that can compass me, and know my drifts,
May say he hath put a girdle 'bout the world,
And sounded all her quicksands.

  Bos. I do not
Think so.

  Ferd. What do you think, then, pray?

  Bos. That you are
Your own chronicle too much, and grossly
Flatter yourself.

  Ferd. Give me thy hand; I thank thee:
I never gave pension but to flatterers,
Till I entertainèd thee. Farewell.
That friend a great man's ruin strongly checks,
Who rails into his belief all his defects.   *[Exeunt.*

SCENE II—*The Bed-chamber of the* DUCHESS

Enter DUCHESS, ANTONIO, *and* CARIOLA.

Duch. Bring me the casket hither, and the glass.—
You get no lodging here to-night, my lord.
  Ant. Indeed, I must persuade one.
  Duch. Very good:
I hope in time 'twill grow into a custom,
That noblemen shall come with cap and knee
To purchase a night's lodging of their wives.
  Ant. I must lie here.
  Duch. Must! you are a lord of mis-rule.
  Ant. Indeed, my rule is only in the night.
  Duch. To what use will you put me?
  Ant. We'll sleep together.
  Duch. Alas,
What pleasure can two lovers find in sleep!
  Cari. My lord, I lie with her often; and I know
She'll much disquiet you.
  Ant. See, you are complained of.
  Cari. For she's the sprawling'st bedfellow.
  Ant. I shall like her the better for that.
  Cari. Sir, shall I ask you a question?
  Ant. Ay, pray thee, Cariola.
  Cari. Wherefore still, when you lie with my lady,
Do you rise so early?
  Ant. Labouring men
Count the clock oftenest, Cariola,
Are glad when their task's ended.
  Duch. I'll stop your mouth.   [*Kisses him.*
  Ant. Nay, that's but one; Venus had two soft doves
To draw her chariot; I must have another—
                                   [*She kisses him again.*
When wilt thou marry, Cariola?
  Cari. Never, my lord.
  Ant. O, fie upon this single life! forego it.
We read how Daphne, for her peevish[24] flight,
Became a fruitless bay-tree; Syrinx turned

[24] *i.e.* Foolish.

To the pale empty reed; Anaxarete
Was frozen into marble: whereas those
Which married, or proved kind unto their friends,
Were by a gracious influence transhaped
Into the olive, pomegranate, mulberry,
Became flowers, precious stones, or eminent stars.

Cari. This is a vain poetry: but I pray you tell me,
If there were proposed me, wisdom, riches, and beauty,
In three several young men, which should I choose.

Ant. 'Tis a hard question: this was Paris' case,
And he was blind in't, and there was great cause;
For how was't possible he could judge right,
Having three amorous goddesses in view,
And they stark naked? 'twas a motion
Were able to benight the apprehension
Of the severest counsellor of Europe.
Now I look on both your faces so well formed,
It puts me in mind of a question I would ask.

Cari. What is't?

Ant. I do wonder why hard-favoured ladies,
For the most part, keep worse-favoured waiting-women
To attend them, and cannot endure fair ones.

Duch. O, that's soon answered.
Did you ever in your life know an ill painter
Desire to have his dwelling next door to the shop
Of an excellent picture-maker? 'twould disgrace
His face-making, and undo him. I prithee,
When were we so merry?—My hair tangles.

Ant. Pray thee, Cariola, let's steal forth the room,
And let her talk to herself: I have divers times
Served her the like, when she hath chafed extremely.
I love to see her angry. Softly, Cariola.

[*Exeunt* ANTONIO *and* CARIOLA.

Duch. Doth not the colour of my hair 'gin to change?
When I wax gray, I shall have all the court
Powder their hair with arras,[25] to be like me.
You have cause to love me; I entered you into my heart
Before you would vouchsafe to call for the keys.

Enter FERDINAND *behind.*

We shall one day have my brothers take you napping;

[25] Orris.

Methinks his presence, being now in court,
Should make you keep your own bed; but you'll say
Love mixed with fear is sweetest. I'll assure you,
You shall get no more children till my brothers
Consent to be your gossips. Have you lost your tongue?
'Tis welcome:
For know, whether I am doomed to live or die,
I can do both like a prince.

 Ferd. Die, then, quickly! *[Giving her a poniard.*
Virtue, where art thou hid? what hideous thing
Is it that doth eclipse thee?

 Duch. Pray, sir, hear me.

 Ferd. Or is it true thou art but a bare name,
And no essential thing?

 Duch. Sir,—

 Ferd. Do not speak.

 Duch. No, sir:
I will plant my soul in mine ears, to hear you.

 Ferd. O most imperfect light of human reason,
That mak'st us so unhappy to foresee
What we can least prevent! Pursue thy wishes,
And glory in them: there's in shame no comfort
But to be past all bounds and sense of shame.

 Duch. I pray, sir, hear me: I am married.

 Ferd. So!

 Duch. Happily, not to your liking: but for that,
Alas, your shears do come untimely now
To clip the bird's wing that's already flown!
Will you see my husband?

 Ferd. Yes, if I could change
Eyes with a basilisk.

 Duch. Sure, you came hither
By his confederacy.

 Ferd. The howling of a wolf
Is music to thee, screech-owl: prithee, peace.—
Whate'er thou art that hast enjoyed my sister,
For I am sure thou hear'st me, for thine own sake
Let me not know thee. I came hither prepared
To work thy discovery; yet am now persuaded
It would beget such violent effects
As would damn us both. I would not for ten millions
I had beheld thee: therefore use all means

I never may have knowledge of thy name;
Enjoy thy lust still, and a wretched life,
On that condition.—And for thee, vile woman,
If thou do wish thy lecher may grow old
In thy embracements, I would have thee build
Such a room for him as our anchorites
To holier use inhabit. Let not the sun
Shine on him till he's dead; let dogs and monkeys
Only converse with him, and such dumb things
To whom nature denies use to sound his name;
Do not keep a paraquito, lest she learn it;
If thou do love him, cut out thine own tongue,
Lest it bewray him.
 Duch. Why might not I marry?
I have not gone about in this to create
Any new world or custom.
 Ferd. Thou art undone;
And thou hast ta'en that massy sheet of lead
That hid thy husband's bones, and folded it
About my heart.
 Duch. Mine bleeds for't.
 Ferd. Thine! thy heart!
What should I name't unless a hollow bullet
Filled with unquenchable wild-fire?
 Duch. You are in this
Too strict; and were you not my princely brother,
I would say, too wilful: my reputation
Is safe.
 Ferd. Dost thou know what reputation is?
I'll tell thee,—to small purpose, since the instruction
Comes now too late.
Upon a time Reputation, Love, and Death,
Would travel o'er the world; and it was concluded
That they should part, and take three several ways.
Death told them, they should find him in great battles,
Or cities plagued with plagues: Love gives them counsel
To inquire for him 'mongst unambitious shepherds,
Where dowries were not talked of, and sometimes
'Mongst quiet kindred that had nothing left
By their dead parents: "Stay," quoth Reputation,
"Do not forsake me; for it is my nature,
If once I part from any man I meet,

I am never found again." And so for you:
You have shook hands with Reputation,
And made him invisible. So, fare you well:
I will never see you more.

 Duch. Why should only I,
Of all the other princes of the world,
Be cased up, like a holy relic? I have youth
And a little beauty.

 Ferd. So you have some virgins
That are witches. I will never see thee more.   [*Exit.*

  Re-enter ANTONIO *with a pistol, and* CARIOLA.

 Duch. You saw this apparition?

 Ant. Yes: we are
Betrayed. How came he hither? I should turn
This to thee, for that.

 Cari. Pray, sir, do; and when
That you have cleft my heart, you shall read there
Mine innocence.

 Duch. That gallery gave him entrance.

 Ant. I would this terrible thing would come again,
That, standing on my guard, I might relate
My warrantable love.—   [*She shows the poniard.*
     Ha! what means this?

 Duch. He left this with me.

 Ant. And it seems did wish
You would use it on yourself.

 Duch. His action
Seemed to intend so much.

 Ant. This hath a handle to't,
As well as a point: turn it towards him,
And so fasten the keen edge in his rank gall.
       [*Knocking within.*
How now! who knocks? more earthquakes?

 Duch. I stand
As if a mine beneath my feet were ready
To be blown up.

 Cari. 'Tis Bosola.

 Duch. Away!
O misery! methinks unjust actions
Should wear these masks and curtains, and not we.

You must instantly part hence: I have fashioned it already

[*Exit* ANTONIO

Enter BOSOLA.

Bos. The duke your brother is ta'en up in a whirlwind;
Hath took horse, and 's rid post to Rome.
    Duch. So late?
    Bos. He told me, as he mounted into the saddle,
You were undone.
    Duch. Indeed, I am very near it.
    Bos. What's the matter?
    Duch. Antonio, the master of our household,
Hath dealt so falsely with me in 's accounts:
My brother stood engaged with me for money
Ta'en up of certain Neapolitan Jews,
And Antonio lets the bonds be forfeit.
    Bos. Strange!—[*Aside.*] This is cunning.
    Duch. And hereupon
My brother's bills at Naples are protested
Against.—Call up our officers.
    Bos. I shall.   [*Exit.*

Re-enter ANTONIO.

Duch. The place that you must fly to is Ancona:
Hire a house there; I'll send after you
My treasure and my jewels. Our weak safety
Runs upon enginous wheels: short syllables
Must stand for periods. I must now accuse you
Of such a feignèd crime as Tasso calls
Magnanima menzogna, a noble lie,
'Cause it must shield our honours.—Hark! they are coming.

Re-enter BOSOLA *and* Officers.

Ant. Will your grace hear me?
    Duch. I have got well by you; you have yielded me
A million of loss: I am like to inherit
The people's curses for your stewardship.
You had the trick in audit-time to be sick,
Till I had signed your quietus; and that cured you
Without help of a doctor.—Gentlemen,
I would have this man be an example to you all;

So shall you hold my favour; I pray, let him;
For h'as done that, alas, you would not think of,
And, because I intend to be rid of him,
I mean not to publish.—Use your fortune elsewhere.

Ant. I am strongly armed to brook my overthrow,
As commonly men bear with a hard year:
I will not blame the cause on't; but do think
The necessity of my malevolent star
Procures this, not her humour. O, the inconstant
And rotten ground of service! you may see,
'Tis even like him, that in a winter night,
Takes a long slumber o'er a dying fire,
A-loth to part from't; yet parts thence as cold
As when he first sat down.

Duch. We do confiscate,
Towards the satisfying of your accounts,
All that you have.

Ant. I am all yours; and 'tis very fit
All mine should be so.

Duch. So, sir, you have your pass.

Ant. You may see, gentlemen, what 'tis to serve
A prince with body and soul.   [*Exit.*

Bos. Here's an example for extortion: what moisture is
drawn out of the sea, when foul weather comes, pours
down, and runs into the sea again.

Duch. I would know what are your opinions
Of this Antonio.

2nd Off. He could not abide to see a pig's head gaping:
I thought your grace would find him a Jew.

3rd Off. I would you had been his officer, for your own
sake.

4th Off. You would have had more money.

1st Off. He stopped his ears with black wool, and to
those came to him for money said he was thick of hearing.

2nd Off. Some said he was an hermaphrodite, for he
could not abide a woman.

4th Off. How scurvy proud he would look when the
treasury was full! Well, let him go.

1st Off. Yes, and the chippings of the buttery fly after
him, to scour his gold chain.

Duch. Leave us.   [*Exeunt* Officers.
What do you think of these?

Bos. That these are rogues that in's prosperity,
But to have waited on his fortune, could have wished
His dirty stirrup rivetted through their noses,
And followed after's mule, like a bear in a ring;
Would have prostituted their daughters to his lust;
'Made their first-born intelligencers; thought none happy
But such as were born under his blest planet,
And wore his livery: and do these lice drop off now?
Well, never look to have the like again:
He hath left a sort of flattering rogues behind him;
Their doom must follow. Princes pay flatterers
In their own money: flatterers dissemble their vices,
And they dissemble their lies; that's justice.
Alas, poor gentleman!
      Duch. Poor! he hath amply filled his coffers.
      Bos. Sure, he was too honest. Pluto,[26] the god of riches,
When he's sent by Jupiter to any man,
He goes limping, to signify that wealth
That comes on God's name comes slowly; but when he's
      sent
On the devil's errand, he rides post and comes in by
      scuttles.
Let me show you what a most unvalued jewel
You have in a wanton humour thrown away,
To bless the man shall find him. He was an excellent
Courtier and most faithful; a soldier that thought it
As beastly to know his own value too little
As devilish to acknowledge it too much.
Both his virtue and form deserved a far better fortune:
His discourse rather delighted to judge itself than show
      itself:
His breast was filled with all perfection,
And yet it seemed a private whispering-room,
It made so little noise of't.
      Duch. But he was basely descended.
      Bos. Will you make yourself a mercenary herald,
Rather to examine men's pedigrees than virtues?
You shall want him:
For know an honest statesman to a prince
Is like a cedar planted by a spring;
The spring bathes the tree's root, the grateful tree

[26] Plutus.

Rewards it with his shadow: you have not done so.
I would sooner swim to the Bermoothes[27] on
Two politicians' rotten bladders, tied
Together with an intelligencer's heart-string,
Than depend on so changeable a prince's favour.
Fare thee well, Antonio! since the malice of the world
Would needs down with thee, it cannot be said yet
That any ill happened unto thee, considering thy fall
Was accompanied with virtue.

    Duch. O, you render me excellent music!

    Bos. Say you?

    Duch. This good one that you speak of is my husband.

    Bos. Do I not dream! can this ambitious age
Have so much goodness in't as to prefer
A man merely for worth, without these shadows
Of wealth and painted honours? possible?

    Duch. I have had three children by him.

    Bos. Fortunate lady!
For you have made your private nuptial bed
The humble and fair seminary of peace.
No question but many an unbeneficed scholar
Shall pray for you for this deed, and rejoice
That some preferment in the world can yet
Arise from merit. The virgins of your land
That have no dowries shall hope your example
Will raise them to rich husbands. Should you want
Soldiers, 'twould make the very Turks and Moors
Turn Christians, and serve you for this act.
Last, the neglected poets of your time,
In honour of this trophy of a man,
Raised by that curious engine, your white hand,
Shall thank you, in your grave, for't; and make that
More reverend than all the cabinets
Of living princes. For Antonio.
His fame shall likewise flow from many a pen,
When heralds shall want coats to sell to men.

    Duch. As I taste comfort in this friendly speech,
So would I find concealment.

    Bos. O, the secret of my prince,
Which I will wear on the inside of my heart!

    Duch. You shall take charge of all my coin and jewels

[27] "The vexed Bermoothes" was the island of Bermuda.

And follow him; for he retires himself
To Ancona.
  Bos. So.
  Duch. Whither, within few days,
I mean to follow thee.
  Bos. Let me think:
I would wish your grace to feign a pilgrimage
To our Lady of Loretto, scarce seven leagues
From fair Ancona; so may you depart
Your country with more honour, and your flight
Will seem a princely progress, retaining
Your usual train about you.
  Duch. Sir, your direction
Shall lead me by the hand.
  Cari. In my opinion,
She were better progress to the baths at Lucca,
Or go visit the Spa
In Germany; for, if you will believe me,
I do not like this jesting with religion,
This feignèd pilgrimage.
  Duch. Thou art a superstitious fool:
Prepare us instantly for our departure.
Past sorrows, let us moderately lament them;
For those to come, seek wisely to prevent them.
              [*Exeunt* Duchess *and* Cariola.
  Bos. A politician is the devil's quilted anvil;
He fashions all sins on him, and the blows
Are never heard: he may work in a lady's chamber,
As here for proof. What rests but I reveal
All to my lord? O, this base quality
Of intelligencer! why, every quality i' the world
Prefers but gain or commendation:
Now for this act I am certain to be raised,
And men that paint weeds to the life are praised.   [*Exit.*

SCENE III—*An Apartment in the* Cardinal's *Palace at Rome*

Enter Cardinal, Ferdinand, Malatesti, Pescara, Delio,
and Silvio.

  Card. Must we turn soldier, then?
  Mal. The emperor,

Hearing your worth that way, ere you attained
This reverend garment, joins you in commission
With the right fortunate soldier the Marquis of Pescara,
And the famous Lannoy.

Card. He that had the honour
Of taking the French king prisoner? [28]

Mal. The same.
Here's a plot[29] drawn for a new fortification
At Naples.

Ferd. This great Count Malatesti, I perceive,
Hath got employment?

Delio. No employment, my lord;
A marginal note in the muster-book, that he is
A voluntary lord.

Ferd. He's no soldier.

Delio. He has worn gunpowder in's hollow tooth for
    the toothache.

Sil. He come to the leaguer[30] with a full intent
To eat fresh beef and garlic, means to stay
Till the scent be gone, and straight return to court.

Delio. He hath read all the late service
As the city chronicle relates it;
And keeps two pewterers going, only to express
Battles in model.

Sil. Then he'll fight by the book.

Delio. By the almanac, I think,
To choose good days and shun the critical;
That's his mistress' scarf.

Sil. Yes, he protests
He would do much for that taffeta.

Delio. I think he would run away from a battle,
To save it from taking prisoner.

Sil. He is horribly afraid
Gunpowder will spoil the perfume on't.

Delio. I saw a Dutchman break his pate once
For calling him pot-gun; he made his head
Have a bore in't like a musket.

Sil. I would he had made a touchhole to't.

---

[28] Francis I., who surrendered to Lannoy at the battle of Pavia.
[29] Plan.
[30] Camp.

He is indeed a guarded [31] sumpter-cloth,
Only for the remove of the court.

Enter BOSOLA.

Pes. Bosola arrived! what should be the business?
Some falling-out amongst the cardinals.
These factions amongst great men, they are like
Foxes, when their heads are divided,
They carry fire in their tails, and all the country
About them goes to wreck for't.

Sil. What's that Bosola?

Delio. I knew him in Padua—a fantastical scholar, like
such who study to know how many knots was in Hercules'
club, of what colour Achilles' beard was, or whether Hector
were not troubled with the toothache. He hath studied
himself half blear-eyed to know the true symmetry of
Cæsar's nose by a shoeing-horn; and this he did to gain
the name of a speculative man.

Pes. Mark Prince Ferdinand:
A very salamander lives in's eye,
To mock the eager violence of fire.

Sil. That cardinal hath made more bad faces with his
oppression than ever Michael Angelo made good ones: he
lifts up's nose, like a foul porpoise before a storm.

Pes. The Lord Ferdinand laughs.

Delio. Like a deadly cannon
That lightens ere it smokes.

Pes. These are your true pangs of death,
The pangs of life, that struggle with great statesmen.

Delio. In such a deformed silence witches whisper their
      charms.

Card. Doth she make religion her riding-hood
To keep her from the sun and tempest?

Ferd. That,
That damns her. Methinks her fault and beauty,
Blended together, show like leprosy,
The whiter, the fouler. I make it a question
Whether her beggarly brats were ever christened.

Card. I will instantly solicit the state of Ancona
To have them banished.

---

[31] Trimmed.

Ferd. You are for Loretto:
I shall not be at your ceremony; fare you well.—
Write to the Duke of Malfi, my young nephew
She had by her first husband, and acquaint him
With's mother's honesty.

   Bos. I will.

   Ferd. Antonio!
A slave that only smelled of ink and counters,
And never in's life looked like a gentleman,
But in the audit-time.—Go, go presently,
Draw me out an hundred and fifty of our horse,
And meet me at the fort-bridge.   [*Exeunt.*

SCENE IV—*The Shrine of our Lady of Loretto*

Enter Two Pilgrims.

   1st Pil. I have not seen a goodlier shrine than this;
Yet I have visited many.

   2nd Pil. The Cardinal of Arragon
Is this day to resign his cardinal's hat:
His sister duchess likewise is arrived
To pay her vow of pilgrimage. I expect
A noble ceremony.

   1st Pil. No question.—They come.

   Here the ceremony of the Cardinal's *instalment, in the
   habit of a soldier, is performed by his delivering up
   his cross, hat, robes, and ring, at the shrine, and the
   investing of him with sword, helmet, shield, and spurs;
   then* ANTONIO, *the* DUCHESS, *and their children, having
   presented themselves at the shrine, are, by a form of
   banishment in dumb-show expressed towards them by
   the* Cardinal *and the state of Ancona, banished: during
   all which ceremony, this ditty is sung, to very solemn
   music, by divers churchmen.*

Arms and honours deck thy story,
To thy fame's eternal glory!
Adverse fortune ever fly thee;
No disastrous fate come nigh thee!
I alone will sing thy praises,
Whom to honour virtue raises;

And thy study, that divine is,
Bent to martial discipline is.
Lay aside all those robes lie by thee;
Crown thy arts with arms, they'll beautify thee.
O worthy of worthiest name, adorned in this manner,
Lead bravely thy forces on under war's warlike banner!
O, mayst thou prove fortunate in all martial courses!
Guide thou still by skill in arts and forces!
Victory attend thee nigh, whilst fame sings loud thy
    powers;
Triumphant conquest crown thy head, and blessings pour
    down showers!

             [*Exeunt all except the* Two Pilgrims.

   1st Pil. Here's a strange turn of state! who would have
    thought
So great a lady would have matched herself
Unto so mean a person? yet the cardinal
Bears himself much too cruel.
   2nd Pil. They are banished.
   1st Pil. But I would ask what power hath this state
Of Ancona to determine of a free prince?
   2nd Pil. They are a free state, sir, and her brother showed
How that the Pope, fore-hearing of her looseness,
Hath seized into the protection of the church
The dukedom which she held as dowager.
   1st Pil. But by what justice?
   2nd Pil. Sure, I think by none,
Only her brother's instigation.
   1st Pil. What was it with such violence he took
Off from her finger?
   2nd Pil. 'Twas her wedding-ring;
Which he vowed shortly he would sacrifice
To his revenge.
   1st Pil. Alas, Antonio!
If that a man be thrust into a well,
No matter who sets hand to't, his own weight
Will bring him sooner to the bottom. Come, let's hence.
Fortune makes this conclusion general,
All things do help the unhappy man to fall.   [*Exeunt.*

SCENE V—*Near Loretto*

Enter DUCHESS, ANTONIO, Children, CARIOLA, *and* Servants.

Duch. Banished Ancona!
Ant. Yes, you see what power
Lightens in great men's breath.
Duch. Is all our train
Shrunk to this poor remainder?
Ant. These poor men,
Which have got little in your service, vow
To take your fortune: but your wiser buntings,
Now they are fledged, are gone.
Duch. They have done wisely.
This puts me in mind of death: physicians thus,
With their hands full of money, use to give o'er
Their patients.
Ant. Right the fashion of the world:
From decayed fortunes every flatterer shrinks;
Men cease to build where the foundation sinks.
Duch. I had a very strange dream to-night.
Ant. What was't?
Duch. Methought I wore my coronet of state,
And on a sudden all the diamonds
Were changed to pearls.
Ant. My interpretation
Is, you'll weep shortly; for to me the pearls
Do signify your tears.
Duch. The birds that live i' the field
On the wild benefit of nature live
Happier than we; for they may choose their mates,
And carol their sweet pleasures to the spring.

Enter BOSOLA *with a letter.*

Bos. You are happily o'erta'en.
Duch. From my brother?
Bos. Yes, from the Lord Ferdinand your brother
All love and safety.
Duch. Thou dost blanch mischief,
Wouldst make it white. See, see, like to calm weather
At sea before a tempest, false hearts speak fair

To those they intend most mischief.   [*Reads*.
"Send Antonio to me; I want his head in a business."
A politic equivocation!
He doth not want your counsel, but your head;
That is, he cannot sleep till you be dead.
And here's another pitfall that's strewed o'er
With roses; mark it, 'tis a cunning one: [*Reads*.
"I stand engaged for your husband for several debts at
Naples: let not that trouble him; I had rather have his
heart than his money:"—
And I believe so too.
 Bos. What do you believe?
 Duch. That he so much distrusts my husband's love,
He will by no means believe his heart is with him
Until he sees it: the devil is not cunning enough
To circumvent us in riddles.
 Bos. Will you reject that noble and free league
Of amity and love which I present you?
 Duch. Their league is like that of some politic kings,
Only to make themselves of strength and power
To be our after-ruin: tell them so.
 Bos. And what from you?
 Ant. Thus tell him; I will not come.
 Bos. And what of this?
 Ant. My brothers have dispersed
Blood-hounds abroad; which till I hear are muzzled,
No truce, though hatched with ne'er such politic skill,
Is safe, that hangs upon our enemies' will.
I'll not come at them.
 Bos. This proclaims your breeding:
Every small thing draws a base mind to fear,
As the adamant draws iron. Fare you well, sir:
You shall shortly hear from's.   [*Exit*.
 Duch. I suspect some ambush:
Therefore by all my love I do conjure you
To take your eldest son, and fly towards Milan.
Let us not venture all this poor remainder
In one unlucky bottom.
 Ant. You counsel safely.
Best of my life, farewell, since we must part:
Heaven hath a hand in't; but no otherwise
Than as some curious artist takes in sunder

A clock or watch, when it is out of frame,
To bring't in better order.

Duch. I know not which is best,
To see you dead, or part with you.—Farewell, boy:
Thou art happy that thou hast not understanding
To know thy misery; for all our wit
And reading brings us to a truer sense
Of sorrow.—In the eternal church, sir,
I do hope we shall not part thus.

Ant. O, be of comfort!
Make patience a noble fortitude,
And think not how unkindly we are used:
Man, like to cassia, is proved best being bruised.

Duch. Must I, like a slave-born Russian,
Account it praise to suffer tyranny?
And yet, O Heaven, thy heavy hand is in't!
I have seen my little boy oft scourge his top,
And compared myself to't: naught made me e'er
Go right but Heaven's scourge-stick.

Ant. Do not weep:
Heaven fashioned us of nothing, and we strive
To bring ourselves to nothing.—Farewell, Cariola,
And thy sweet armful.—If I do never see thee more,
Be a good mother to your little ones,
And save them from the tiger: fare you well.

Duch. Let me look upon you once more, for that speech
Came from a dying father: your kiss is colder
Than that I have seen an holy anchorite
Give to a dead man's skull.

Ant. My heart is turned to a heavy lump of lead,
With which I sound my danger: fare you well.

[*Exeunt* ANTONIO *and his* Son

Duch. My laurel is all withered.

Cari. Look, madam, what a troop of armèd men
Make towards us.

Duch. O, they are very welcome:
When Fortune's wheel is over-charged with princes,
The weight makes it move swift: I would have my ruin
Be sudden.

Re-enter BOSOLA *visarded, with a* Guard.

I am your adventure, am I not?

Bos. You are: you must see your husband no more.

Duch. What devil art thou that counterfeit'st Heaven's
thunder?

Bos. Is that terrible? I would have you tell me whether
Is that note worse that frights the silly birds
Out of the corn, or that which doth allure them
To the nets? you have hearkened to the last too much.

Duch. O misery! like to a rusty o'er-charged cannon,
Shall I never fly in pieces?—Come, to what prison?

Bos. To none.

Duch. Whither, then?

Bos. To your palace.

Duch. I have heard
That Charon's boat serves to convey all o'er
The dismal lake, but brings none back again.

Bos. Your brothers mean you safety and pity.

Duch. Pity!
With such a pity men preserve alive
Pheasants and quails, when they are not fat enough
To be eaten.

Bos. These are your children?

Duch. Yes.

Bos. Can they prattle?

Duch. No;
But I intend, since they were born accursed,
Curses shall be their first language.

Bos. Fie, madam!
Forget this base, low fellow,—

Duch. Were I a man,
I'd beat that counterfeit face into thy other.

Bos. One of no birth.

Duch. Say that he was born mean,
Man is most happy when's own actions
Be arguments and examples of his virtue.

Bos. A barren, beggarly virtue.

Duch. I prithee, who is greatest? can you tell?
Sad tales befit my woe: I'll tell you one.
A salmon, as she swam unto the sea,
Met with a dog-fish, who encounters her
With this rough language: "Why art thou so bold
To mix thyself with our high state of floods,
Being no eminent courtier, but one

That for the calmest and fresh time o' the year
Dost live in shallow rivers, rank'st thyself
With silly smelts and shrimps? and darest thou
Pass by our dog-ship without reverence?"
"O!" quoth the salmon, "sister, be at peace:
Thank Jupiter we both have passed the net!
Our value never can be truly known,
Till in the fisher's basket we be shown:
I' the market then my price may be the higher,
Even when I am nearest to the cook and fire."
So to great men the moral may be stretched;
Men oft are valued high, when they're most wretched.—
But come, whither you please. I am armed 'gainst misery;
Bent to all sways of the oppressor's will:
There's no deep valley but near some great hill.   [*Exeunt.*

ACT THE FOURTH

SCENE I—*An Apartment in the* DUCHESS' *Palace at Malfi*

Enter FERDINAND *and* BOSOLA.

FERD. How doth our sister duchess bear herself
In her imprisonment?
   Bos. Nobly: I'll describe her.
She's sad as one long used to't, and she seems
Rather to welcome the end of misery
Than shun it; a behaviour so noble
As gives a majesty to adversity:
You may discern the shape of loveliness
More perfect in her tears than in her smiles:
She will muse four hours together; and her silence,
Methinks, expresseth more than if she spake.
   Ferd. Her melancholy seems to be fortified
With a strange disdain.
   Bos. 'Tis so; and this restraint,
Like English mastiffs that grow fierce with tying,
Makes her too passionately apprehend
Those pleasures she's kept from.
   Ferd. Curse upon her!
I will no longer study in the book

Of another's heart. Inform her what I told you.   [*Exit.*

Enter DUCHESS.[32]

Bos. All comfort to your grace!

Duch. I will have none.
Pray thee, why dost thou wrap thy poisoned pills
In gold and sugar?

Bos. Your elder brother, the Lord Ferdinand,
Is come to visit you, and sends you word,
'Cause once he rashly made a solemn vow
Never to see you more, he comes i' the night;
And prays you gently neither torch nor taper
Shine in your chamber: he will kiss your hand,
And reconcile himself; but for his vow
He dares not see you.

Duch. At his pleasure.—
Take hence the lights.—He's come.

Enter FERDINAND.

Ferd. Where are you?

Duch. Here, sir.

Ferd. This darkness suits you well.

Duch. I would ask you pardon.

Ferd. You have it;
For I account it the honorabl'st revenge,
Where I may kill, to pardon.—Where are your cubs?

Duch. Whom?

Ferd. Call them your children;
For though our national law distinguish bastards
From true legitimate issue, compassionate nature
Makes them all equal.

Duch. Do you visit me for this?
You violate a sacrament o' the church
Shall make you howl in hell for't.

Ferd. It had been well,
Could you have lived thus always; for, indeed,
You were too much i' the light:—but no more;
I come to seal my peace with you. Here's a hand
                                        [*Gives her a dead man's hand.*

---

[32] Dyce suggests that here the audience had to imagine a change of scene—
to the lodging of the Duchess, who is confined to certain apartments in her
own palace.

To which you have vowed much love; the ring upon't
You gave.

Duch. I affectionately kiss it.

Ferd. Pray, do, and bury the print of it in your heart.
I will leave this ring with you for a love-token;
And the hand as sure as the ring; and do not doubt
But you shall have the heart too: when you need a friend,
Send it to him that owned it; you shall see
Whether he can aid you.

Duch. You are very cold:
I fear you are not well after your travel.—
Ha! lights!—O, horrible!

Ferd. Let her have lights enough.   [*Exit.*

Duch. What witchcraft doth he practise, that he hath left
A dead man's hand here?

> [*Here is discovered, behind a traverse,*[33] *the artificial
> figures of* ANTONIO *and his* Children, *appearing
> as if they were dead.*

Bos. Look you, here's the piece from which 'twas ta'en.
He doth present you this sad spectacle,
That, now you know directly they are dead,
Hereafter you may wisely cease to grieve
For that which cannot be recoverèd.

Duch. There is not between Heaven and earth one wish
I stay for after this: it wastes me more
Than were't my picture, fashioned out of wax,
Stuck with a magical needle, and then buried
In some foul dunghill; and yond's an excellent property
For a tyrant, which I would account mercy.

Bos. What's that?

Duch. If they would bind me to that lifeless trunk,
And let me freeze to death.

Bos. Come, you must live.

Duch. That's the greatest torture souls feel in hell,
In hell, that they must live, and cannot die.
Portia, I'll new kindle thy coals again,
And revive the rare and almost dead example
Of a loving wife.

Bos. O, fie! despair? remember
You are a Christian.

[33] Curtain.

Duch. The church enjoins fasting:
I'll starve myself to death.

Bos. Leave this vain sorrow.
Things being at the worst begin to mend: the bee
When he hath shot his sting into your hand,
May then play with your eyelid.

Duch. Good comfortable fellow,
Persuade a wretch that's broke upon the wheel
To have all his bones new set; entreat him live
To be executed again. Who must despatch me?
I account this world a tedious theatre,
For I do play a part in't 'gainst my will.

Bos. Come, be of comfort; I will save your life.

Duch. Indeed, I have not leisure to tend
So small a business.

Bos. Now, by my life, I pity you.

Duch. Thou art a fool, then,
To waste thy pity on a thing so wretched
As cannot pity itself. I am full of daggers.
Puff, let me blow these vipers from me.

Enter Servant.

What are you?

Serv. One that wishes you long life.

Duch. I would thou wert hanged for the horrible curse
Thou hast given me: I shall shortly grow one
Of the miracles of pity. I'll go pray;—
No, I'll go curse.

Bos. O, fie!

Duch. I could curse the stars.

Bos. O, fearful.

Duch. And those three smiling seasons of the year
Into a Russian winter: nay, the world
To its first chaos.

Bos. Look you, the stars shine still.

Duch. O, but you must
Remember, my curse hath a great way to go.—
Plagues, that make lanes through largest families,
Consume them!—

Bos. Fie, lady!

Duch. Let them, like tyrants,

Never be remembered but for the ill they have done;
Let all the zealous prayers of mortified
Churchmen forget them!—

   Bos. O, uncharitable!

   Duch. Let Heaven a little while cease crowning martyrs,
To punish them!—
Go, howl them this, and say, I long to bleed:
It is some mercy when men kill with speed.   [*Exit.*

           Re-enter FERDINAND.

   Ferd. Excellent, as I would wish; she's plagued in art:
These presentations are but framed in wax
By the curious master in that quality,
Vincentio Lauriola, and she takes them
For true substantial bodies.

   Bos. Why do you do this?

   Ferd. To bring her to despair.

   Bos. Faith, end here,
And go no farther in your cruelty:
Send her a penitential garment to put on
Next to her delicate skin, and furnish her
With beads and prayer-books.

   Ferd. Damn her! that body of hers,
While that my blood ran pure in 't, was more worth
Than that which thou wouldst comfort, called a soul.
I will send her masks of common courtezans,
Have her meat served up by bawds and ruffians,
And, 'cause she'll needs be mad, I am resolved
To remove forth the common hospital
All the mad-folk, and place them near her lodging;
There let them practise together, sing and dance,
And act their gambols to the full o' the moon:
If she can sleep the better for it, let her.
Your work is almost ended.

   Bos. Must I see her again?

   Ferd. Yes.

   Bos. Never.

   Ferd. You must.

   Bos. Never in mine own shape;
That's forfeited by my intelligence
And this last cruel lie: when you send me next,
The business shall be comfort.

Ferd. Very likely;
Thy pity is nothing of kin to thee. Antonio
Lurks about Milan: thou shalt shortly thither,
To feed a fire as great as my revenge,
Which never will slack till it have spent his fuel:
Intemperate agues make physicians cruel.   [*Exeunt.*

SCENE II—*Another Room in the* DUCHESS' *Lodging*

Enter DUCHESS *and* CARIOLA.

Duch. What hideous noise was that?
Cari. 'Tis the wild consort[34]
Of madmen, lady, which your tyrant brother
Hath placed about your lodging: this tyranny,
I think, was never practised till this hour.
Duch. Indeed, I thank him: nothing but noise and folly
Can keep me in my right wits; whereas reason
And silence make me stark mad. Sit down;
Discourse to me some dismal tragedy.
Cari. O, 'twill increase your melancholy.
Duch. Thou art deceived:
To hear of greater grief would lessen mine.
This is a prison?
Cari. Yes, but you shall live
To shake this durance off.
Duch. Thou art a fool:
The robin-redbreast and the nightingale
Never live long in cages.
Cari. Pray, dry your eyes.
What think you of, madam?
Duch. Of nothing;
When I muse thus, I sleep.
Cari. Like a madman, with your eyes open?
Duch. Dost thou think we shall know one another
In the other world?
Cari. Yes, out of question.
Duch. O, that it were possible we might
But hold some two days' conference with the dead!
From them I should learn somewhat, I am sure,

[34] Band.

I never shall know here. I'll tell thee a miracle;
I am not mad yet, to my cause of sorrow:
The Heaven o'er my head seems made of molten brass,
The earth of flaming sulphur, yet I am not mad.
I am acquainted with sad misery
As the tanned galley-slave is with his oar;
Necessity makes me suffer constantly,
And custom makes it easy. Who do I look like now?

   Cari. Like to your picture in the gallery,
A deal of life in show, but none in practice;
Or rather like some reverend monument
Whose ruins are even pitied.

   Duch. Very proper;
And Fortune seems only to have her eyesight
To behold my tragedy.—How now!
What noise is that?

Enter Servant.

   Serv. I am come to tell you
Your brother hath intended you some sport.
A great physician, when the Pope was sick
Of a deep melancholy, presented him
With several sorts of madmen, which wild object
Being full of change and sport, forced him to laugh,
And so the imposthume broke: the self-same cure
The duke intends on you.

   Duch. Let them come in.

   Serv. There's a mad lawyer; and a secular priest;
A doctor that hath forfeited his wits
By jealousy; an astrologian
That in his works said such a day o' the month
Should be the day of doom, and, failing of't,
Ran mad; an English tailor crazed i' the brain
With the study of new fashions; a gentleman-usher
Quite beside himself with care to keep in mind
The number of his lady's salutations
Or "How do you" she employed him in each morning;
A farmer, too, an excellent knave in grain,
Mad 'cause he was hindered transportation:
And let one broker that's mad loose to these,
You'd think the devil were among them.

Duch. Sit, Cariola.—Let them loose when you please,
For I am chained to endure all your tyranny.

Enter Madmen.

*Here this Song is sung to a dismal kind of music by
a* Madman.

O, let us howl some heavy note,
    Some deadly dogged howl,
Sounding as from the threatening throat
    Of beasts and fatal fowl!
As ravens, screech-owls, bulls, and bears,
    We'll bell, and bawl our parts,
Till irksome noise have cloyed your ears
    And còrrosived your hearts.
At last, whenas our quire wants breath,
    Our bodies being blest,
We'll sing, like swans, to welcome death,
    And die in love and rest.

1st Madman. Doom's-day not come yet! I'll draw it nearer
by a perspective, or make a glass that shall set all the world
on fire upon an instant. I cannot sleep; my pillow is stuffed
with a litter of porcupines.

2nd Madman. Hell is a mere glass-house, where the devils
are continually blowing up women's souls on hollow irons,
and the fire never goes out.

3rd Madman. I will lie with every woman in my parish
the tenth night; I will tythe them over like haycocks.

4th Madman. Shall my pothecary out-go me because I
am a cuckold? I have found out his roguery; he makes
alum of his wife's urine, and sells it to Puritans that have
sore throats with overstraining.

1st Madman. I have skill in heraldry.

2nd Madman. Hast?

1st Madman. You do give for your crest a woodcock's
head with the brains picked out on't; you are a very ancient
gentleman.

3rd Madman. Greek is turned Turk: we are only to be
saved by the Helvetian translation.

1st Madman. Come on, sir, I will lay the law to you.

2nd Madman. O, rather lay a corrosive: the law will eat
to the bone.

3rd Madman. He that drinks but to satisfy nature is damned.

4th Madman. If I had my glass here, I would show a sight should make all the women here call me mad doctor.

1st Madman. What's he? a rope-maker?

2nd Madman. No, no, no, a snuffling knave that, while he shows the tombs, will have his hand in a wench's placket.

3rd Madman. Woe to the caroche[35] that brought home my wife from the masque at three o'clock in the morning! it had a large feather-bed in it.

4th Madman. I have pared the devil's nails forty times, roasted them in raven's eggs, and cured agues with them.

3rd Madman. Get me three hundred milchbats, to make possets to procure sleep.

4th Madman. All the college may throw their caps at me: I have made a soap-boiler costive; it was my master-piece.

> [*Here a dance of* Eight Madmen, *with music
> answerable thereto; after which,* Bosola, *like
> an* Old Man, *enters.*

Duch. Is he mad too?

Serv. Pray, question him. I'll leave you.

> [*Exeunt* Servant *and* Madmen.

Bos. I am come to make thy tomb.

Duch. Ha! my tomb!
Thou speak'st as if I lay upon my deathbed,
Gasping for breath: dost thou perceive me sick?

Bos. Yes, and the more dangerously, since thy sickness is insensible.

Duch. Thou art not mad, sure: dost know me?

Bos. Yes.

Duch. Who am I?

Bos. Thou art a box of worm-seed, at best but a salvatory of green mummy. What's this flesh? a little crudded milk, fantastical puff-paste. Our bodies are weaker than those paper-prisons boys use to keep flies in; more contemptible, since ours is to preserve earth-worms. Didst thou ever see a lark in a cage? Such is the soul in the body: this world is like her little turf of grass, and the Heaven o'er our heads,

35 Coach.

like her looking-glass, only gives us a miserable knowledge
of the small compass of our prison.

Duch. Am not I thy duchess?

Bos. Thou art some great woman, sure, for riot begins
to sit on thy forehead (clad in grey hairs) twenty years
sooner than on a merry milkmaid's. Thou sleepest worse
than if a mouse should be forced to take up her lodging
in a cat's ear: a little infant that breeds its teeth, should it
lie with thee, would cry out, as if thou wert the more unquiet bedfellow.

Duch. I am Duchess of Malfi still.

Bos. That makes thy sleeps so broken:
Glories, like glow-worms, afar off shine bright,
But looked to near, have neither heat nor light.

Duch. Thou art very plain.

Bos. My trade is to flatter the dead, not the living;
I am a tomb-maker.

Duch. And thou comest to make my tomb?

Bos. Yes.

Duch. Let me be a little merry:—of what stuff wilt thou
make it?

Bos. Nay, resolve me first, of what fashion?

Duch. Why do we grow fantastical in our deathbed? do
we affect fashion in the grave?

Bos. Most ambitiously. Princes' images on their tombs do
not lie, as they were wont, seeming to pray up to Heaven;
but with their hands under their cheeks, as if they died of
the toothache: they are not carved with their eyes fixed
upon the stars; but as their minds were wholly bent upon
the world, the self-same way they seem to turn their faces.

Duch. Let me know fully therefore the effect
Of this thy dismal preparation,
This talk fit for a charnel.

Bos. Now I shall:—

Enter Executioners, *with a coffin, cords, and a bell.*

Here is a present from your princely brothers;
And may it arrive welcome, for it brings
Last benefit, last sorrow.

Duch. Let me see it:
I have so much obedience in my blood,

I wish it in their veins to do them good.

   Bos. This is your last presence-chamber.

   Cari. O my sweet lady!

   Duch. Peace; it affrights not me.

   Bos. I am the common bellman,

That usually is sent to condemned persons
The night before they suffer.

   Duch. Even now thou said'st

Thou wast a tomb-maker.

   Bos. 'Twas to bring you

By degrees to mortification. Listen.

        Hark, now every thing is still
        The screech-owl and the whistler shrill
        Call upon our dame aloud,
        And bid her quickly don her shroud!
        Much you had of land and rent;
        Your length in clay's now competent:
        A long war disturbed your mind;
        Here your perfect peace is signed.
        Of what is't fools make such vain keeping?
        Sin their conception, their birth weeping,
        Their life a general mist of error,
        Their death a hideous storm of terror.
        Strew your hair with powders sweet,
        Don clean linen, bathe your feet,
        And (the foul fiend more to check)
        A crucifix let bless your neck:
        'Tis now full tide 'tween night and day;
        End your groan, and come away.

   Cari. Hence, villains, tyrants, murderers! alas!

What will you do with my lady?—Call for help.

   Duch. To whom? to our next neighbours? they are mad-
     folks.

   Bos. Remove that noise.

   Duch. Farewell, Cariola.

In my last will I have not much to give:
A many hungry guests have fed upon me;
Thine will be a poor reversion.

   Cari. I will die with her.

   Duch. I pray thee, look thou giv'st my little boy

Some syrup for his cold, and let the girl
Say her prayers ere she sleep.

[CARIOLA *is forced out by the* Executioners.
                                    Now what you please:
What death?

Bos. Strangling; here are your executioners.

Duch. I forgive them:
The apoplexy, catarrh, or cough o' the lungs,
Would do as much as they do.

Bos. Doth not death fright you?

Duch. Who would be afraid on't,
Knowing to meet such excellent company
In the other world?

Bos. Yet, methinks,
The manner of your death should much afflict you:
This cord should terrify you.

Duch. Not a whit:
What would it pleasure me to have my throat cut
With diamonds? or to be smotherèd
With cassia? or to be shot to death with pearls?
I know death hath ten thousand several doors
For men to take their exits; and 'tis found
They go on such strange geometrical hinges,
You may open them both ways; any way, for Heaven sake,
So I were out of your whispering. Tell my brothers
That I perceive death, now I am well awake,
Best gift is they can give or I can take.
I would fain put off my last woman's fault,
I'd not be tedious to you.

1st Execut. We are ready.

Duch. Dispose my breath how please you; but my body
Bestow upon my women, will you?

1st Execut. Yes.

Duch. Pull, and pull strongly, for your able strength
Must pull down Heaven upon me:—
Yet stay; Heaven-gates are not so highly arched
As princes' palaces; they that enter there
Must go upon their knees [*Kneels*].—Come, violent death,
Serve for mandragora to make me sleep!—
Go tell my brothers, when I am laid out,
They then may feed in quiet.

                    [*The* Executioners *strangle the* DUCHESS.[36]

---

[36] "She has lived among horrors till she is become 'native and endowed unto
that element.' She speaks the dialect of despair, her tongue has a smatch of

Bos. Where's the waiting woman?
Fetch her: some other strangle the children.

> [CARIOLA *and* Children *are brought in by the*
> Executioners; *who presently strangle the*
> Children.

Look you, there sleeps your mistress.

Cari. O, you are damned
Perpetually for this! My turn is next,
Is't not so ordered?

Bos. Yes, and I am glad
You are so well prepared for't.

Cari. You are deceived, sir,
I am not prepared for't, I will not die;
I will first come to my answer, and know
How I have offended.

Bos. Come, despatch her.—
You kept her counsel; now you shall keep ours.

Cari. I will not die, I must not; I am contracted
To a young gentleman.

1st Execut. Here's your wedding-ring.

Cari. Let me but speak with the duke; I'll discover
Treason to his person.

Bos. Delays;—throttle her.

1st Execut. She bites and scratches.

Cari. If you kill me now,
I am damned; I have not been at confession
This two years.

Bos. [*To* Executioners.] When?

Cari. I am quick with child.

Bos. Why, then,
Your credit's saved.

> [*The* Executioners *strangle* CARIOLA.
> Bear her into the next room;

Tartarus and the souls in bale. What are 'Luke's iron crown,' the brazen bull
of Perillus, Procrustes' bed, to the waxen images which counterfeit death, to
the wild masque of madmen, the tomb-maker, the bell-man, the living person's
dirge, the mortification by degrees! To move a horror skilfully, to touch a
soul to the quick, to lay upon fear as much as it can bear, to wean and
weary a life till it is ready to drop, and then step in with mortal instruments
to take its last forfeit; this only a Webster can do. Writers of an inferior genius
may 'upon horror's head horrors accumulate,' but they cannot do this. They
mistake quantity for quality, they 'terrify babes with painted devils,' but they
know not how a soul is capable of being moved; their terrors want dignity,
their affrightments are without decorum.''—C. Lamb, *Spec. of Eng. Dram. Poets.*

Let these lie still.
    [*Exeunt the* Executioners *with the body of* CARIOLA.

Enter FERDINAND.

  Ferd. Is she dead?
  Bos. She is what
You'd have her. But here begin your pity:
                  [*Shows the* Children *strangled.*
Alas, how have these offended?
  Ferd. The death
Of young wolves is never to be pitied.
  Bos. Fix your eye here.
  Ferd. Constantly.
  Bos. Do you not weep?
Other sins only speak; murder shrieks out:
The element of water moistens the earth,
But blood flies upwards and bedews the heavens.
  Ferd. Cover her face; mine eyes dazzle: she died **young.**
  Bos. I think not so; her infelicity
Seemed to have years too many.
  Ferd. She and I were twins;
And should I die this instant, I had lived
Her time to a minute.
  Bos. It seems she was born first:
You have bloodily approved the ancient truth,
That kindred commonly do worse agree
Than remote strangers.
  Ferd. Let me see her face
Again. Why didst not thou pity her? what
An excellent honest man mightst thou have **been,**
If thou hadst born her to some sanctuary!
Or, bold in a good cause, opposed thyself,
With thy advancèd sword above thy head,
Between her innocence and my revenge!
I bade thee, when I was distracted of my wits,
Go kill my dearest friend, and thou hast done't.
For let me but examine well the cause:
What was the meanness of her match to me?
Only I must confess I had a hope,
Had she continued widow, to have gained
An infinite mass of treasure by her death:
And what was the main cause? her marriage,

That drew a stream of gall quite through my heart.
For thee, as we observe in tragedies
That a good actor many times is cursed
For playing a villain's part, I hate thee for't,
And, for my sake, say, thou hast done much ill well.

Bos. Let me quicken your memory, for I perceive
You are falling into ingratitude: I challenge
The reward due to my service.

Ferd. I'll tell thee
What I'll give thee.

Bos. Do.

Ferd. I'll give thee a pardon
For this murder.

Bos. Ha!

Ferd. Yes, and 'tis
The largest bounty I can study to do thee.
By what authority didst thou execute
This bloody sentence?

Bos. By yours.

Ferd. Mine! was I her judge?
Did any ceremonial form of law
Doom her to not-being? did a còmplete jury
Deliver her conviction up i' the court?
Where shalt thou find this judgment registered,
Unless in hell? See, like a bloody fool,
Thou'st forfeited thy life, and thou shalt die for't.

Bos. The office of justice is perverted quite
When one thief hangs another. Who shall dare
To reveal this?

Ferd. O, I'll tell thee;
The wolf shall find her grave, and scrape it up,
Not to devour the corpse, but to discover
The horrid murder.[37]

Bos. You, not I, shall quake for't.

Ferd. Leave me.

Bos. I will first receive my pension.

Ferd. You are a villain.

Bos. When your ingratitude
Is judge, I am so.

Ferd. O horror,
That not the fear of him which binds the devils

[37] This was a common superstition of the time.

Can prescribe man obedience!—
Never look upon me more.

Bos. Why, fare thee well.
Your brother and yourself are worthy men:
You have a pair of hearts are hollow graves,
Rotten, and rotting others; and your vengeance,
Like two chained bullets, still goes arm in arm:
You may be brothers; for treason, like the plague,
Doth take much in a blood. I stand like one
That long hath ta'en a sweet and golden dream:
I am angry with myself, now that I wake.

Ferd. Get thee into some unknown part o' the world,
That I may never see thee.

Bos. Let me know
Wherefore I should be thus neglected. Sir,
I served your tyranny, and rather strove
To satisfy yourself than all the world:
And though I loathed the evil, yet I loved
You that did counsel it; and rather sought
To appear a true servant than an honest man.

Ferd. I'll go hunt the badger by owl-light:
'Tis a deed of darkness.   [*Exit.*

Bos. He's much distracted. Off, my painted honour!
While with vain hopes our faculties we tire,
We seem to sweat in ice and freeze in fire.
What would I do, were this to do again?
I would not change my peace of conscience
For all the wealth of Europe.—She stirs; here's life:—
Return, fair soul, from darkness, and lead mine
Out of this sensible hell:—she's warm, she breathes:—
Upon thy pale lips I will melt my heart,
To store them with fresh colour.—Who's there!
Some cordial drink!—Alas! I dare not call:
So pity would destroy pity.—Her eye opes,
And Heaven in it seems to ope, that late was shut,
To take me up to mercy.

Duch. Antonio!

Bos. Yes, madam, he is living;
The dead bodies you saw were but feigned statues:
He's reconciled to your brothers; the Pope hath wrought
The atonement.

Duch. Mercy!   [*Dies.*

Bos. O, she's gone again! there the cords of life broke.
O sacred innocence, that sweetly sleeps
On turtles' feathers, whilst a guilty conscience
Is a black register wherein is writ
All our good deeds and bad, a perspective
That shows us hell! That we cannot be suffered
To do good when we have a mind to it!
This is manly sorrow;
These tears, I am very certain, never grew
In my mother's milk: my estate is sunk
Below the degree of fear: where were
These penitent fountains while she was living?
O, they were frozen up! Here is a sight
As direful to my soul as is the sword
Unto a wretch hath slain his father. Come,
I'll bear thee hence,
And execute thy last will; that's deliver
Thy body to the reverend dispose
Of some good women: that the cruel tyrant
Shall not deny me. Then I'll post to Milan,
Where somewhat I will speedily enact
Worth my dejection.   [*Exit.*

ACT THE FIFTH

SCENE I—*A Public Place in Milan*

Enter ANTONIO *and* DELIO.

ANT. What think you of my hope of reconcilement
To the Arragonian brethren?
   Delio. I misdoubt it;
For though they have sent their letters of safe-conduct
For your repair to Milan, they appear
But nets to entrap you. The Marquis of Pescara,
Under whom you hold certain land in cheat,
Much 'gainst his noble nature hath been moved
To seize those lands; and some of his dependants
Are at this instant making it their suit
To be invested in your revenues.

I cannot think they mean well to your life
That do deprive you of your means of life,
Your living.

Ant. You are still an heretic
To any safety I can shape myself.

Delio. Here comes the marquis: I will make myself
Petitioner for some part of your land,
To know whither it is flying.

Ant. I pray do.

Enter PESCARA.

Delio. Sir, I have a suit to you.

Pes. To me?

Delio. An easy one:
There is the citadel of Saint Bennet,
With some demesnes, of late in the possession
Of Antonio Bologna,—please you bestow them on me.

Pes. You are my friend; but this is such a suit,
Nor fit for me to give, nor you to take.

Delio. No, sir?

Pes. I will give you ample reason for't
Soon in private:—here's the cardinal's mistress.

Enter JULIA.

Julia. My lord, I am grown your poor petitioner,
And should be an ill beggar, had I not
A great man's letter here, the cardinal's,
To court you in my favour.   [*Gives a letter.*

Pes. He entreats for you
The citadel of Saint Bennet, that belonged
To the banished Bologna.

Julia. Yes.

Pes. I could not have thought of a friend I could rather
Pleasure with it: 'tis yours.

Julia. Sir, I thank you;
And he shall know how doubly I am engaged
Both in your gift, and speediness of giving
Which makes your grant the greater.   [*Exit.*

Ant. How they fortify
Themselves with my ruin!

Delio. Sir, I am
Little bound to you.

Pes. Why?

Delio. Because you denied this suit to me, and gave't
To such a creature.

Pes. Do you know what it was?
It was Antonio's land; not forfeited
By course of law, but ravished from his throat
By the cardinal's entreaty: it were not fit
I should bestow so main a piece of wrong
Upon my friend; 'tis a gratification
Only due to a strumpet, for it is injustice.
Shall I sprinkle the pure blood of innocents
To make those followers I call my friends
Look ruddier upon me? I am glad
This land, ta'en from the owner by such wrong,
Returns again unto so foul an use
As salary for his lust. Learn, good Delio,
To ask noble things of me, and you shall find
I'll be a noble giver.

Delio. You instruct me well.

Ant. Why, here's a man now would fright impudence
From sauciest beggars.

Pes. Prince Ferdinand's come to Milan,
Sick, as they give out, of an apoplexy;
But some say 'tis a frenzy: I am going
To visit him.   [*Exit.*

Ant. 'Tis a noble old fellow.

Delio. What course do you mean to take, Antonio?

Ant. This night I mean to venture all my fortune,
Which is no more than a poor lingering life,
To the cardinal's worst of malice: I have got
Private access to his chamber; and intend
To visit him about the mid of night,
As once his brother did our noble duchess.
It may be that the sudden apprehension
Of danger,—for I'll go in mine own shape,—
When he shall see it fraught[38] with love and duty,
May draw the poison out of him, and work
A friendly reconcilement: if it fail,
Yet it shall rid me of this infamous calling;
For better fall once than be ever falling.

[38] Fraught.

Delio. I'll second you in all danger; and, howe'er,
My life keeps rank with yours.

Ant. You are still my loved and best friend.   [*Exeunt.*

SCENE II—*A Gallery in the* Cardinal's *Palace at Milan*

Enter PESCARA *and* Doctor.

Pes. Now, doctor, may I visit your patient?

Doc. If't please your lordship: but he's instantly
To take the air here in the gallery
By my direction.

Pes. Pray thee, what's his disease?

Doc. A very pestilent disease, my lord,
They call lycanthropia.

Pes. What's that?
I need a dictionary to't.

Doc. I'll tell you.
In those that are possessed with't there o'erflows
Such melancholy humour they imagine
Themselves to be transformed into wolves;
Steal forth to churchyards in the dead of night,
And dig dead bodies up: as two nights since
One met the duke 'bout midnight in a lane
Behind Saint Mark's church, with the leg of a man
Upon his shoulder; and he howled fearfully;
Said he was a wolf, only the difference
Was, a wolf's skin was hairy on the outside,
His on the inside; bade them take their swords,
Rip up his flesh, and try: straight I was sent for,
And, having ministered to him, found his grace
Very well recovered.

Pes. I am glad on't.

Doc. Yet not without some fear
Of a relapse. If he grow to his fit again,
I'll go a nearer way to work with him
Than ever Paracelsus dreamed of; if
They'll give me leave, I'll buffet his madness out of him.
Stand aside; he comes.

Enter FERDINAND, *Cardinal,* MALATESTI, *and* BOSOLA.

Ferd. Leave me.

Mal. Why doth your lordship love this solitariness?

Ferd. Eagles commonly fly alone: they are crows, daws, and starlings that flock together. Look, what's that follows me?

Mal. Nothing, my lord.

Ferd. Yes.

Mal. 'Tis your shadow.

Ferd. Stay it; let it not haunt me.

Mal. Impossible, if you move, and the sun shine.

Ferd. I will throttle it.

            [Throws himself down on his shadow.

Mal. O, my lord, you are angry with nothing.

Ferd. You are a fool: how is't possible I should catch my shadow, unless I fall upon't? When I go to hell, I mean to carry a bribe; for, look you, good gifts evermore make way for the worst persons.

Pes. Rise, good my lord.

Ferd. I am studying the art of patience.

Pes. 'Tis a noble virtue.

Ferd. To drive six snails before me from this town to Moscow; neither use goad nor whip to them, but let them take their own time;—the patient'st man i' the world match me for an experiment;—and I'll crawl after like a sheep-biter.

Card. Force him up.   *[They raise him.*

Ferd. Use me well, you were best. What I have done, I have done: I'll confess nothing.

Doc. Now let me come to him.—Are you mad, my lord? are you out of your princely wits?

Ferd. What's he?

Pes. Your doctor.

Ferd. Let me have his beard sawed off, and his eyebrows filed more civil.

Doc. I must do mad tricks with him, for that's the only way on't.—I have brought your grace a salamander's skin to keep you from sun-burning.

Ferd. I have cruel sore eyes.

Doc. The white of a cockatrix's egg is present remedy.

Ferd. Let it be a new laid one, you were best.—

Hide me from him: physicians are like kings,—
They brook no contradiction.

Doc. Now he begins to fear me: now let me alone with
him.

Card. How now! put off your gown!

Doc. Let me have some forty urinals filled with rose-
water: he and I'll go pelt one another with them.—Now
he begins to fear me.—Can you fetch a frisk, sir?—Let him
go, let him go, upon my peril: I find by his eye he stands
in awe of me; I'll make him as tame as a dormouse.

Ferd. Can you fetch your frisks, sir!—I will stamp him
into a cullis, flay off his skin, to cover one of the anat-
omies[39] this rogue hath set i' the cold yonder in Barber-
Surgeon's-hall.—Hence, hence! you are all of you like beasts
for sacrifice: there's nothing left of you but tongue and
belly, flattery and lechery.   [*Exit.*

Pes. Doctor, he did not fear you throughly.

Doc. True; I was somewhat too forward.

Bos. Mercy upon me, what a fatal judgment
Hath fall'n upon this Ferdinand!

Pes. Knows your grace
What accident hath brought unto the prince
This strange distraction?

Card. [*Aside.*] I must feign somewhat.—Thus they say
it grew.
You have heard it rumoured, for these many years
None of our family dies but there is seen
The shape of an old woman, which is given
By tradition to us to have been murdered
By her nephews for her riches. Such a figure
One night, as the prince sat up late at's book,
Appeared to him; when crying out for help,
The gentlemen of's chamber found his grace
All on a cold sweat, altered much in face
And language: since which apparition,
He hath grown worse and worse, and I much fear
He cannot live.

Bos. Sir, I would speak with you.

Pes. We'll leave your grace,
Wishing to the sick prince, our noble lord,
All health of mind and body.

[39] Skeletons.

Card. You are most welcome.

[*Exeunt* PESCARA, MALATESTI, *and* Doctor.
Are you come? so.—[*Aside.*] This fellow must not know
By any means I had intelligence
In our duchess' death; for, though I counselled it,
The full of all the engagement seemed to grow
From Ferdinand.—Now, sir, how fares our sister?
I do not think but sorrow makes her look
Like to an oft-dyed garment: she shall now
Taste comfort from me. Why do you look so wildly?
O, the fortune of your master here the prince
Dejects you; but be you of happy comfort:
If you'll do one thing for me I'll entreat,
Though he had a cold tombstone o'er his bones,
I'd make you what you would be.

Bos. Any thing;
Give it me in a breath, and let me fly to't:
They that think long small expedition win,
For musing much o' the end cannot begin.

Enter JULIA.

Julia. Sir, will you come in to supper?
Card. I am busy; leave me.
Julia. [*Aside.*] What an excellent shape hath that fellow!
[*Exit.*

Card. 'Tis thus. Antonio lurks here in Milan:
Inquire him out, and kill him. While he lives,
Our sister cannot marry; and I have thought
Of an excellent match for her. Do this, and style me
Thy advancement.

Bos. But by what means shall I find him out?
Card. There is a gentleman called Delio
Here in the camp, that hath been long approved
His loyal friend. Set eye upon that fellow;
Follow him to mass; may be Antonio,
Although he do account religion
But a school-name, for fashion of the world
May accompany him; or else go inquire out
Delio's confessor, and see if you can bribe
Him to reveal it. There are a thousand ways
A man might find to trace him; as to know

What fellows haunt the Jews for taking up
Great sums of money, for sure he's in want;
Or else to go to the picture-makers, and learn
Who bought her picture lately: some of these
Happily may take.

    Bos. Well, I'll not freeze i' the business:
I would see that wretched thing, Antonio,
Above all sights i' the world.

    Card. Do, and be happy.   *[Exit.*

    Bos. This fellow doth breed basilisks in's eyes,
He's nothing else but murder; yet he seems
Not to have notice of the duchess' death.
'Tis his cunning: I must follow his example;
There cannot be a surer way to trace
Than that of an old fox.

Re-enter JULIA.

    Julia. So, sir, you are well met.

    Bos. How now!

    Julia. Nay, the doors are fast enough:
Now, sir, I will make you confess your treachery.

    Bos. Treachery!

    Julia. Yes, confess to me
Which of my women 'twas you hired to put
Love-powder into my drink?

    Bos. Love-powder!

    Julia. Yes, when I was at Malfi.
Why should I fall in love with such a face else?
I have already suffered for thee so much pain,
The only remedy to do me good
Is to kill my longing.

    Bos. Sure, your pistol holds
Nothing but perfumes or kissing-comfits.[40]
Excellent lady!
You have a pretty way on't to discover
Your longing. Come, come, I'll disarm you,
And arm you thus: yet this is wondrous strange.

    Julia. Compare thy form and my eyes together,
You'll find my love no such great miracle.
Now you'll say

[40] Sugar-plums perfumed for sweetening the breath.

I am wanton: this nice modesty in ladies
Is but a troublesome familiar
That haunts them.

   Bos. Know you me, I am a blunt soldier.

   Julia. The better:
Sure, there wants fire where there are no lively sparks
Of roughness.

   Bos. And I want compliment.

   Julia. Why, ignorance
In courtship cannot make you do amiss,
If you have a heart to do well.

   Bos. You are very fair.

   Julia. Nay, if you lay beauty to my charge,
I must plead unguilty.

   Bos. Your bright eyes
Carry a quiver of darts in them sharper
Than sunbeams.

   Julia. You will mar me with commendation,
Put yourself to the charge of courting me,
Whereas now I woo you.

   Bos. [*Aside.*] I have it, I will work upon this creature.—
Let us grow most amorously familiar:
If the great cardinal now should see me thus,
Would he not count me a villain?

   Julia. No; he might count me a wanton,
Not lay a scruple of offence on you;
For if I see and steal a diamond,
The fault is not i' the stone, but in me the thief
That purloins it. I am sudden with you:
We that are great women of pleasure use to cut off
These uncertain wishes and unquiet longings,
And in an instant join the sweet delight
And the pretty excuse together. Had you been i' the street,
Under my chamber-window, even there
I should have courted you.

   Bos. O, you are an excellent lady!

   Julia. Bid me do somewhat for you presently
To express I love you.

   Bos. I will; and if you love me,
Fail not to effect it.
The cardinal is grown wondrous melancholy;

Demand the cause, let him not put you off
With feigned excuse; discover the main ground on't.
Julia. Why would you know this?
Bos. I have depended on him,
And I hear that he is fall'n in some disgrace
With the emperor: if he be, like the mice
That forsake falling houses, I would shift
To other dependance.
Julia. You shall not need
Follow the wars: I'll be your maintenance.
Bos. And I your loyal servant: but I cannot
Leave my calling.
Julia. Not leave an ungrateful
General for the love of a sweet lady!
You are like some cannot sleep in feather-beds,
But must have blocks for their pillows.
Bos. Will you do this?
Julia. Cunningly.
Bos. To-morrow I'll expect the intelligence.
Julia. To-morrow! get you into my cabinet;
You shall have it with you. Do not delay me,
No more than I do you: I am like one
That is condemned; I have my pardon promised,
But I would see it sealed. Go, get you in:
You shall see me wind my tongue about his heart
Like a skein of silk.   [*Exit* BOSOLA.

Re-enter Cardinal.

Card. Where are you?

Enter Servants.

Servants. Here.
Card. Let none, upon your lives, have conference
With the Prince Ferdinand, unless I know it.—
[*Aside.*] In this distraction he may reveal
The murder.   [*Exeunt* Servants.
                    Yond's my lingering consumption:
I am weary of her, and by any means
Would be quit of.
Julia. How now, my lord! what ails you?
Card. Nothing.

Julia. O, you are much altered:
Come, I must be your secretary, and remove
This lead from off your bosom: what's the matter?
   Card. I may not tell you.
   Julia. Are you so far in love with sorrow
You cannot part with part of it? or think you
I cannot love your grace when you are sad
As well as merry? or do you suspect
I, that have been a secret to your heart
These many winters, cannot be the same
Unto your tongue?
   Card. Satisfy thy longing,—
The only way to make thee keep my counsel
Is, not to tell thee.
   Julia. Tell your echo this,
Or flatterers, that like echoes still report
What they hear though most imperfect, and not me;
For if that you be true unto yourself,
I'll know.
   Card. Will you rack me?
   Julia. No, judgment shall
Draw it from you: it is an equal fault,
To tell one's secrets unto all or none.
   Card. The first argues folly.
   Julia. But the last tyranny.
   Card. Very well: why, imagine I have committed
Some secret deed which I desire the world
May never hear of.
   Julia. Therefore may not I know it?
You have concealed for me as great a sin
As adultery. Sir, never was occasion
For perfect trial of my constancy
Till now: sir, I beseech you—
   Card. You'll repent it.
   Julia. Never.
   Card. It hurries thee to ruin: I'll not tell thee.
Be well advised, and think what danger 'tis
To receive a prince's secrets: they that do,
Had need have their breasts hooped with adamant
To contain them. I pray thee, yet be satisfied;
Examine thine own frailty; 'tis more easy
To tie knots than unloose them: 'tis a secret

That, like a lingering poison, may chance lie
Spread in thy veins, and kill thee seven year hence.

Julia. Now you dally with me.

Card. No more; thou shalt know it.
By my appointment the great Duchess of Malfi
And two of her young children, four nights since,
Were strangled.

Julia. O Heaven! sir, what have you done!

Card. How now? how settles this? think you your bosom
Will be a grave dark and obscure enough
For such a secret?

Julia. You have undone yourself, sir.

Card. Why?

Julia. It lies not in me to conceal it.

Card. No?
Come, I will swear you to't upon this book.

Julia. Most religiously.

Card. Kiss it.   [*She kisses the book.*
Now you shall never utter it; thy curiosity
Hath undone thee: thou'rt poisoned with that book;
Because I knew thou couldst not keep my counsel,
I have bound thee to't by death.

Re-enter BOSOLA.

Bos. For pity-sake, hold!

Card. Ha, Bosola!

Julia. I forgive you
This equal piece of justice you have done;
For I betrayed your counsel to that fellow:
He overheard it; that was the cause I said
It lay not in me to conceal it.

Bos. O foolish woman,
Couldst not thou have poisoned him?

Julia. 'Tis weakness,
Too much to think what should have been done. I go,
I know not whither.   [*Dies.*

Card. Wherefore com'st thou hither?

Bos. That I might find a great man like yourself,
Not out of his wits as the Lord Ferdinand,
To remember my service.

Card. I'll have thee hewed in pieces.

Bos. Make not yourself such a promise of that life
Which is not yours to dispose of.

Card. Who placed thee here?

Bos. Her lust, as she intended.

Card. Very well:
Now you know me for your fellow-murderer.

Bos. And wherefore should you lay fair marble colours,
Upon your rotten purposes to me?
Unless you imitate some that do plot great treasons,
And when they have done, go hide themselves i' the graves
Of those were actors in't?

Card. No more; there is
A fortune attends thee.

Bos. Shall I go sue to Fortune any longer?
'Tis the fool's pilgrimage.

Card. I have honours in store for thee.

Bos. There are many ways that conduct to seeming
    honour,
And some of them very dirty ones.

Card. Throw to the devil
Thy melancholy. The fire burns well;
What need we keep a stirring of't, and make
A greater smother? Thou wilt kill Antonio?

Bos. Yes.

Card. Take up that body.

Bos. I think I shall
Shortly grow the common bier for churchyards.

Card. I will allow thee some dozen of attendants
To aid thee in the murder.

Bos. O, by no means. Physicians that apply horse-leeches,
to any rank swelling use to cut off their tails, that the
blood may run through them the faster: let me have no
train when I go to shed blood, lest it make me have a
greater when I ride to the gallows.

Card. Come to me after midnight, to help to remove
That body to her own lodging: I'll give out
She died o' the plague; 'twill breed the less inquiry
After her death.

Bos. Where's Castruccio her husband?

Card. He's rode to Naples, to take possession
Of Antonio's citadel.

Bos. Believe me, you have done a very happy turn.

Card. Fail not to come: there is the master-key
Of our lodgings; and by that you may conceive
What trust I plant in you.

   Bos. You shall find me ready.   [*Exit* Cardinal.
O poor Antonio, though nothing be so needful
To thy estate as pity, yet I find
Nothing so dangerous; I must look to my footing:
In such slippery ice-pavements men had need
To be frost-nailed well, they may break their necks else;
The precedent's here afore me. How this man
Bears up in blood! seems fearless! Why, 'tis well:
Security some men call the suburbs of hell,
Only a dead wall between. Well, good Antonio,
I'll seek thee out; and all my care shall be
To put thee into safety from the reach
Of these most cruel biters that have got
Some of thy blood already. It may be,
I'll join with thee in a most just revenge:
The weakest arm is strong enough that strikes
With the sword of justice. Still methinks the duchess
Haunts me: there, there—'Tis nothing but my melancholy.
O Penitence, let me truly taste thy cup,
That throws men down only to raise them up!   [*Exit.*

SCENE III—*A Fortification at Milan*

Enter ANTONIO *and* DELIO.

   Delio. Yond's the cardinal's window. This fortification
Grew from the ruins of an ancient abbey;
And to yond side o' the river lies a wall,
Piece of a cloister, which in my opinion
Gives the best echo that you ever heard,
So hollow and so dismal, and withal
So plain in the distinction of our words,
That many have supposed it is a spirit
That answers.

   Ant. I do love these ancient ruins.
We never tread upon them but we set
Our foot upon some reverend history:
And, questionless, here in this open court,

Which now lies naked to the injuries
Of stormy weather, some men lie interred
Loved the church so well, and gave so largely to't,
They thought it should have canopied their bones
Till doomsday; but all things have their end:
Churches and cities, which have diseases like to men,
Must have like death that we have.

    Echo. "Like death that we have."

    Delio. Now the echo hath caught you.

    Ant. It groaned, methought, and gave
A very deadly accent.

    Echo. "Deadly accent."

    Delio. I told you 'twas a pretty one: you may make it
A huntsman, or a falconer, a musician,
Or a thing of sorrow.

    Echo. "A thing of sorrow."

    Ant. Ay, sure, that suits it best.

    Echo. "That suits it best."

    Ant. 'Tis very like my wife's voice.

    Echo. "Ay, wife's voice."

    Delio. Come, let us walk further from't.
I would not have you go to the cardinal's to-night:
Do not.

    Echo. "Do not."

    Delio. Wisdom doth not more moderate wasting sorrow
Than time: take time for't; be mindful of thy safety.

    Echo. "Be mindful of thy safety."

    Ant. Necessity compels me:
Make scrutiny throughout the passages
Of your own life, you'll find it impossible
To fly your fate.

    Echo. "O, fly your fate."

    Delio. Hark! the dead stones seem to have pity on you,
And give you good counsel.

    Ant. Echo, I will not talk with thee,
For thou art a dead thing.

    Echo. "Thou art a dead thing."

    Ant. My duchess is asleep now,
And her little ones, I hope sweetly: O Heaven,
Shall I never see her more?

    Echo. "Never see her more."

    Ant. I marked not one repetition of the echo

But that; and on the sudden a clear light
Presented me a face folded in sorrow.
    Delio. Your fancy merely.
    Ant. Come, I'll be out of this ague,
For to live thus is not indeed to live;
It is a mockery and abuse of life:
I will not henceforth save myself by halves;
Lose all, or nothing.
    Delio. Your own virtue save you!
I'll fetch your eldest son, and second you:
It may be that the sight of his own blood
Spread in so sweet a figure may beget
The more compassion. However, fare you well.
Though in our miseries Fortune have a part,
Yet in our noble sufferings she hath none:
Contempt of pain, that we may call our own.   [*Exeunt.*

SCENE IV—*An Apartment in the* Cardinal's *Palace*

Enter Cardinal, PESCARA, MALATESTI, RODERIGO, *and*
GRISOLAN.

    Card. You shall not watch to-night by the sick prince;
His grace is very well recovered.
    Mal. Good my lord, suffer us.
    Card. O, by no means;
The noise, and change of object in his eye,
Doth more distract him: I pray, all to bed;
And though you hear him in his violent fit,
Do not rise, I entreat you.
    Pes. So, sir; we shall not.
    Card. Nay, I must have you promise
Upon your honours, for I was enjoined to't
By himself; and he seemed to urge it sensibly.
    Pes. Let our honours bind this trifle.
    Card. Nor any of your followers.
    Mal. Neither.
    Card. It may be, to make trial of your promise.
When he's asleep, myself will rise and feign
Some of his mad tricks, and cry out for help,
And feign myself in danger.

Mal. If your throat were cutting,
I'd not come at you, now I have protested against it.

Card. Why, I thank you.

Gris. 'Twas a foul storm to-night.

Rod. The Lord Ferdinand's chamber shook like an osier.

Mal. 'Twas nothing but pure kindness in the devil,
To rock his own child.   [*Exeunt all except the* Cardinal.

Card. The reason why I would not suffer these
About my brother, is, because at midnight
I may with better privacy convey
Julia's body to her own lodging. O, my conscience!
I would pray now; but the devil takes away my heart
For having any confidence in prayer.
About this hour I appointed Bosola
To fetch the body: when he hath served my turn,
He dies.   [*Exit.*

Enter BOSOLA.

Bos. Ha! 'twas the cardinal's voice; I heard him name
Bosola and my death. Listen; I hear one's footing.

Enter FERDINAND.

Ferd. Strangling is a very quiet death.

Bos. [*Aside.*] Nay, then, I see I must stand upon my
    guard.

Ferd. What say you to that? whisper softly; do you
agree to't? So; it must be done i' the dark: the cardinal
would not for a thousand pounds the doctor should see it.
                                  [*Exit.*

Bos. My death is plotted; here's the consequence of
    murder.
We value not desert nor Christian breath,
When we know black deeds must be cured with death.

Enter ANTONIO and Servant.

Serv. Here stay, sir, and be confident, I pray:
I'll fetch you a dark lantern.   [*Exit.*

Ant. Could I take him at his prayers,
There were hope of pardon.

Bos. Fall right, my sword!—   [*Stabs him.*
I'll not give thee so much leisure as to pray.

Ant. O, I am gone! Thou hast ended a long suit
In a minute.

Bos. What art thou?

Ant. A most wretched thing,
That only have thy benefit in death,
To appear myself.

Re-enter Servant *with a lantern.*

Serv. Where are you, sir?

Ant. Very near my home.—Bosola!

Serv. O, misfortune!

Bos. Smother thy pity, thou art dead else.—Antonio!
The man I would have saved 'bove mine own life!
We are merely the stars' tennis-balls, struck and bandied
Which way please them.—O good Antonio,
I'll whisper one thing in thy dying ear
Shall make thy heart break quickly! thy fair duchess and
        two sweet children—

Ant. Their very names
Kindle a little life in me.

Bos. Are murdered.

Ant. Some men have wished to die
At the hearing of sad things; I am glad
That I shall do't in sadness: [41] I would not now
Wish my wounds balmed nor healed, for I have no use
To put my life to. In all our quest of greatness,
Like wanton boys, whose pastime is their care,
We follow after bubbles blown in the air.
Pleasure of life, what is't? only the good hours
Of an ague; merely a preparative to rest,
To endure vexation. I do ask
The process of my death; only commend me
To Delio.

Bos. Break, heart!

Ant. And let my son fly the courts of princes.   [*Dies.*

Bos. Thou seem'st to have loved Antonio?

Serv. I brought him hither,
To have reconciled him to the cardinal.

Bos. I do not ask thee that.
Take him up, if thou tender thine own life,

[41] *i.e.* Earnest.

And bear him where the lady Julia
Was wont to lodge.—O, my fate moves swift;
I have this cardinal in the forge already;
Now I'll bring him to the hammer. O direful misprision!
I will not imitate things glorious,
No more than base; I'll be mine own example.—
On, on, and look thou represent, for silence,
The thing thou bear'st.   [*Exeunt.*

SCENE V—*Another Apartment in the same*

Enter Cardinal, *with a book.*

Card. I am puzzled in a question about hell:
He says, in hell there's one material fire,
And yet it shall not burn all men alike.
Lay him by. How tedious is a guilty conscience!
When I look into the fish-ponds in my garden,
Methinks I see a thing armed with a rake,
That seems to strike at me.

Enter Bosola, *and* Servant *bearing* Antonio's *body.*

                                         Now, art thou come?
Thou look'st ghastly:
There sits in thy face some great determination
Mixed with some fear.

Bos. Thus it lightens into action:
I am come to kill thee.

Card. Ha!—Help! our guard!

Bos. Thou art deceived;
They are out of thy howling.

Card. Hold; and I will faithfully divide
Revenues with thee.

Bos. Thy prayers and proffers
Are both unseasonable.

Card. Raise the watch! we are betrayed!

Bos. I have confined your flight:
I'll suffer your retreat to Julia's chamber,
But no further.

Card. Help! we are betrayed!

Enter, above, PESCARA, MALATESTI, RODERIGO, *and* GRISOLAN.

Mal. Listen.

Card. My dukedom for rescue!

Rod. Fie upon his counterfeiting!

Mal. Why, 'tis not the cardinal.

Rod. Yes, yes, 'tis he:
But I'll see him hanged ere I'll go down to him.

Card. Here's a plot upon me; I am assaulted! I am lost,
Unless some rescue.

Gris. He doth this pretty well;
But it will not serve to laugh me out of mine honour.

Card. The sword's at my throat!

Rod. You would not bawl so loud then.

Mal. Come, come, let's go
To bed: he told us thus much aforehand.

Pes. He wished you should not come at him; but,
     believe't,
The accent of the voice sounds not in jest:
I'll down to him, howsoever, and with engines
Force ope the doors.   [*Exit above.*

Rod. Let's follow him aloof,
And note how the cardinal will laugh at him.

     [*Exeunt, above,* MALATESTI, RODERIGO, *and* GRISOLAN.

Bos. There's for you first,
'Cause you shall not unbarricade the door
To let in rescue.   [*Kills the* Servant.

Card. What cause hast thou to pursue my life?

Bos. Look there.

Card. Antonio!

Bos. Slain by my hand unwittingly.
Pray, and be sudden: when thou killed'st thy sister,
Thou took'st from Justice her most equal balance,
And left her naught but her sword.

Card. O, mercy!

Bos. Now it seems thy greatness was only outward;
For thou fall'st faster of thyself than calamity
Can drive thee. I'll not waste longer time; there!

                                        [*Stabs him.*

Card. Thou hast hurt me.

Bos. Again!   [*Stabs him again.*

Card. Shall I die like a leveret,

Without any resistance?—Help, help, help!
I am slain!

Enter FERDINAND.

Ferd. The alarum! give me a fresh horse;
Rally the vaunt-guard, or the day is lost.
Yield, yield! I give you the honour of arms,
Shake my sword over you; will you yield?
  Card. Help me; I am your brother!
  Ferd. The devil!
My brother fight upon the adverse party!
          [*He wounds the* Cardinal, *and, in the scuffle,
                 gives* BOSOLA *his death-wound.*
There flies your ransom.
  Card. O justice!
I suffer now for what hath former bin:
Sorrow is held the eldest child of sin.
  Ferd. Now you're brave fellows. Cæsar's fortune was
harder than Pompey's; Cæsar died in the arms of prosperity,
Pompey at the feet of disgrace. You both died in the field.
The pain's nothing: pain many times is taken away with
the apprehension of greater, as the toothache with the sight
of the barber that comes to pull it out: there's philosophy
for you.
  Bos. Now my revenge is perfect.—Sink, thou main cause
                                    [*Kills* FERDINAND.
Of my undoing!—The last part of my life
Hath done me best service.
  Ferd. Give me some wet hay; I am broken-winded.
I do account this world but a dog kennel:
I will vault credit and affect high pleasures
Beyond death.
  Bos. He seems to come to himself,
Now he's so near the bottom.
  Ferd. My sister, O my sister! there's the cause on't.
Whether we fall by ambition, blood, or lust,
Like diamonds we are cut with our own dust.   [*Dies.*
  Card. Thou hast thy payment too.
  Bos. Yes, I hold my weary soul in my teeth;
'Tis ready to part from me. I do glory

That thou, which stood'st like a huge pyramid
Begun upon a large and ample base,
Shalt end in a little point, a kind of nothing.

Enter below, PESCARA, MALATESTI, RODERIGO, *and* GRISOLAN.

 Pes. How now, my lord!
 Mal. O sad disaster!
 Rod. How comes this?
 Bos. Revenge for the Duchess of Malfi murdered
By the Arragonian brethren; for Antonio
Slain by this hand; for lustful Julia
Poisoned by this man; and lastly for myself,
That was an actor in the main of all
Much 'gainst mine own good nature, yet i' the end
Neglected.
 Pes. How now, my lord!
 Card. Look to my brother:
He gave us these large wounds, as we were struggling
Here i' the rushes.[42] And now, I pray, let me
Be laid by and never thought of.   [*Dies.*
 Pes. How fatally, it seems, he did withstand
His own rescue!
 Mal. Thou wretched thing of blood
How came Antonio by his death?
 Bos. In a mist; I know not how:
Such a mistake as I have often seen
In a play. O, I am gone!
We are only like dead walls or vaulted graves,
That, ruined, yield no echo. Fare you well.
It may be pain, but no harm, to me to die
In so good a quarrel. O, this gloomy world!
In what a shadow, or deep pit of darkness,
Doth womanish and fearful mankind live!
Let worthy minds ne'er stagger in distrust
To suffer death or shame for what is just:
Mine is another voyage.   [*Dies.*
 Pes. The noble Delio, as I came to the palace,
Told me of Antonio's being here, and showed me
A pretty gentleman, his son and heir.

---

[42] With which it was the custom to strew the floors.

Enter DELIO *and* ANTONIO's Son.

Mal. O sir, you come too late!

Delio. I heard so, and
Was armed for't, ere I came. Let us make noble use
Of this great ruin; and join all our force
To establish this young hopeful gentleman
In's mother's right. These wretched eminent things
Leave no more fame behind 'em, than should one
Fall in a frost, and leave his print in snow;
As soon as the sun shines, it ever melts,
Both form and matter. I have ever thought
Nature doth nothing so great for great men
As when she's pleased to make them lords of truth:
Integrity of life is fame's best friend,
Which nobly, beyond death, shall crown the end.

[*Exeunt.*

THE ATHEIST'S TRAGEDY;

or, the Honest Man's Revenge

CYRIL TOURNEUR's *Atheist's Tragedy, or, the Honest Man's Revenge,* was first printed in 1611, "as in divers places it hath often been acted." It was probably written earlier than *The Revenger's Tragedy.*

It was not printed again until 1792, and was subsequently included in Churton Collins's edition of Tourneur's works.

DRAMATIS PERSONÆ.

MONTFERRERS, a Baron.
BELFOREST, a Baron.
D'AMVILLE, Brother of MONTFERRERS.
CHARLEMONT, Son of MONTFERRERS.
ROUSARD, elder Son of D'AMVILLE.
SEBASTIAN, younger Son of D'AMVILLE.
LANGUEBEAU SNUFFE, a Puritan, Chaplain to BELFOREST.
BORACHIO, D'AMVILLE's instrument.
FRESCO, Servant to CATAPLASMA.
Serjeant in war.
Soldiers, Servants, Watchmen, Judges, Officers.

LEVIDULCIA, Wife of BELFOREST.
CASTABELLA, Daughter of BELFOREST.
CATAPLASMA, a Maker of Periwigs and Attires.
SOQUETTE, a seeming Gentlewoman to CATAPLASMA.

SCENE—FRANCE.

THE ATHEIST'S TRAGEDY

ACT THE FIRST

SCENE I—*In the Grounds of* D'AMVILLE'S *Mansion*

Enter D'AMVILLE, BORACHIO, *and* Attendants.

D'AM. I saw my nephew Charlemont but now
Part from his father. Tell him I desire
To speak with him.   [*Exit* Servant.
Borachio, thou art read
In nature and her large philosophy.
Observ'st thou not the very self-same course
Of revolution, both in man and beast?

Bor. The same, for birth, growth, state, decay and death;
Only a man's beholding to his nature
For the better composition o' the two.

D'Am. But where that favour of his nature is
Not full and free, you see a man becomes
A fool, as little-knowing as a beast.

Bor. That shows there's nothing in a man above
His nature; if there were, considering 'tis
His being's excellency, 'twould not yield
To nature's weakness.

D'Am. Then, if Death casts up
Our total sum of joy and happiness,
Let me have all my senses feasted in
The abundant fulness of delight at once,
And, with a sweet insensible increase
Of pleasing surfeit, melt into my dust.

Bor. That revolution is too short, methinks.
If this life comprehends our happiness,
How foolish to desire to die so soon!
And if our time runs home unto the length
Of nature, how improvident it were
To spend our substance on a minute's pleasure,
And after, live an age in misery!

D'Am. So thou conclud'st that pleasure only flows
Upon the stream of riches?
   Bor. Wealth is lord
Of all felicity.
   D'Am. 'Tis, oracle.
For what's a man that's honest without wealth?
   Bor. Both miserable and contemptible.
   D'Am. He's worse, Borachio. For if charity
Be an essential part of honesty,
And should be practised first upon ourselves,
Which must be granted, then your honest man
That's poor, is most dishonest, for he is
Uncharitable to the man whom he
Should most respect. But what doth this touch me
That seem to have enough?—thanks industry.
'Tis true, had not my body spread itself
Into posterity, perhaps I should
Desire no more increase of substance, than
Would hold proportion with mine own dimensions.
Yet even in that sufficiency of state,
A man has reason to provide and add.
For what is he hath such a present eye,
And so prepared a strength, that can foresee,
And fortify his substance and himself
Against those accidents, the least whereof
May rob him of an age's husbandry?
And for my children, they are as near to me
As branches to the tree whereon they grow;
And may as numerously be multiplied.
As they increase, so should my providence;
For from my substance they receive the sap,
Whereby they live and flourish.
   Bor. Sir, enough.
I understand the mark whereat you aim.

Enter CHARLEMONT.

D'Am. Silence, we are interrupted. Charlemont.
   Charl. Good morrow, uncle.
   D'Am. Noble Charlemont,
Good morrow. Is not this the honoured day
You purposed to set forward to the war?

Charl. My inclination did intend it so.

D'Am. And not your resolution?

Charl. Yes, my lord;
Had not my father contradicted it.

D'Am. O noble war! Thou first original
Of all man's honour, how dejectedly
The baser spirit of our present time
Hath cast itself below the ancient worth
Of our forefathers, from whose noble deeds
Ignobly we derive our pedigrees.

Charl. Sir, tax not me for his unwillingness.
By the command of his authority
My disposition's forced against itself.

D'Am. Nephew, you are the honour of our blood.
The troop of gentry, whose inferior worth
Should second your example, are become
Your leaders; and the scorn of their discourse
Turns smiling back upon your backwardness.

Charl. You need not urge my spirit by disgrace,
'Tis free enough; my father hinders it.
To curb me, he denies me maintenance
To put me in the habit of my rank.
Unbind me from that strong necessity,—
And call me coward, if I stay behind.

D'Am. For want of means? Borachio, where's the gold?
I'd disinherit my posterity
To purchase honour. 'Tis an interest
I prize above the principal of wealth.
I'm glad I had the occasion to make known
How readily my substance shall unlock
Itself to serve you. Here's a thousand crowns.

Charl. My worthy uncle, in exchange for this
I leave my bond; so I am doubly bound;
By that, for the repayment of this gold,
And by this gold, to satisfy your love.

D'Am. Sir, 'tis a witness only of my love,
And love doth always satisfy itself.
Now to your father, labour his consent,
My importunity shall second yours.
We will obtain it.

Charl. If entreaty fail,
The force of reputation shall prevail.   [*Exit.*

D'Am. Go call my sons, that they may take their leaves
Of noble Charlemont. Now, my Borachio!

Bor. The substance of our former argument
Was wealth.

D'Am. The question, how to compass it.

Bor. Young Charlemont is going to the war.

D'Am. O, thou begin'st to take me!

Bor. Mark me then.
Methinks the pregnant wit of man might make
The happy absence of this Charlemont
A subject of commodious providence.
He has a wealthy father, ready even
To drop into his grave. And no man's power,
When Charlemont is gone, can interpose
'Twixt you and him.

D'Am. Thou hast apprehended both
My meaning and my love. Now let thy trust,
For undertaking and for secrecy
Hold measure with thy amplitude of wit;
And thy reward shall parallel thy worth.

Bor. My resolution has already bound
Me to your service.

D'Am. And my heart to thee.

Enter Rousard *and* Sebastian.

Here are my sons.—
There's my eternity. My life in them
And their succession shall for ever live.
And in my reason dwells the providence
To add to life as much of happiness.
Let all men lose, so I increase my gain,
I have no feeling of another's pain. [*Exeunt.*

SCENE II—*An Apartment in* Montferrers' *Mansion*

Enter Montferrers *and* Charlemont.

Mont. I prithee, let this current of my tears
Divert thy inclination from the war,
For of my children thou art only left
To promise a succession to my house.

And all the honour thou canst get by arms
Will give but vain addition to thy name;
Since from thy ancestors thou dost derive
A dignity sufficient, and as great
As thou hast substance to maintain and bear.
I prithee, stay at home.

  Charl. My noble father,
The weakest sigh you breathe hath power to turn
My strongest purpose, and your softest tear
To melt my resolution to as soft
Obedience; but my affection to the war
Is as hereditary as my blood
To every life of all my ancestry.
Your predecessors were your precedents,
And you are my example. Shall I serve
For nothing but a vain parenthesis
I' the honoured story of your family?
Or hang but like an empty scutcheon
Between the trophies of my predecessors,
And the rich arms of my posterity?
There's not a Frenchman of good blood and youth,
But either out of spirit or example
Is turned a soldier. Only Charlemont
Must be reputed that same heartless thing
That cowards will be bold to play upon.

      Enter D'AMVILLE, ROUSARD, *and* SEBASTIAN.

  D'Am. Good morrow, my lord.
  Mont. Morrow, good brother.
  Charl. Good morrow, uncle.
  D'Am. Morrow, kind nephew.
What, ha' you washed your eyes wi' tears this morning?
Come, by my soul, his purpose does deserve
Your free consent;—your tenderness dissuades him.
What to the father of a gentleman
Should be more tender than the maintenance
And the increase of honour to his house?
My lord, here are my boys. I should be proud
That either this were able, or that inclined
To be my nephew's brave competitor.

  Mont. Your importunities have overcome.
Pray God my forced grant prove not ominous!

D'Am. We have obtained it.—Ominous! in what?
It cannot be in anything but death.
And I am of a confident belief
That even the time, place, manner of our deaths
Do follow Fate with that necessity
That makes us sure to die. And in a thing
Ordained so certainly unalterable,
What can the use of providence prevail?

Enter BELFOREST, LEVIDULCIA, CASTABELLA, *and* Attendants.

Bel. Morrow, my Lord Montferrers, Lord D'Amville.
Good morrow, gentlemen. Cousin Charlemont,
Kindly good morrow. Troth, I was afeared
I should ha' come too late to tell you that
I wish your undertakings a success
That may deserve the measure of their worth.

Charl. My lord, my duty would not let me go
Without receiving your commandëments.

Bel. Accompliments are more for ornament
Than use. We should employ no time in them
But what our serious business will admit.

Mont. Your favour had by his duty been prevented
If we had not withheld him in the way.

D'Am. He was a coming to present his service;
But now no more. The book invites to breakfast.
Wilt please your lordship enter?—Noble lady!

[*Exeunt all except* CHARLEMONT *and* CASTABELLA.

Charl. My noble mistress, this accompliment
Is like an elegant and moving speech,
Composed of many sweet persuasive points,
Which second one another, with a fluent
Increase and confirmation of their force,
Reserving still the best until the last,
To crown the strong impulsion of the rest
With a full conquest of the hearer's sense;
Because the impression of the last we speak
Doth always longest and most constantly
Possess the entertainment of remembrance.
So all that now salute my taking leave
Have added numerously to the love
Wherewith I did receive their courtesy.
But you, dear mistress, being the last and best

That speaks my farewell, like the imperious close
Of a most sweet oration, wholly have
Possessed my liking, and shall ever live
Within the soul of my true memory.
So, mistress, with this kiss I take my leave.

   Cast. My worthy servant, you mistake the intent
Of kissing. 'Twas not meant to separate
A pair of lovers, but to be the seal
Of love; importing by the joining of
Our mutual and incorporated breaths,
That we should breathe but one contracted life.
Or stay at home, or let me go with you.

   Charl. My Castabella, for myself to stay,
Or you to go, would either tax my youth
With a dishonourable weakness, or
Your loving purpose with immodesty.

Enter LANGUEBEAU SNUFFE.

And, for the satisfaction of your love,
Here comes a man whose knowledge I have made
A witness to the contract of our vows,
Which my return, by marriage, shall confirm.

   Lang. I salute you both with the spirit of copulation, already informed of your matrimonial purposes, and will testimony to the integrity—

   Cast. O the sad trouble of my fearful soul!
My faithful servant, did you never hear
That when a certain great man went to the war,
The lovely face of Heaven was masqued with sorrow,
The sighing winds did move the breast of earth,
The heavy clouds hung down their mourning heads,
And wept sad showers the day that he went hence
As if that day presaged some ill success
That fatally should kill his happiness.
And so it came to pass. Methinks my eyes
(Sweet Heaven forbid!) are like those weeping clouds,
And as their showers presaged, so do my tears.
Some sad event will follow my sad fears.

   Charl. Fie, superstitious! Is it bad to kiss?

   Cast. May all my fears hurt me no more than this!

   Lang. Fie, fie, fie! these carnal kisses do stir up the concupiscences of the flesh.

Enter BELFOREST *and* LEVIDULCIA.

Lev. O! here's your daughter under her servant's lips.

Charl. Madam, there is no cause you should mistrust
The kiss I gave; 'twas but a parting one.

Lev. A lusty blood! Now by the lip of love,
Were I to choose your joining one for me—

Bel. Your father stays to bring you on the way.
Farewell. The great commander of the war
Prosper the course you undertake! Farewell.

Charl. My lord, I humbly take my leave.—Madam,
I kiss your hand.—And your sweet lip.—[*To* CASTABELLA.]
    Farewell.

    [*Exeunt* BELFOREST, LEVIDULCIA, *and* CASTABELLA.
Her power to speak is perished in her tears.
Something within me would persuade my stay.
But reputation will not yield unto't.
Dear sir, you are the man whose honest trust
My confidence hath chosen for my friend.
I fear my absence will discomfort her.
You have the power and opportunity
To moderate her passion. Let her grief
Receive that friendship from you, and your love
Shall not repent itself of courtesy.

Lang. Sir, I want words and protestation to insinuate
into your credit; but in plainness and truth, I will qualify
her grief with the spirit of consolation.

Charl. Sir, I will take your friendship up at use,
And fear not that your profit shall be small;
Your interest shall exceed your principal.   [*Exit.*

Re-enter D'AMVILLE *with* BORACHIO.

D'Am. Monsieur Languebeau! happily encountered. The
honesty of your conversation makes me request more interest in your familiarity.

Lang. If your lordship will be pleased to salute me without ceremony, I shall be willing to exchange my service
for your favour; but this worshipping kind of entertainment
is a superstitious vanity; in plainness and truth, I love it
not.

D'Am. I embrace your disposition, and desire to give

you as liberal assurance of my love as my Lord Belforest, your deserved favourer.

Lang. His lordship is pleased with my plainness and truth of conversation.

D'Am. It cannot displease him. In the behaviour of his noble daughter Castabella a man may read her worth and your instruction.

Lang. That gentlewoman is most sweetly modest, fair, honest, handsome, wise, well-born, and rich.

D'Am. You have given me her picture in small.

Lang. She's like your diamond; a temptation in every man's eye, yet not yielding to any light impression herself.

D'Am. The praise is hers, but the comparison your own.
[*Gives him the ring.*

Lang. You shall forgive me that, sir.

D'Am. I will not do so much at your request as forgive you it. I will only give you it, sir. By——you will make me swear.

Lang. O! by no means. Profane not your lips with the foulness of that sin. I will rather take it. To save your oath, you shall lose your ring.—Verily, my lord, my praise came short of her worth. She exceeds a jewel. This is but only for ornament: she both for ornament and use.

D'Am. Yet unprofitably kept without use. She deserves a worthy husband, sir. I have often wished a match between my elder son and her. The marriage would join the houses of Belforest and D'Amville into a noble alliance.

Lang. And the unity of families is a work of love and charity.

D'Am. And that work an employment well becoming the goodness of your disposition.

Lang. If your lordship please to impose it upon me I will carry it without any second end; the surest way to satisfy your wish.

D'Am. Most joyfully accepted. Rousard! Here are letters to my Lord Belforest, touching my desire to that purpose.

Enter ROUSARD, *looking sickly.*

Rousard, I send you a suitor to Castabella. To this gentleman's discretion I commit the managing of your suit. His good success shall be most thankful to your trust. Follow his instructions; he will be your leader.

Lang. In plainness and truth.

Rous. My leader! Does your lordship think me too weak
to give the onset myself?

Lang. I will only assist your proceedings.

Rous. To say true, so I think you had need; for a sick
man can hardly get a woman's good will without help.

Lang. Charlemont, thy gratuity and my promises were
    both
But words, and both, like words, shall vanish into air
For thy poor empty hand I must be mute;
This gives me feeling of a better suit.

> [*Exeunt* LANGUEBEAU *and* ROUSARD.

D'Am. Borachio, didst precisely note this man?

Bor. His own profession would report him pure.

D'Am. And seems to know if any benefit
Arises of religion after death.
Yet but compare's profession with his life;—
They so directly contradict themselves,
As if the end of his instructions were
But to divert the world from sin, that he
More easily might ingross it to himself.
By that I am confirmed an atheist.
Well! Charlemont is gone; and here thou seest
His absence the foundation of my plot.

Bor. He is the man whom Castabella loves.

D'Am. That was the reason I propounded him
Employment, fixed upon a foreign place,
To draw his inclination out o' the way.

Bor. It has left the passage of our practice free.

D'Am. This Castabella is a wealthy heir;
And by her marriage with my elder son
My house is honoured and my state increased.
This work alone deserves my industry;
But if it prosper, thou shalt see my brain
Make this but an induction to a point
So full of profitable policy,
That it would make the soul of honesty
Ambitious to turn villain.

Bor. I bespeak
Employment in't. I'll be an instrument
To grace performance with dexterity.

D'Am. Thou shalt. No man shall rob thee of the honour.

Go presently and buy a crimson scarf
Like Charlemont's: prepare thee a disguise
I' the habit of a soldier, hurt and lame;
And then be ready at the wedding feast,
Where thou shalt have employment in a work
Will please thy disposition.

Bor. As I vowed,
Your instrument shall make your project proud.

D'Am. This marriage will bring wealth. If that succeed,
I will increase it though my brother bleed.　　　[*Exeunt.*

SCENE III—*An Apartment in* BELFOREST'S *Mansion*

Enter CASTABELLA *avoiding the importunity of* ROUSARD.

Cast. Nay, good sir; in troth, if you knew how little it pleases me, you would forbear it.

Rous. I will not leave thee till thou'st entertained me for thy servant.

Cast. My servant! You are sick you say. You would tax me of indiscretion to entertain one that is not able to do me service.

Rous. The service of a gentlewoman consists most in chamber work, and sick men are fittest for the chamber. I prithee give me a favour.

Cast. Methinks you have a very sweet favour of your own.

Rous. I lack but your black eye.

Cast. If you go to buffets among the boys, they'll give you one.

Rous. Nay, if you grow bitter I'll dispraise your black
　　　eye.
The gray-eyed morning makes the fairest day.

Cast. Now that you dissemble not, I could be willing to give you a favour. What favour would you have?

Rous. Any toy, any light thing.

Cast. Fie! Will you be so uncivil to ask a light thing at a gentlewoman's hand?

Rous. Wilt give me a bracelet o' thy hair then?

Cast. Do you want hair, sir?

Rous. No, faith, I'll want no hair, so long as I can have it for money.

Cast. What would you do with my hair then?

Rous. Wear it for thy sake, sweetheart.

Cast. Do you think I love to have my hair worn off?

Rous. Come, you are so witty now and so sensible.

[*Kisses her.*

Cast. Tush, I would I wanted one o' my senses now!

Rous. Bitter again? What's that? Smelling?

Cast. No, no, no. Why now y'are satisfied, I hope. I have given you a favour.

Rous. What favour? A kiss? I prithee give me another.

Cast. Show me that I gave it you then.

Rous. How should I show it?

Cast. You are unworthy of a favour if you will not bestow the keeping of it one minute.

Rous. Well, in plain terms, dost love me? That's the purpose of my coming.

Cast. Love you? Yes, very well.

Rous. Give me thy hand upon't.

Cast. Nay, you mistake me. If I love you very well I must not love you now. For now y'are not very well, y'are sick.

Rous. This equivocation is for the jest now.

Cast. I speak't as 'tis now in fashion, in earnest. But I shall not be in quiet for you, I perceive, till I have given you a favour. Do you love me?

Rous. With all my heart.

Cast. Then with all my heart I'll give you a jewel to hang in your ear.—Hark ye—I can never love you.   [*Exit.*

Rous. Call you this a jewel to hang in mine ear? 'Tis no light favour, for I'll be sworn it comes somewhat heavily to me. Well, I will not leave her for all this. Methinks it animates a man to stand to't, when a woman desires to be rid of him at the first sight.   [*Exit.*

SCENE IV—*Another Apartment in the same*

Enter BELFOREST *and* LANGUEBEAU SNUFFE.

Bel. I entertain the offer of this match
With purpose to confirm it presently.
I have already moved it to my daughter.

Her soft excuses savoured at the first,
Methought, but of a modest innocence
Of blood, whose unmoved stream was never drawn
Into the current of affection. But when I
Replied with more familiar arguments,
Thinking to make her apprehension bold,—
Her modest blush fell to a pale dislike,
And she refused it with such confidence,
As if she had been prompted by a love
Inclining firmly to some other man;
And in that obstinacy she remains.

  Lang. Verily, that disobedience doth not become a child.
It proceedeth from an unsanctified liberty. You will be
accessory to your own dishonour if you suffer it.

  Bel. Your honest wisdom has advised me well.
Once more I'll move her by persuasive means.
If she resist, all mildness set apart,
I will make use of my authority.

  Lang. And instantly, lest fearing your constraint
Her contrary affection teach her some
Device that may prevent you.

  Bel. To cut off every opportunity
Procrastination may assist her with
This instant night she shall be married.

  Lang. Best.

Enter CASTABELLA.

  Cast. Please it your lordship, my mother attends
I' the gallery, and desires your conference. [*Exit* BELFOREST.
This means I used to bring me to your ear.
                                    [*To* LANGUEBEAU.
Time cuts off circumstance; I must be brief.
To your integrity did Charlemont
Commit the contract of his love and mine;
Which now so strong a hand seeks to divide,
That if your grave advice assist me not,
I shall be forced to violate my faith.

  Lang. Since Charlemont's absence I have weighed his love
with the spirit of consideration; and in sincerity I find it
to be frivolous and vain. Withdraw your respect; his affection deserveth it not.

  Cast. Good sir, I know your heart cannot profane

The holiness you make profession of
With such a vicious purpose as to break
The vow your own consent did help to make.

Lang. Can he deserve your love who in neglect
Of your delightful conversation and
In obstinate contempt of all your prayers
And tears, absents himself so far from your
Sweet fellowship, and with a purpose so
Contracted to that absence that you see
He purchases your separation with
The hazard of his blood and life, fearing to want
Pretence to part your companies.—
'Tis rather hate that doth division move.
Love still desires the presence of his love.—
Verily he is not of the family of love.

Cast. O do not wrong him! 'Tis a generous mind
That led his disposition to the war:
For gentle love and noble courage are
So near allied, that one begets another;
Or Love is sister and Courage is the brother.
Could I affect him better than before,
His soldier's heart would make me love him more.

Lang. But, Castabella—

Enter LEVIDULCIA.

Lev. Tush, you mistake the way into a woman.
The passage lies not through her reason but her blood.
          [*Exit* LANGUEBEAU. CASTABELLA *about to follow.*
Nay, stay! How wouldst thou call the child,
That being raised with cost and tenderness
To full hability of body and means,
Denies relief unto the parents who
Bestowed that bringing up?

Cast. Unnatural.

Lev. Then Castabella is unnatural.
Nature, the loving mother of us all,
Brought forth a woman for her own relief
By generation to revive her age;
Which, now thou hast hability and means
Presented, most unkindly dost deny.

Cast. Believe me, mother, I do love a man.

Lev. Preferr'st the affection of an absent love

Before the sweet possession of a man;
The barren mind before the fruitful body,
Where our creation has no reference
To man but in his body, being made
Only for generation; which (unless
Our children can be gotten by conceit)
Must from the body come? If Reason were
Our counsellor, we would neglect the work
Of generation for the prodigal
Expense it draws us to of that which is
The wealth of life. Wise Nature, therefore, hath
Reserved for an inducement to our sense
Our greatest pleasure in that greatest work;
Which being offered thee, thy ignorance
Refuses, for the imaginary joy
Of an unsatisfied affection to
An absent man whose blood once spent i' the war
Then he'll come home sick, lame, and impotent,
And wed thee to a torment, like the pain
Of Tantalus, continuing thy desire
With fruitless presentation of the thing
It loves, still moved, and still unsatisfied.

   Enter BELFOREST, D'AMVILLE, ROUSARD, SEBASTIAN,
                  LANGUEBEAU, *&c.*

   Bel. Now, Levidulcia, hast thou yet prepared
My daughter's love to entertain this man
Her husband, here?
   Lev. I'm but her mother i' law;
Yet if she were my very flesh and blood
I could advise no better for her[1] good.
   Rous. Sweet wife,
Thy joyful husband thus salutes thy cheek.
   Cast. My husband? O! I am betrayed.—
Dear friend of Charlemont, your purity
Professes a divine contempt o' the world;
O be not bribed by that you so neglect,
In being the world's hated instrument,
To bring a just neglect upon yourself!
                         [*Kneels from one to another.*
Dear father, let me but examine my

---
[1] The quarto drops the "her."

Affection.—Sir, your prudent judgment can
Persuade your son that 'tis improvident
To marry one whose disposition he
Did ne'er observe.—Good sir, I may be of
A nature so unpleasing to your mind,
Perhaps you'll curse the fatal hour wherein
You rashly married me.

    D'Am. My Lord Belforest,
I would not have her forced against her choice.

    Bel. Passion o' me, thou peevish girl! I charge
Thee by my blessing, and the authority
I have to claim thy obedience, marry him.

    Cast. Now, Charlemont! O my presaging tears!
This sad event hath followed my sad fears.

    Sebas. A rape, a rape, a rape!

    Bel. How now!

    D'Am. What's that?

    Sebas. Why what is't but a rape to force a wench
To marry, since it forces her to lie
With him she would not?

    Lang. Verily his tongue is an unsanctified member.

    Sebas. Verily
Your gravity becomes your perished soul
As hoary mouldiness does rotten fruit.

    Bel. Cousin, y'are both uncivil and profane.

    D'Am. Thou disobedient villain, get thee out of my sight.
Now, by my soul, I'll plague thee for this rudeness.

    Bel. Come, set forward to the church.

                          [Exeunt all except SEBASTIAN.

    Sebas. And verify the proverb—The nearer the church the
further from God.—Poor wench! For thy sake may his
hability die in his appetite, that thou beest not troubled
with him thou lovest not! May his appetite move thy desire
to another man, so he shall help to make himself cuckold!
And let that man be one that he pays wages to; so thou
shalt profit by him thou hatest. Let the chambers be matted,
the hinges oiled, the curtain rings silenced, and the chambermaid hold her peace at his own request, that he may sleep
the quieter; and in that sleep let him be soundly cuckolded.
And when he knows it, and seeks to sue a divorce, let him
have no other satisfaction than this: He lay by and slept:

the law will take no hold of her because he winked at it.
[*Exit.*

ACT THE SECOND

SCENE I—*The Banqueting Room in* BELFOREST'S *Mansion*

Night time. A Banquet set out. Music.

Enter D'AMVILLE, BELFOREST, LEVIDULCIA, ROUSARD, CASTA-
    BELLA, LANGUEBEAU SNUFFE, *at one side. At the other
    side enter* CATAPLASMA *and* SOQUETTE, *ushered by*
    FRESCO.

LEV. Mistress Cataplasma, I expected you an hour since.

Cata. Certain ladies at my house, madam, detained me;
otherwise I had attended your ladyship sooner.

Lev. We are beholden to you for your company. My
lord, I pray you bid these gentlewomen welcome; they're
my invited friends.

D'Am. Gentlewomen, y'are welcome. Pray sit down.

Lev. Fresco, by my Lord D'Amville's leave, I prithee go
into the buttery. Thou shalt find some o' my men there.
If they bid thee not welcome they are very loggerheads.

Fres. If your loggerheads will not, your hogsheads shall,
madam, if I get into the buttery.   [*Exit.*

D'Am. That fellow's disposition to mirth should be our
present example. Let's be grave, and meditate when our
affairs require our seriousness. 'Tis out of season to be
heavily disposed.

Lev. We should be all wound up into the key of mirth.

D'Am. The music there!

Bel. Where's my Lord Montferrers? Tell him here's a
room attends him.

Enter MONTFERRERS.

Mont. Heaven given your marriage that I am deprived
of, joy!

D'Am. My Lord Belforest, Castabella's health!
[D'AMVILLE *drinks.*

Set ope the cellar doors, and let this health
Go freely round the house.—Another to
Your son, my lord; to noble Charlemont—
He is a soldier—Let the instruments
Of war congratulate his memory. [*Drums and trumpets.*

Enter a Servant.

Ser. My lord, here's one, i' the habit of a soldier, says he
is newly returned from Ostend, and has some business of
import to speak.

D'Am. Ostend! let him come in. My soul foretells
He brings the news will make our music full.
My brother's joy would do't, and here comes he
Will raise it.

Enter BORACHIO *disguised.*

Mont. O my spirit, it does dissuade
My tongue to question him, as if it knew
His answer would displease.

D'Am. Soldier, what news?
We heard a rumour of a blow you gave
The enemy.[2]

Bor. 'Tis very true, my lord.

Bel. Canst thou relate it?

Bor. Yes.

D'Am. I prithee do.

Bor. The enemy, defeated of a fair
Advantage by a flatt'ring stratagem,
Plants all the artillery against the town;
Whose thunder and lightning made our bulwarks shake,
And threatened in that terrible report
The storm wherewith they meant to second it.
The assault was general. But, for the place
That promised most advantage to be forced,
The pride of all their army was drawn forth
And equally divided into front
And rear. They marched, and coming to a stand,
Ready to pass our channel at an ebb,
We advised it for our safest course, to draw
Our sluices up and mak't impassable.
Our governor opposed and suffered them

---

[2] At the siege of Ostend, which is described in Borachio's speech.

To charge us home e'en to the rampier's foot.
But when their front was forcing up our breach
At push o' pike, then did his policy
Let go the sluices, and tripped up the heels
Of the whole body of their troop that stood
Within the violent current of the stream.
Their front, beleaguered 'twixt the water and
The town, seeing the flood was grown too deep
To promise them a safe retreat, exposed
The force of all their spirits (like the last
Expiring gasp of a strong-hearted man)
Upon the hazard of one charge, but were
Oppressed, and fell. The rest that could not swim
Were only drowned; but those that thought to 'scape
By swimming, were by murderers that flanked
The level of the flood, both drowned and slain.

    D'Am. Now, by my soul, soldier, a brave service.

    Mont. O what became of my dear Charlemont?

    Bor. Walking next day upon the fatal shore,
Among the slaughtered bodies of their men
Which the full-stomached sea had cast upon
The sands, it was my unhappy chance to light
Upon a face, whose favour[3] when it lived,
My astonished mind informed me I had seen.
He lay in's armour, as if that had been
His coffin; and the weeping sea, like one
Whose milder temper doth lament the death
Of him whom in his rage he slew, runs up
The shore, embraces him, kisses his cheek,
Goes back again, and forces up the sands
To bury him, and every time it parts
Sheds tears upon him, till at last (as if
It could no longer endure to see the man
Whom it had slain, yet loth to leave him) with
A kind of unresolved unwilling pace,
Winding her waves one in another, like
A man that folds his arms or wrings his hands
For grief, ebbed from the body, and descends
As if it would sink down into the earth,
And hide itself for shame of such a deed.[4]

---

[3] Appearance. This meaning passes into that of countenance.

[4] This way of description, which seems unwilling ever to leave off weaving
parenthesis within parenthesis, was brought to its height by Sir Philip Sidney.

D'Am. And, soldier, who was this?

Mont. O Charlemont!

Bor. Your fear hath told you that, whereof my grief
Was loth to be the messenger.

    Cast. O God!   *[Exit.*

D'Am. Charlemont drowned! Why how could that be,
    since
It was the adverse party that received
The overthrow?

Bor. His forward spirit pressed into the front,
And being engaged within the enemy
When they retreated through the rising stream,
I' the violent confusion of the throng
Was overborne, and perished in the flood.
And here's the sad remembrance of his life—the scarf,
Which, for his sake, I will for ever wear.

Mont. Torment me not with witnesses of that
Which I desire not to believe, yet must.

D'Am. Thou art a screech-owl and dost come i' the night
To be the cursèd messenger of death.
Away! depart my house, or, by my soul,
You'll find me a more fatal enemy
Than ever was Ostend. Begone; dispatch!

Bor. Sir, 'twas my love.

D'Am. Your love to vex my heart
With that I hate?
Hark, do you hear, you knave?
O thou'rt a most delicate, sweet, eloquent villain!   *[Aside.*

Bor. Was't not well counterfeited?   *[Aside.*

D'Am. Rarely.—[*Aside.*] Begone. I will not here reply.

Bor. Why then, farewell. I will not trouble you.   *[Exit.*

D'Am. So. The foundation's laid. Now by degrees
                                      [Aside.
The work will rise and soon be perfected.
O this uncertain state of mortal man!

Bel. What then? It is the inevitable fate
Of all things underneath the moon.

D'Am. 'Tis true.
Brother, for health's sake overcome your grief.

Mont. I cannot, sir. I am incapable

He seems to have set the example to Shakespeare. Many beautiful instances may
be found all over the *Arcadia*. These bountiful wits always give full measure,
pressed down and overflowing.—*Charles Lamb.*

Of comfort. My turn will be next. I feel
Myself not well.

D'Am. You yield too much to grief.

Lang. All men are mortal. The hour of death is uncertain.
Age makes sickness the more dangerous, and grief is subject to distraction. You know not how soon you may be
deprived of the benefit of sense. In my understanding,
therefore,
You shall do well if you be sick to set
Your state in present order. Make your will.

D'Am. I have my wish. Lights for my brother.

Mont. I'll withdraw a while,
And crave the honest counsel of this man.

Bel. With all my heart. I pray attend him, sir.

                         [*Exeunt* MONTFERRERS *and* SNUFFE.

This next room, please your lordship.

D'Am. Where you will.

                         [*Exeunt* BELFOREST *and* D'AMVILLE.

Lev. My daughter's gone. Come, son, Mistress Cataplasma,
come, we'll up into her chamber. I'd fain see how she entertains the expectation of her husband's bedfellowship.

Rous. 'Faith, howsoever she entertains it, I
Shall hardly please her; therefore let her rest.

Lev. Nay, please her hardly, and you please her best.

                                      [*Exeunt.*

SCENE II—*The Hall in the same*

Enter three Servants, *drunk, drawing in* FRESCO.

1st Ser. Boy! fill some drink, boy.

Fres. Enough, good sir; not a drop more by this light.

2nd Ser. Not by this light? Why then put out the candles
and we'll drink i' the dark, and t'-to 't, old boy.

Fres. No, no, no, no, no.

3rd Ser. Why then take thy liquor. A health, Fresco!

                                      [*Kneels.*

Fres. Your health will make me sick, sir.

1st Ser. Then 'twill bring you o' your knees, I hope, sir.

Fres. May I not stand and pledge it, sir?

2nd Ser. I hope you will do as we do.

Fres. Nay then, indeed I must not stand, for you cannot.

3rd Ser. Well said, old boy.

Fres. Old boy! you'll make me a young child anon; for if I continue this I shall scarce be able to go alone.

1st Ser. My body is as weak as water, Fresco.

Fres. Good reason, sir. The beer has sent all the malt up into your brain and left nothing but the water in your body.

Enter D'AMVILLE *and* BORACHIO, *closely observing their drunkenness.*

D'Am. Borachio, seest those fellows?

Bor. Yes, my lord.

D'Am. Their drunkenness, that seems ridiculous,
Shall be a serious instrument to bring
Our sober purposes to their success.

Bor. I am prepared for the execution, sir.

D'Am. Cast off this habit and about it straight.

Bor. Let them drink healths and drown their brains i' the
          flood;
I promise them they shall be pledged in blood.   [*Exit.*

1st Ser. You ha' left a damnable snuff here.

2nd Ser. Do you take that in snuff, sir?

1st Ser. You are a damnable rogue then—

                              [*Together by the ears.*

D'Am. Fortune, I honour thee. My plot still rises
According to the model of mine own desires.
Lights for my brother——What ha' you drunk yourselves
          mad, you knaves?

1st Ser. My lord, the jacks abused me.

D'Am. I think they are the jacks[5] indeed that have abused thee. Dost hear? That fellow is a proud knave. He has abused thee. As thou goest over the fields by-and-by in lighting my brother home, I'll tell thee what shalt do. Knock him over the pate with thy torch. I'll bear thee out in't.

1st Ser. I will singe the goose by this torch.   [*Exit.*

D'Am. [*To 2nd Servant.*] Dost hear, fellow? Seest thou
          that proud knave.
I have given him a lesson for his sauciness.
He's wronged thee. I will tell thee what shalt do:
As we go over the fields by-and-by

[5] Play on the double meaning—clown, leathern flagon—of the word "jack."

Clap him suddenly o'er the coxcomb with
Thy torch. I'll bear thee out in't.

2nd Ser. I will make him understand as much. [*Exit.*

Enter LANGUEBEAU SNUFFE.

D'Am. Now, Monsieur Snuffe, what has my brother
done?

Lang. Made his will, and by that will made you his heir
with this proviso, that as occasion shall hereafter move him,
he may revoke, or alter it when he pleases.

D'Am. Yes. Let him if he can.—I'll make it sure
From his revoking. [*Aside.*

Enter MONTFERRERS *and* BELFOREST *attended with lights.*

Mont. Brother, now good night.

D'Am. The sky is dark; we'll bring you o'er the fields.
Who can but strike, wants wisdom to maintain;
He that strikes safe and sure, has heart and brain. [*Exeunt.*

SCENE III—*An Apartment in the same*

Enter CASTABELLA.

Cas. O love, thou chaste affection of the soul,
Without the adulterate mixture of the blood,
That virtue, which to goodness addeth good,—
The minion of Heaven's heart. Heaven! is't my fate
For loving that thou lov'st, to get thy hate,
Or was my Charlemont thy chosen love,
And therefore hast received him to thyself?
Then I confess thy anger's not unjust.
I was thy rival. Yet to be divorced
From love, has been a punishment enough
(Sweet Heaven!) without being married unto hate,
Hadst thou been pleased,—O double misery,—
Yet, since thy pleasure hath inflicted it,
If not my heart, my duty shall submit.

Enter LEVIDULCIA, ROUSARD, CATAPLASMA, SOQUETTE, *and*
FRESCO *with a lanthorn.*

Lev. Mistress Cataplasma, good night. I pray when your

man has brought you home, let him return and light me to
my house.

Cata. He shall instantly wait upon your ladyship.

Lev. Good Mistress Cataplasma! for my servants are all
drunk, I cannot be beholden to 'em for their attendance.

                 [*Exeunt* CATAPLASMA, SOQUETTE, *and* FRESCO.
O here's your bride!

Rous. And melancholic too, methinks.

Lev. How can she choose? Your sickness will
Distaste the expected sweetness o' the night
That makes her heavy.

Rous. That should make her light.

Lev. Look you to that.

Cast. What sweetness speak you of?
The sweetness of the night consists in rest.

Rous. With that sweetness thou shalt be surely blest
Unless my groaning wake thee. Do not moan.

Lev. She'd rather you would wake, and make her groan.

Rous. Nay 'troth, sweetheart, I will not trouble thee.
Thou shalt not lose thy maidenhead to-night.

Cast. O might that weakness ever be in force,
I never would desire to sue divorce.

Rous. Wilt go to bed?

Cast. I will attend you, sir.

Rous. Mother, good night.

Lev. Pleasure be your bedfellow.

                 [*Exeunt* ROUSARD *and* CASTABELLA.
Why sure their generation was asleep
When she begot those dormice, that she made
Them up so weakly and imperfectly.
One wants desire, the t'other ability,
When my affection even with their cold bloods
(As snow rubbed through an active hand does make
The flesh to burn) by agitation is
Inflamed, I could embrace and entertain
The air to cool it.

            Enter SEBASTIAN.

Sebas. That but mitigates
The heat; rather embrace and entertain
A younger brother; he can quench the fire.

Lev. Can you so, sir? Now I beshrew your ear.

Why, bold Sebastian, how dare you approach
So near the presence of your displeased father?
   Sebas. Under the protection of his present absence.
   Lev. Belike you knew he was abroad then?
   Sebas. Yes.
Let me encounter you so: I'll persuade
Your means to reconcile me to his loves.
   Lev. Is that the way? I understand you not.
But for your reconcilement meet me at home;
I'll satisfy your suit.
   Sebas. Within this half-hour?   [*Exit.*
   Lev. Or within this whole hour. When you will.—
A lusty blood! has both the presence and spirit of a man.
I like the freedom of his behaviour.
—Ho!—Sebastian! Gone?—Has set
My blood o' boiling i' my veins. And now,
Like water poured upon the ground that mixes
Itself with every moisture it meets, I could
Clasp with any man.

Enter Fresco *with a lanthorn.*

O, Fresco, art thou come?
If t'other fail, then thou art entertained.
Lust is a spirit, which whosoe'er doth raise,
The next man that encounters boldly, lays.   [*Exeunt.*

SCENE IV—*A Country Road near a Gravel Pit. Night time*

Enter Borachio *warily and hastily over the Stage
with a stone in either hand.*

   Bor. Such stones men use to raise a house upon,
But with these stones I go to ruin one.   [*Descends.*

Enter two Servants *drunk, fighting with their torches;*
   D'Amville, Montferrers, Belforest, *and* Languebeau Snuffe.

   Bel. Passion o' me, you drunken knaves! you'll put
The lights out.
   D'Am. No, my lord; they are but in jest.
   1st Ser. Mine's out.

D'Am. Then light it at his head,—that's light enough.—
'Fore God, they are out. You drunken rascals, back
And light 'em.

Bel. 'Tis exceeding dark.   [*Exeunt* Servants.
D'Am. No matter;
I am acquainted with the way. Your hand.
Let's easily walk. I'll lead you till they come.

Mont. My soul's oppressed with grief. 'T lies heavy at
My heart. O my departed son, ere long
I shall be with thee!

                [D'AMVILLE *thrusts him down into the gravel pit.*
D'Am. Marry, God forbid!
Mont. O, O, O!
D'Am. Now all the host of Heaven forbid! Knaves!
        Rogues!
Bel. Pray God he be not hurt. He's fallen into the gravel
        pit.
D'Am. Brother! dear brother! Rascals! villains! knaves!

Re-enter Servants *with lights.*

Eternal darkness damn you! come away!
Go round about into the gravel pit,
And help my brother up. Why what a strange
Unlucky night is this! Is't not, my lord?
I think that dog that howled the news of grief,
That fatal screech-owl, ushered on this mischief.

                [*Exit* Servants *and re-enter with the murdered body.*
Lang. Mischief indeed, my lord. Your brother's dead!
Bel. He's dead?
Ser. He's dead!
D'Am. Dead be your tongues! Drop out
Mine eye-balls and let envious Fortune play
At tennis with 'em. Have I lived to this?
Malicious Nature, hadst thou borne me blind,
Thou hadst yet been something favourable to me.
No breath? no motion? Prithee tell me, Heaven,
Hast shut thine eye to wink at murder; or
Hast put this sable garment on to mourn
At's death?
Not one poor spark in the whole spacious sky
Of all that endless number would vouchsafe
To shine?—You viceroys to the king of Nature,

Whose constellations govern mortal births,
Where is that fatal planet ruled at his
Nativity? that might ha' pleased to light him out,
As well as into the world, unless it be
Ashamèd I have been the instrument
Of such a good man's cursèd destiny.—

    Bel. Passion transports you. Recollect yourself.
Lament him not. Whether our deaths be good
Or bad, it is not death, but life that tries.
He lived well; therefore, questionless, well dies.

    D'Am. Ay, 'tis an easy thing for him that has
No pain, to talk of patience. Do you think
That Nature has no feeling?

    Bel. Feeling? Yes.
But has she purposed anything for nothing?
What good receives this body by your grief?
Whether is't more unnatural, not to grieve
For him you cannot help with it, or hurt
Yourself with grieving, and yet grieve in vain?

    D'Am. Indeed, had he been taken from me like
A piece o' dead flesh, I should neither ha' felt it
Nor grieved for't. But come hither, pray look here.
Behold the lively tincture of his blood!
Neither the dropsy nor the jaundice in't,
But the true freshness of a sanguine red,
For all the fog of this black murderous night
Has mixed with it. For anything I know
He might ha' lived till doomsday, and ha' done
More good than either you or I. O brother!
He was a man of such a native goodness,
As if regeneration had been given
Him in his mother's womb. So harmless
That rather than ha' trod upon a worm
He would ha' shunned the way.
So dearly pitiful that ere the poor
Could ask his charity with dry eyes he gave 'em
Relief with tears—with tears—yes, faith, with tears.

    Bel. Take up the corpse. For wisdom's sake let reason
fortify this weakness.

    D'Am. Why, what would you ha' me do? Foolish Nature
Will have her course in spite o' wisdom. But
I have e'en done. All these words were

But a great wind; and now this shower of tears
Has laid it, I am calm again. You may
Set forward when you will. I'll follow you
Like one that must and would not.

Lang. Our opposition will but trouble him.

Bel. The grief that melts to tears by itself is spent; Passion
resisted grows more violent.

[*Exeunt all except* D'AMVILLE. BORACHIO *ascends.*

D'Am. Here's a sweet comedy. 'T begins with *O Dolentis*[6]
and concludes with ha, ha, he!

Bor. Ha, ha, he!

D'Am. O my echo! I could stand
Reverberating this sweet musical air
Of joy till I had perished my sound lungs
With violent laughter. Lonely night-raven,
Thou hast seized a carcase.

Bor. Put him out on's pain.
I lay so fitly underneath the bank,
From whence he fell, that ere his faltering tongue
Could utter double O, I knocked out's brains
With this fair ruby, and had another stone,
Just of this form and bigness, ready; that
I laid i' the broken skull upon the ground
For's pillow, against the which they thought he fell
And perished.

D'Am. Upon this ground I'll build my manor house;
And this shall be the chiefest corner stone.

Bor. 'T has crown the most judicious murder that
The brain of man was e'er delivered of.

D'Am. Ay, mark the plot. Not any circumstance
That stood within the reach of the design
Of persons, dispositions, matter, time, or place
But by this brain of mine was made
An instrumental help; yet nothing from
The induction to the accomplishment seemed forced,
Or done o' purpose, but by accident.

Bor. First, my report that Charlemont was dead,
Though false, yet covered with a mask of truth.

D'Am. Ay, and delivered in as fit a time
When all our minds so wholly were possessed

---

[6] With the O of one in pain. An odd and tragical application of a rule from
the Latin Grammar.—*Collins.*

With one affair, that no man would suspect
A thought employed for any second end.
 Bor. Then the precisian[7] to be ready, when
Your brother spake of death, to move his will.
 D'Am. His business called him thither, and it fell
Within his office unrequested to't.
From him it came religiously, and saved
Our project from suspicion which if I
Had moved, had been endangered.
 Bor. Then your healths,
Though seeming but the ordinary rites
And ceremonies due to festivals—
 D'Am. Yet used by me to make the servants drunk,
An instrument the plot could not have missed.
'Twas easy to set drunkards by the ears,
They'd nothing but their torches to fight with,
And when those lights were out—
 Bor. Then darkness did
Protect the execution of the work
Both from prevention and discovery.
 D'Am. Here was a murder bravely carried through
The eye of observation, unobserved.
 Bor. And those that saw the passage of it made
The instruments, yet knew not what they did.
 D'Am. That power of rule philosophers ascribe
To him they call the Supreme of the stars
Making their influences governors
Of sublunary creatures, when themselves
Are senseless of their operations.
What!   *[Thunder and lightning.*
Dost start at thunder? Credit my belief
'Tis a mere effect of Nature—an exhalation hot
And dry involved within a watery vapour
I' the middle region of the air; whose coldness,
Congealing that thick moisture to a cloud,
The angry exhalation, shut within
A prison of contrary quality,
Strives to be free and with the violent
Eruption through the grossness of that cloud,
Makes this noise we hear.
 Bor. 'Tis a fearful noise.

[7] Sanctified Puritan.

D'Am. 'Tis a brave noise, and methinks
Graces our accomplished project as
A peal of ordnance does a triumph. It speaks
Encouragement. Now Nature shows thee how
It favoured our performance, to forbear
This noise when we set forth, because it should
Not terrify my brother's going home,
Which would have dashed our purpose,—to forbear
This lightning in our passage lest it should
Ha' warned him o' the pitfall.
Then propitious Nature winked
At our proceedings: now it doth express
How that forbearance favoured our success.

Bor. You have confirmed me. For it follows well
That Nature, since herself decay doth hate,
Should favour those that strengthen their estate.

D'Am. Our next endeavour is, since on the false
Report that Charlemont is dead depends
The fabric of the work, to credit that
With all the countenance we can.

Bor. Faith, sir,
Even let his own inheritance, whereof
You have dispossessed him, countenance the act.
Spare so much out of that to give him a
Solemnity of funeral. 'Twill quit
The cost, and make your apprehension of
His death appear more confident and true.

D'Am. I'll take thy counsel. Now farewell, black Night;
Thou beauteous mistress of a murderer.
To honour thee that hast accomplished all
I'll wear thy colours at his funeral.   [*Exeunt.*

SCENE V—LEVIDULCIA's *Apartment*

Enter LEVIDULCIA *manned*[8] *by* FRESCO.

Lev. Thou art welcome into my chamber, Fresco.
Prithee shut the door.—Nay, thou mistakest me.
Come in and shut it.

Fres. 'Tis somewhat late, madam.

[8] To man is to attend or escort.

Lev. No matter. I have somewhat to say to thee. What, is not thy mistress towards a husband yet?

Fres. Faith, madam, she has suitors, but they will not suit her, methinks. They will not come off lustily, it seems.

Lev. They will not come on lustily, thou wouldst say.

Fres. I mean, madam, they are not rich enough.

Lev. But ay, Fresco, they are not bold enough. Thy mistress is of a lively attractive blood, Fresco, and in truth she is of my mind for that. A poor spirit is poorer than a poor purse. Give me a fellow that brings not only temptation with him, but has the activity of wit and audacity of spirit to apply every word and gesture of a woman's speech and behaviour to his own desire, and make her believe she's the suitor herself; never give back till he has made her yield to it.

Fres. Indeed among our equals, madam; but otherwise we shall be put horribly out o' countenance.

Lev. Thou art deceived, Fresco. Ladies are as courteous as yeomen's wives, and methinks they should be more gentle. Hot diet and soft ease makes 'em like wax always kept warm, more easy to take impression.—Prithee, untie my shoe.—What, art thou shamefaced too? Go roundly to work, man. My leg is not gouty: 'twill endure the feeling, I warrant thee. Come hither, Fresco; thine ear. S'dainty, I mistook the place, I missed thine ear and hit thy lip.

Fres. Your ladyship has made me blush.

Lev. That shows thou art full o' lusty blood and thou knowest not how to use it. Let me see thy hand. Thou shouldst not be shamefaced by thy hand, Fresco. Here's a brawny flesh and a hairy skin, both signs of an able body. I do not like these phlegmatic, smooth-skinned, soft-fleshed fellows. They are like candied suckets[9] when they begin to perish, which I would always empty my closet of, and give 'em my chambermaid.—I have some skill in palmistry: by this line that stands directly against me thou shouldst be near a good fortune, Fresco, if thou hadst the grace to entertain it.

Fres. O what is that, madam, I pray?

Lev. No less than the love of a fair lady, if thou dost not lose her with faint-heartedness.

[9] Preserves, sweetmeats.

Fres. A lady, madam? Alas, a lady is a great thing: I cannot compass her.

Lev. No? Why, I am a lady. Am I so great I cannot be compassed? Clasp my waist, and try.

Fres. I could find i' my heart, madam—

[SEBASTIAN *knocks within.*

Lev. 'Uds body, my husband! Faint-hearted fool! I think thou wert begotten between the North Pole and the congealed passage.[10] Now, like an ambitious coward that betrays himself with fearful delay, you must suffer for the treason you never committed. Go, hide thyself behind yon arras instantly.   [FRESCO *hides himself.*

Enter SEBASTIAN.

Sebastian! What do you here so late?

Sebas. Nothing yet, but I hope I shall.   [*Kisses her.*

Lev. Y'are very bold.

Sebas. And you very valiant, for you met me at full career.[11]

Lev. You come to ha' me move your father's reconciliation. I'll write a word or two i' your behalf.

Sebas. A word or two, madam? That you do for me will not be contained in less than the compass of two sheets. But in plain terms shall we take the opportunity of privateness.

Lev. What to do?

Sebas. To dance the beginning of the world after the English manner.

Lev. Why not after the French or Italian?

Sebas. Fie! they dance it preposterously; backward!

Lev. Are you so active to dance?

Sebas. I can shake my heels.

Lev. Y'are well made for't.

Sebas. Measure me from top to toe you shall not find me differ much from the true standard of proportion.

[BELFOREST *knocks within.*

Lev. I think I am accursed, Sebastian. There's one at the door has beaten opportunity away from us. In brief, I love thee, and it shall not be long before I give thee a testimony of it. To save thee now from suspicion do no

[10] A reference to Arctic voyages.
[11] In full course. A metaphor from the jousting-ground.

more but draw thy rapier, chafe thyself, and when he
comes in, rush by without taking notice of him. Only seem
to be angry, and let me alone for the rest[12]

Enter BELFOREST.

Sebas. Now by the hand of Mercury—   [*Exit.*

Bel. What's the matter, wife?

Lev. Oh, oh, husband!

Bel. Prithee what ail'st thou, woman?

Lev. O feel my pulse. It beats, I warrant you.
Be patient a little, sweet husband: tarry but till my breath
come to me again and I'll satisfy you.

Bel. What ails Sebastian? He looks so distractedly.

Lev. The poor gentleman's almost out on's wits, I think.
You remember the displeasure his father took against him
about the liberty of speech he used even now, when your
daughter went to be married?

Bel. Yes. What of that?

Lev. 'T has crazed him sure. He met a poor man i' the
street even now. Upon what quarrel I know not, but he
pursued him so violently that if my house had not been his
rescue he had surely killed him.

Bel. What a strange desperate young man is that!

Lev. Nay, husband, he grew so in rage, when he saw the
man was conveyed from him, that he was ready even to
have drawn his naked weapon upon me. And had not your
knocking at the door prevented him, surely he'd done something to me.

Bel. Where's the man?

Lev. Alas, here! I warrant you the poor fearful soul is
scarce come to himself again yet.—If the fool have any wit
he will apprehend me. [*Aside.*]—Do you hear, sir? You
may be bold to come forth: the fury that haunted you is
gone.

[FRESCO *peeps fearfully forth from behind the arras.*

Fres. Are you sure he is gone?

Bel. He's gone, he's gone, I warrant thee.

Fres. I would I were gone too. H's shook me almost into
a dead palsy.

Bel. How fell the difference between you?

[12] This trick of a woman, caught with a lover, to deceive her husband is frequently employed by the Italian novelists.

Fres. I would I were out at the back door.

Bel. Thou art safe enough. Prithee tell's the falling out.

Fres. Yes, sir, when I have recovered my spirits. My memory is almost frighted from me.—Oh, so, so, so!—Why, sir, as I came along the street, sir—this same gentleman came stumbling after me and trod o' my heel.—I cried O. Do you cry, sirrah? says he. Let me see your heel; if it be not hurt I'll make you cry for something. So he claps my head between his legs and pulls off my shoe. I having shifted no socks in a sen'night, the gentleman cried foh! and said my feet were base and cowardly feet, they stunk for fear. Then he knocked my shoe about my pate, and I cried O once more. In the meantime comes a shag-haired dog by, and rubs against his shins. The gentleman took the dog in shag-hair to be some watchman in a rug gown, and swore he would hang me up at the next door with my lanthorn in my hand, that passengers might see their way as they went, without rubbing against gentlemen's shins. So, for want of a cord, he took his own garters off, and as he was going to make a noose, I watched my time and ran away. And as I ran, indeed I bid him hang himself in his own garters. So he, in choler, pursued me hither, as you see.

Bel. Why, this savours of distraction.

Lev. Of mere distraction.

Fres. Howsoever it savours, I am sure it smell like a lie.
                                                      [*Aside.*

Bel. Thou may'st go forth at the back door, honest fellow; the way is private and safe.

Fres. So it had need, for your fore-door here is both common and dangerous.   [*Exit* BELFOREST.

Lev. Good night, honest Fresco.

Fres. Good night, madam. If you get me kissing o' ladies again!—   [*Exit.*

Lev. This falls out handsomely.
But yet the matter does not well succeed,
Till I have brought it to the very deed.   [*Exit.*

SCENE VI—*A Camp*

Enter CHARLEMONT *in arms, a* Musketeer, *and a* Serjeant.

Charl. Serjeant, what hour o' the night is't?
Serj. About one.
Charl. I would you would relieve me, for I am
So heavy that I shall ha' much ado
To stand out my perdu.   [*Thunder and lightning.*
  Serj. I'll e'en but walk
The round, sir, and then presently return.
  Sol. For God's sake, serjeant, relieve me. Above five hours
together in so foul a stormy night as this!
  Serj. Why 'tis a music, soldier. Heaven and earth are
now in consort, when the thunder and the cannon play
one to another.   [*Exit* Serjeant.
  Charl. I know not why I should be thus inclined
To sleep. I feel my disposition pressed
With a necessity of heaviness.
Soldier, if thou hast any better eyes,
I prithee wake me when the serjeant comes.
  Sol. Sir, 'tis so dark and stormy that I shall
Scarce either see or hear him, ere he comes
Upon me.
  Charl. I cannot force my self to wake.—   [*Sleeps.*

Enter the Ghost of MONTFERRERS.

Mont. Return to France, for thy old father's dead,
And thou by murder disinherited.
Attend with patience the success of things,
But leave revenge unto the King of kings.   [*Exit.*
                          [CHARLEMONT *starts and wakes.*
  Charl. O my affrighted soul, what fearful dream
Was this that waked me? Dreams are but the raised
Impressions of premediated things
By serious apprehension left upon
Our minds; or else the imaginary shapes
Of objects proper to the complexion, or
The dispositions of our bodies. These
Can neither of them be the cause why I
Should dream thus; for my mind has not been moved
With any one conception of a thought
To such a purpose; nor my nature wont

To trouble me with fantasies of terror.
It must be something that my Genius would
Inform me of. Now gracious Heaven forbid!
Oh! let my spirit be deprived of all
Foresight and knowledge, ere it understand
That vision acted, or divine that act
To come. Why should I think so? Left I not
My worthy father i' the kind regard
Of a most loving uncle? Soldier, saw'st
No apparition of a man?

   Sol. You dream,
Sir. I saw nothing.

   Charl. Tush! these idle dreams
Are fabulous. Our boyling fantasies
Like troubled waters falsify the shapes
Of things retained in them, and make 'em seem
Confounded when they are distinguished. So,
My actions daily conversant with war,
The argument of blood and death had left
Perhaps the imaginary presence of
Some bloody accident upon my mind,
Which, mixed confusedly with other thoughts,
Whereof the remembrance of my father might
Be one presented, all together seem
Incorporate, as if his body were
The owner of that blood, the subject of
That death, when he's at Paris and that blood
Shed here. It may be thus. I would not leave
The war, for reputation's sake, upon
An idle apprehension, a vain dream.

Enter the Ghost.

   Sol. Stand! Stand, I say! No? Why then have at thee,
Sir. If you will not stand, I'll make you fall.   [*Fires.*
Nor stand nor fall? Nay then, the devil's dam
Has broke her husband's head, for sure it is
A spirit.
I shot it through, and yet it will not fall.   [*Exit.*
       [*The Ghost approaches* CHARLEMONT *who
          fearfully avoids it.*

   Charl. O pardon me, my doubtful heart was slow
To credit that which I did fear to know.   [*Exeunt*

ACT THE THIRD

SCENE I—*Inside a Church*

Enter the funeral of MONTFERRERS.

D'AM. Set down the body. Pay Earth what she lent.
But she shall bear a living monument
To let succeeding ages truly know
That she is satisfied what he did owe,
Both principal and use; because his worth
Was better at his death than at his birth.

> [*A dead march. Enter the funeral of*
> CHARLEMONT *as a Soldier.*

And with his body place that memory
Of noble Charlemont, his worthy son;
And give their graves the rites that do belong
To soldiers. They were soldiers both. The father
Held open war with sin, the son with blood:
This in a war more gallant, that more good.

> [*The first volley.*

There place their arms, and here their epitaphs
And may these lines survive the last of graves.   [*Reads.*

"*The Epitaph of* MONTFERRERS.

"Here lie the ashes of that earth and fire,
  Whose heat and fruit did feed and warm the poor!
And they (as if they would in sighs expire,
  And into tears dissolve) his death deplore.
He did that good freely for goodness' sake
  Unforced, for generousness he held so dear
That he feared but Him that did him make
  And yet he served Him more for love than fear.
So's life provided that though he did die
  A sudden death, yet died not suddenly.

"*The Epitaph of* CHARLEMONT.

"His body lies interred within this mould,
  Who died a young man yet departed old,

And in all strength of youth that man can have
Was ready still to drop into his grave.
For aged in virtue, with a youthful eye
He welcomed it, being still prepared to die,
And living so, though young deprived of breath
He did not suffer an untimely death,
But we may say of his brave blessed decease
He died in war, and yet he died in peace."

[The second volley.

O might that fire revive the ashes of
This phœnix! yet the wonder would not be
So great as he was good, and wondered at
For that. His life's example was so true
A practique of religion's theory
That her divinity seemed rather the
Description than the instruction of his life.
And of his goodness was his virtuous son
A worthy imitator. So that on
These two Herculean pillars where their arms
Are placed there may be writ *Non ultra*.[13] For
Beyond their lives, as well for youth as age,
Nor young nor old, in merit or in name,
Shall e'er exceed their virtues or their fame.

[The third volley.

'Tis done. Thus fair accompliments make foul
Deeds gracious. Charlemont, come now when thou wilt,
I've buried under these two marble stones
Thy living hopes, and thy dead father's bones.   *[Exeunt.*

Enter CASTABELLA *mourning, to the monument of*
CHARLEMONT.

Cast. O thou that knowest me justly Charlemont's,
Though in the forced possession of another,
Since from thine own free spirit we receive it
That our affections cannot be compelled
Though our actions may, be not displeased if on
The altar of his tomb I sacrifice
My tears. They are the jewels of my love
Dissolved into grief, and fall upon
His blasted Spring, as April dew upon

13 An allusion, of course, to the Straits of Gibraltar, where Hercules was supposed to have set up columns forbidding further exploration of the ocean.

A sweet young blossom shaked before the time.

Enter CHARLEMONT *with a Servant.*

Charl. Go see my trunks disposed of. I'll but walk
A turn or two i' the' church and follow you.   [*Exit Servant.*
O! here's the fatal monument of my
Dead father first presented to mine eye.
What's here?—"In memory of Charlemont?"
Some false relation has abused belief.
I am deluded. But I thank thee, Heaven.
For ever let me be deluded thus.
My Castabella mourning o'er my hearse?
Sweet Castabella, rise. I am not dead.

Cast. O Heaven defend me!   [*Falls in a swoon.*

Charl. I—Beshrew my rash
And inconsiderate passion.—Castabella!
That could not think—my Castabella!—that
My sudden presence might affright her sense.—
I prithee, my affection, pardon me.   [*She rises.*
Reduce thy understanding to thine eye.
Within this habit, which thy misinformed
Conceit takes only for a shape, live both
The soul and body of thy Charlemont.

Cast. I feel a substance warm, and soft, and moist,
Subject to the capacity of sense.[14]

Charl. Which spirits are not; for their essence is
Above the nature and the order of
Those elements whereof our senses are
Created. Touch my lip. Why turn'st thou from me?

Cast. Grief above griefs! That which should woe relieve
Wished and obtained, gives greater cause to grieve.

Charl. Can Castabella think it cause of grief
That the relation of my death prove false?

Cast. The presence of the person we affect,
Being hopeless to enjoy him, makes our grief
More passionate than if we saw him not.

Charl. Why not enjoy? Has absence changed thee.

Cast. Yes.
From maid to wife.

Charl. Art married?

Cast. O! I am.

[14] *i.e.* Tangible, yielding impressions to the senses of another person.

Charl. Married?—Had not my mother been a woman,
I should protest against the chastity
Of all thy sex. How can the merchant or
The mariners absent whole years from wives
Experienced in the satisfaction of
Desire, promise themselves to find their sheets
Unspotted with adultery at their
Return, when you that never had the sense
Of actual temptation could not stay
A few short months?

Cast. O! do but hear me speak.

Charl. But thou wert wise, and did'st consider that
A soldier might be maimed, and so perhaps
Lose his ability to please thee.

Cast. No.

That weakness pleases me in him I have.

Charl. What, married to a man unable too?
O strange incontinence! Why, was thy blood
Increased to such a pleurisy of lust,[15]
That of necessity there must a vein
Be opened, though by one that had no skill
To do't?

Cast. Sir, I beseech you hear me.

Charl. Speak.

Cast. Heaven knows I am unguilty of this act.

Charl. Why? Wert thou forced to do't?

Cast. Heaven knows I was.

Charl. What villain did it?

Cast. Your uncle D'Amville.
And he that dispossessed my love of you
Hath disinherited you of possession.

Charl. Disinherited? wherein have I deserved
To be deprived of my dear father's love?

Cast. Both of his love and him. His soul's at rest;
But here your injured patience may behold
The signs of his lamented memory.

[CHARLEMONT *finds his* Father's *monument.*]
He's found it. When I took him for a ghost
I could endure the torment of my fear
More eas'ly than I can his sorrows hear.   [*Exit.*

---

[15] So in *Two Noble Kinsmen* pleurisy is used for plethora—"The pleurisy of people."

Charl. Of all men's griefs must mine be singular?
Without example? Here I met my grave.
And all men's woes are buried i' their graves
But mine. In mine my miseries are born.
I prithee, sorrow, leave a little room
In my confounded and tormented mind
For understanding to deliberate
The cause or author of this accident.—
A close advantage of my absence made
To dispossess me both of land and wife,
And all the profit does arise to him
By whom my absence was first moved and urged.
These circumstances, uncle, tell me you
Are the suspected author of those wrongs,
Whereof the lightest is more heavy than
The strongest patience can endure to bear.　　　　　*[Exit.*

SCENE II—*An Apartment in* D'Amville's *Mansion*

Enter D'Amville, Sebastian, *and* Languebeau.

D'Am. Now, sir, your business?

Sebas. My annuity.

D'Am. Not a denier.[16]

Sebas. How would you ha' me live?

D'Am. Why; turn crier. Cannot you turn crier?

Sebas. Yes.

D'Am. Then do so: y' have a good voice for't.
Y'are excellent at crying of a rape.[17]

Sebas. Sir, I confess in particular respect to yourself I
was somewhat forgetful. General honesty possessed me.

D'Am. Go, th'art the base corruption of my blood;
And, like a tetter, growest unto my flesh.

Sebas. Inflict any punishment upon me. The severity shall
not discourage me if it be not shameful, so you'll but put
money i' my purse. The want of money makes a free
spirit more mad than the possession does an usurer.

D'Am. Not a farthing.

---

[16] *i.e.* A farthing.
[17] See on page 238, Sebastian's exclamation, "A rape!" near end of Act 1,
sc. 4.

Sebas. Would you ha' me turn purse-taker? 'Tis the next
way to do't. For want is like the rack: it draws a man
to endanger himself to the gallows rather than endure it.

Enter CHARLEMONT. D'AMVILLE *counterfeits to take him
for a* Ghost.

D'Am. What art thou? Stay—Assist my troubled sense—
My apprehension will distract me—Stay.

　　　　　　　[LANGUEBEAU SNUFFE *avoids him fearfully.*
Sebas. What art thou? Speak.

Charl. The spirit of Charlemont.

D'Am. O! stay. Compose me. I dissolve.

Lang. No. 'Tis profane. Spirits are invisible. 'Tis the
fiend i' the likeness of Charlemont. I will have no conversation with Satan.   [*Exit.*

Sebas. The spirit of Charlemont? I'll try that.

　　　　　　　[*He strikes, and the blow is returned.*
'Fore God thou sayest true: th'art all spirit.

D'Am. Go, call the officers.   [*Exit.*

Charl. Th'art a villain, and the son of a villain.

Sebas. You lie.

Charl. Have at thee.   [*They fight,* SEBASTIAN *falls.*

Enter the Ghost *of* MONTFERRERS.

Revenge, to thee I'll dedicate this work.

Mont. Hold, Charlemont.
Let him revenge my murder and thy wrongs
To whom the justice of revenge belongs.   [*Exit.*

Charl. You torture me between the passion of
My blood and the religion of my soul.

Sebas. [*Rising.*] A good honest fellow!

Re-enter D'AMVILLE *with* Officers

D'Am. What, wounded? Apprehend him. Sir, is this
Your salutation for the courtesy
I did you when we parted last? You have
Forgot I lent you a thousand crowns. First, let
Him answer for this riot. When the law
Is satisfied for that, an action for
His debt shall clap him up again. I took
You for a spirit and I'll conjure you
Before I ha' done.

Charl. No, I'll turn conjuror. Devil!
Within this circle, in the midst of all
Thy force and malice, I conjure thee do
Thy worst.

D'Am. Away with him!

[*Exeunt* Officers *with* CHARLEMONT.

Sebas. Sir, I have got
A scratch or two here for your sake. I hope
You'll give me money to pay the surgeon.

D'Am. Borachio, fetch me a thousand crowns. I am
Content to countenance the freedom of
Your spirit when 'tis worthily employed.
'A God's name, give behaviour the full scope
Of generous liberty, but let it not
Disperse and spend itself in courses of
Unbounded licence. Here, pay for your hurts.   [*Exit.*

Sebas. I thank you, sir.—Generous liberty!—that is to
say, freely to bestow my abilities to honest purposes. Methinks I should not follow that instruction now, if having
the means to do an honest office for an honest fellow, I
should neglect it. Charlemont lies in prison for a thousand
crowns. Honesty tells me 'twere well done to release Charlemont. But discretion says I had much ado to come by this,
and when this shall be gone I know not where to finger
any more, especially if I employ it to this use, which
is like to endanger me into my father's perpetual displeasure.
And then I may go hang myself, or be forced to do that
will make another save me the labour. No matter, Charlemont, thou gavest me my life, and that's somewhat of a
purer earth than gold, fine as it is. 'Tis no courtesy, I do
thee but thankfulness. I owe it thee, and I'll pay it. He
fought bravely, but the officers dragged him villainously.
Arrant knaves! for using him so discourteously; may the
sins o' the poor people be so few that you sha' not be able
to spare so much out of your gettings as will pay for the
hire of a lame starved hackney to ride to an execution,
but go a-foot to the gallows and be hanged. May elder
brothers turn good husbands, and younger brothers get good
wives, that there be no need of debt books nor use of
serjeants. May there be all peace, but i' the war and all
charity, but i' the devil, so that prisons may be turned to
hospitals, though the officers live o' the benevolence. If this

curse might come to pass, the world would say, "Blessed
be he that curseth."   [*Exit.*

SCENE III—*Inside a Prison*

CHARLEMONT *discovered.*

Charl. I grant thee, Heaven, thy goodness doth command
Our punishments, but yet no further than
The measure of our sins. How should they else
Be just? Or how should that good purpose of
Thy justice take effect by bounding men
Within the confines of humanity,
When our afflictions do exceed our crimes?
Then they do rather teach the barbarous world
Examples that extend her cruelties
Beyond their own dimensions, and instruct
Our actions to be much more barbarous.
O my afflicted soul! How torment swells
Thy apprehension with profane conceit,
Against the sacred justice of my God!
Our own constructions are the authors of
Our misery. We never measure our
Conditions but with men above us in
Estate. So while our spirits labour to
Be higher than our fortunes, they are more base.
Since all those attributes which make men seem
Superior to us, are man's subjects and
Were made to serve him. The repining man
Is of a servile spirit to deject
The value of himself below their estimation.

Enter SEBASTIAN *with the Keeper.*

Sebas. Here. Take my sword.—How now, my wild
swagerer? Y'are tame enough now, are you not? The penury
of a prison is like a soft consumption. 'Twill humble the
pride o' your mortality, and arm your soul in complete
patience to endure the weight of affliction without feeling
it. What, hast no music in thee? Th' hast trebles and basses
enough. Treble injury and base usage. But trebles and

basses make poor music without means.[18] Thou wantest
means, dost? What? Dost droop? art dejected?

Charl. No, sir. I have a heart above the reach
Of thy most violent maliciousness;
A fortitude in scorn of thy contempt
(Since Fate is pleased to have me suffer it)
That can bear more than thou hast power t' inflict.
I was a baron. That thy father has
Deprived me of. Instead of that I am
Created king. I've lost a signiory[19]
That was confined within a piece of earth,
A wart upon the body of the world,
But now I am an emperor of a world,
This little world of man. My passions are
My subjects, and I can command them laugh,
Whilst thou dost tickle 'em to death with misery.

Sebas. 'Tis bravely spoken, and I love thee for't.
Thou liest here for a thousand crowns. Here are a
thousand to redeem thee. Not for the ransom o' my
life thou gavest me,—that I value not at one crown—
'tis none o' my deed. Thank my father for't. 'Tis
his goodness. Yet he looks not for thanks. For he
does it under hand, out of a reserved disposition to
do thee good without ostentation.—Out o' great
heart you'll refuse't now; will you?

Charl. No. Since I must submit myself to Fate,
I never will neglect the offer of
One benefit, but entertain them as
Her favours and the inductions to some end
Of better fortune. As whose instrument,
I thank thy courtesy.

Sebas. Well, come along.   [*Exeunt.*

---

[18] "Means" are here equivalent to voices intermediate between treble and bass,
as tenors. Collins adduces a passage from Lyly's *Galathea* (Act v, sc. 3), where
there is a similar play on words.
[19] *i.e.* A lordship, Ital. *Signoria*; Fr. *Seigneurie.*

SCENE IV—*An Apartment in* D'AMVILLE's *Mansion*

Enter D'AMVILLE *and* CASTABELLA.

D'Am. Daughter, you do not well to urge me. I
Ha' done no more than justice. Charlemont
Shall die and rot in prison, and 'tis just.

Cast. O father, mercy is an attribute
As high as justice, an essential part
Of his unbounded goodness, whose divine
Impression, form, and image man should bear!
And, methinks, man should love to imitate
His mercy, since the only countenance
Of justice were destruction, if the sweet
And loving favour of his mercy did
Not mediate between it and our weakness.

D'Am. Forbear. You will displease me. He shall rot.

Cast. Dear sir, since by your greatness you
Are nearer Heaven in place, be nearer it
In goodness. Rich men should transcend the poor
As clouds the earth, raised by the comfort of
The sun to water dry and barren grounds.
If neither the impression in your soul
Of goodness, nor the duty of your place
As goodness' substitute can move you, then
Let nature, which in savages, in beasts,
Can stir to pity, tell you that he is
Your kinsman.—

D'Am. You expose your honesty
To strange construction. Why should you so urge
Release for Charlemont? Come, you profess
More nearness to him than your modesty
Can answer. You have tempted my suspicion.
I tell thee he shall starve, and die, and rot.

Enter CHARLEMONT *and* SEBASTIAN.

Charl. Uncle, I thank you.

D'Am. Much good do it you.—Who did release him?

Sebas. I.   [*Exit* CASTABELLA.

D'Am. You are a villain.

Sebas. Y'are my father.   [*Exit* SEBASTIAN.

D'Am. I must temporize.—   [*Aside*
Nephew, had not his open freedom made
My disposition known, I would ha' borne
The course and inclination of my love
According to the motion of the sun,
Invisibly enjoyed and understood.

Charl. That shows your good works are directed to
No other end than goodness. I was rash,
I must confess. But—

D'Am. I will excuse you.
To lose a father and, as you may think,
Be disinherited, it must be granted
Are motives to impatience. But for death,
Who can avoid it? And for his estate,
In the uncertainty of both your lives
'Twas done discreetly to confer't upon
A known successor being the next in blood.
And one, dear nephew, whom in time to come
You shall have cause to thank. I will not be
Your dispossessor but your guardian.
I will supply your father's vacant place
To guide your green improvidence of youth,
And make you ripe for your inheritance.

Charl. Sir, I embrace your generous promises.

Enter ROUSARD *looking sickly, and* CASTABELLA.

Rous. Embracing! I behold the object that
Mine eye affects. Dear cousin Charlemont!

D'Am. My elder son! He meets you happily.
For with the hand of our whole family
We interchange the indenture[20] of our loves.

Charl. And I accept it. Yet not so joyfully
Because y'are sick.

D'Am. Sir, his affection's sound
Though he be sick in body.

Rous. Sick indeed.
A general weakness did surprise my health
The very day I married Castabella,
As if my sickness were a punishment
That did arrest me for some injury

<hr/>

[20] *i.e.* Bond, contract.

I then committed. Credit me, my love,
I pity thy ill fortune to be matched
With such a weak, unpleasing bedfellow.

    Cast. Believe me, sir, it never troubles me.
I am as much respectless to enjoy
Such pleasure, as ignorant what it is.

    Charl. Thy sex's wonder. Unhappy Charlemont!

    D'Am. Come, let's to supper. There we will confirm
The eternal bond of our concluded love.   [*Exeunt.*

ACT THE FOURTH

SCENE I—*A Room in* CATAPLASMA's *House*

Enter CATAPLASMA *and* SOQUETTE *with needlework.*

CATAPLASMA. Come, Soquette, your work! let's examine your
work. What's here? a medlar with a plum tree growing
hard by it; the leaves o' the plum tree falling off; the gum
issuing out o' the perished joints; and the branches some of
'em dead, and some rotten; and yet but a young plum tree.
In good sooth very pretty.

    Soqu. The plum tree, forsooth, grows so near the medlar
that the medlar sucks and draws all the sap from it and the
natural strength o' the ground, so that it cannot prosper.

    Cata. How conceited you are! [21] But here th'ast made a
tree to bear no fruit. Why's that?

    Soqu. There grows a savin tree next it, forsooth. [22]

    Cata. Forsooth you are a little too witty in that.

Enter SEBASTIAN.

    Sebas. But this honeysuckle winds about this white thorn
very prettily and lovingly, sweet Mistress Cataplasma.

    Cata. Monsieur Sebastian! in good sooth very uprightly
welcome this evening.

    Sebas. What, moralizing upon this gentlewoman's needle-
work? Let's see.

---

[21] What pretty fancies you have.

[22] Savin, an irritant poison, has long been in popular use to induce abortion
in women.

Cata. No, sir. Only examining whether it be done to the true nature and life o' the thing.

Sebas. Here y' have set a medlar with a bachelor's button o' one side and a snail o' the tother. The bachelor's button should have held his head up more pertly towards the medlar: the snail o' the tother side should ha' been wrought with an artificial laziness, doubling his tail and putting out his horn but half the length. And then the medlar falling (as it were) from the lazy snail and ending towards the pert bachelor's button, their branches spreading and winding one within another as if they did embrace. But here's a moral. A poppring[23] pear tree growing upon the bank of a river seeming continually to look downwards into the water as if it were enamoured of it, and ever as the fruit ripens lets it fall for love (as it were) into her lap. Which the wanton stream, like a strumpet, no sooner receives but she carries it away and bestows it upon some other creature she maintains, still seeming to play and dally under the poppring so long that it has almost washed away the earth from the root, and now the poor tree stands as if it were ready to fall and perish by that whereon it spent all the substance it had.

Cata. Moral for you that love those wanton running waters.

Sebas. But is not my Lady Levidulcia come yet?

Cata. Her purpose promised us her company ere this. Sirrah, your lute and your book.

Sebas. Well said. A lesson o' the lute, to entertain the time with till she comes.

Cata. Sol, fa, mi, la.——*Mi, mi, mi.*——Precious! Dost not see *mi* between the two crochets? Strike me full there. ——So——forward. This is a sweet strain, and thou finger'st it beastly. *Mi* is a *laerg*[24] there, and the prick that stands before *mi* a long; always halve your note.——Now——Run your division pleasingly with these quavers. Observe all your graces i' the touch.——Here's a sweet close——strike it full; it sets off your music delicately.

Enter LANGUEBEAU SNUFFE *and* LEVIDULCIA.

Lang. Purity be in this house.

23 Also spelt *popering*. A particular species of pear.
24 This is obscure, but it probably refers to the Italian music phrase *largo*.

Cata. 'Tis now entered; and welcome with your good ladyship.

Sebas. Cease that music. Here's a sweeter instrument.

Lev. Restrain your liberty. See you not Snuffe?

Sebas. What does the stinkard here? put Snuffe out. He's offensive.

Lev. No. The credit of his company defends my being abroad from the eye of suspicion.

Cata. Wilt please your ladyship go up into the closet? There are those falls and tires[25] I told you of.

Lev. Monsieur Snuffe, I shall request your patience. My stay will not be long.   [*Exit with* SEBASTIAN.

Lang. My duty, madam.——Falls and tires! I begin to suspect what falls and tires you mean. My lady and Sebastian the fall and the tire, and I the shadow. I perceive the purity of my conversation is used but for a property to cover the uncleanness of their purposes. The very contemplation o' the thing makes the spirit of the flesh begin to wriggle in my blood. And here my desire has met with an object already. This gentlewoman, methinks, should be swayed with the motion, living in a house where moving example is so common.——Mistress Cataplasma, my lady, it seems, has some business that requires her stay. The fairness o' the evening invites me into the air. Will it please you give this gentlewoman leave to leave her work and walk a turn or two with me for honest recreation?

Cata. With all my heart, sir. Go, Soquette: give ear to his instructions. You may get understanding by his company, I can tell you.

Lang. In the way of holiness, Mistress Cataplasma.

Cata. Good Monsieur Snuffe!—I will attend your return.

Lang. Your hand, gentlewoman.—[*To* SOQUETTE.]
The flesh is humble till the spirit move it.
But when 'tis raised it will command above it.   [*Exeunt.*

SCENE II—*An Apartment in* D'AMVILLE'S *Mansion*

Enter D'AMVILLE, CHARLEMONT, *and* BORACHIO.

D'Am. Your sadness and the sickness of my son

[25] Articles of millinery: veils and headdresses.

Have made our company and conference
Less free and pleasing than I purposed it.

　　Charl. Sir, for the present I am much unfit
For conversation or society.
With pardon I will rudely take my leave.

　　D'Am. Good night, dear nephew.　　[*Exit* CHARLEMONT.
Seest thou that same man?

　　Bor. Your meaning, sir?

　　D'Am. That fellow's life, Borachio,
Like a superfluous letter in the law,
Endangers our assurance.[26]

　　Bor. Scrape him out.

　　D'Am. Wilt do't?

　　Bor. Give me your purpose—I will do't.

　　D'Am. Sad melancholy has drawn Charlemont
With meditation on his father's death
Into the solitary walk behind the church.

　　Bor. The churchyard? 'Tis the fittest place for death.
Perhaps he's praying. Then he's fit to die.
We'll send him charitably to his grave.

　　D'Am. No matter how thou tak'st him. First take this—
　　　　　　　　　　　　　　　[*Gives him a pistol.*
Thou knowest the place. Observe his passages,
And with the most advantage make a stand,
That, favoured by the darkness of the night,
His breast may fall upon thee at so near
A distance that he sha' not shun the blow.
The deed once done, thou may'st retire with safety.
The place is unfrequented, and his death
Will be imputed to the attempt of thieves.

　　Bor. Be careless. Let your mind be free and clear.
This pistol shall discharge you of your fear.　　　[*Exit.*

　　D'Am. But let me call my projects to account
For what effect and end have I engaged
Myself in all this blood? To leave a state
To the succession of my proper blood.
But how shall that succession be continued?
Not in my elder son, I fear. Disease
And weakness have disabled him for issue.
For the other,—his loose humour will endure

---

[26] The simile is from legal documents in which one superfluous letter might
nullify a deed.

No bond of marriage. And I doubt his life,
His spirit is so boldly dangerous.
O pity that the profitable end
Of such a prosperous murder should be lost!
Nature forbid! I hope I have a body
That will not suffer me to lose my labour
For want of issue yet. But then't must be
A bastard.—Tush! they only father bastards
That father other men's begettings. Daughter!
Be it mine own. Let it come whence it will,
I am resolved. Daughter!

Enter Servant.

Ser. My lord.
D'Am. I prithee call my daughter.

Enter Castabella.

Cast. Your pleasure, sir.
D'Am. Is thy husband i' bed?
Cast. Yes, my lord.
D'Am. The evening's fair. I prithee walk a turn or two.
Cast. Come, Jaspar.
D'Am. No.
We'll walk but to the corner o' the church;
And I have something to speak privately.
Cast. No matter; stay.   [*Exit* Servant.
D'Am. This falls out happily.   [*Exeunt.*

SCENE III—*The Churchyard*

Enter Charlemont.—Borachio *dogging him.*
The clock strikes twelve.

Charl. Twelve.
Bor. 'Tis a good hour: 'twill strike one anon.
Charl. How fit a place for contemplation is this dead of
night, among the dwellings of the dead.—This grave—
Perhaps the inhabitant was in his lifetime the possessor of
his own desires. Yet in the midst of all his greatness and
his wealth he was less rich and less contented than in this
poor piece of earth lower and lesser than a cottage. For here

he neither wants nor cares. Now that his body savours of
corruption
He enjoys a sweeter rest than e'er he did
Amongst the sweetest pleasures of this life,
For here there's nothing troubles him.—And there
—In that grave lies another. He, perhaps,
Was in his life as full of misery
As this of happiness. And here's an end
Of both. Now both their states are equal. O
That man with so much labour should aspire
To worldly height, when in the humble earth
The world's condition's at the best, or scorn
Inferior men, since to be lower than
A worm is to be higher than a king.

    Bor. Then fall and rise.

        [Discharges the pistol, which misses fire.

    Charl. What villain's hand was that?

Save thee, or thou shalt perish.   *[They fight.*

    Bor. Zounds! unsaved

I think.   *[Falls.*

    Charl. What? Have I killed him? Whatsoe'er thou beest,
I would thy hand had prospered. For I was
Unfit to live and well prepared to die.
What shall I do? Accuse myself? Submit
Me to the law? And that will quickly end
This violent increase of misery.
But 'tis a murder to be accessory
To mine own death. I will not. I will take
This opportunity to 'scape. It may
Be Heaven reserves me to some better end.   *[Exit.*

Enter LANGUEBEAU SNUFFE *and* SOQUETTE.

    Soqu. Nay, good sir, I dare not. In good sooth I come of
a generation both by father and mother that were all as
fruitful as costermongers' wives.

    Lang. Tush! then a tympany[27] is the greatest danger can
be feared. Their fruitfulness turns but to a certain kind of
phlegmatic windy disease.

    Soqu. I must put my understanding to your trust, sir. I
would be loth to be deceived.

    Lang. No, conceive thou sha't not. Yet thou shalt profit

₂₇ A flatulent swelling of the abdomen.

by my instruction too. My body is not every day drawn dry, wench.

Soqu. Yet methinks, sir, your want of use should rather make your body like a well,—the lesser 'tis drawn, the sooner it grows dry.

Lang. Thou shalt try that instantly.

Soqu. But we want place and opportunity.

Lang. We have both. This is the back side of the house which the superstitious call St. Winifred's church, and is verily a convenient unfrequented place.—
Where under the close curtains of the night—

Soqu. You purpose i' the dark to make me light.

        [SNUFFE *pulls out a sheet, a hair, and a beard.*
But what ha' you there?

Lang. This disguise is for security's sake, wench. There's a talk, thou know'st, that the ghost of old Montferrers walks. In this church he was buried. Now if any stranger fall upon us before our business be ended, in this disguise I shall be taken for that ghost, and never be called to examination, I warrant thee. Thus we shall 'scape both prevention and discovery. How do I look in this habit, wench?

Soqu. So like a ghost that notwithstanding I have some foreknowledge of you, you make my hair stand almost on end.

Lang. I will try how I can kiss in this beard. O, fie, fie, fie! I will put it off and then kiss, and then put it on. I can do the rest without kissing.

Re-enter CHARLEMONT *doubtfully, with his sword drawn; he comes upon them before they are aware. They run out different ways, leaving the disguise behind.*

Charl. What ha' we here? A sheet! a hair! a beard!
What end was this disguise intended for?
No matter what. I'll not expostulate
The purpose of a friendly accident.[28]
Perhaps it may accommodate my 'scape.
—I fear I am pursued. For more assurance,
I'll hide me here i' th' charnel house,
This convocation-house of dead men's skulls.

        [*In getting into the charnel house he takes hold of a death's head; it slips, and he staggers.*

---

[28] Too narrowly dispute the reason of an accident favourable to myself.

Death's head, deceivest my hold?
Such is the trust to all mortality.

[Hides himself in the charnel house.

Enter D'AMVILLE *and* CASTABELLA.

Cast. My lord, the night grows late. Your lordship spake
Of something you desired to move in private.

D'Am. Yes. Now I'll speak it. The argument is love.
The smallest ornament of thy sweet form
(That abstract of all pleasure) can command
The senses into passion and thy entire
Perfection is my object, yet I love thee
With the freedom of my reason. I can give
Thee reason for my love.

Cast.   Love me, my lord?
I do believe it, for I am the wife
Of him you love.

D'Am.   'Tis true. By my persuasion thou wert forced
To marry one unable to perform
The office of a husband. I was the author
Of the wrong.
My conscience suffer under't, and I would
Disburthen it by satisfaction.

Cast.   How?

D'Am. I will supply that pleasure to thee which he cannot.

Cast. Are ye a devil or a man?

D'Am. A man, and such a man as can return
Thy entertainment with as prodigal
A body as the covetous desire,
Or woman ever was delighted with.
So that, besides the full performance of
Thy empty husband's duty, thou shalt have
The joy of children to continue the
Succession of thy blood. For the appetite
That steals her pleasure, draws the forces of
The body to an united strength, and puts 'em
Altogether into action, never fails
Of procreation. All the purposes
Of man aim but at one of these two ends—
Pleasure or profit; and in this one sweet
Conjunction of our loves they both will meet.
Would it not grieve thee that a stranger to

Thy blood should lay the first foundation of
His house upon the ruins of thy family?

 Cast. Now Heaven defend me! May my memory
Be utterly extinguished, and the heir
Of him that was my father's enemy
Raise his eternal monument upon
Our ruins, ere the greatest pleasure or
The greatest profit ever tempt me to
Continue it by incest.

 D'Am. Incest? Tush!
These distances affinity observes
Are articles of bondage cast upon
Our freedoms by our own objections.
Nature allows a general liberty
Of generation to all creatures else.
Shall man,
To whose command and use all creatures were
Made subject, be less free than they?

 Cast. O God!
Is Thy unlimited and infinite
Omnipotence less free because thou doest
No ill?
Or if you argue merely out of nature,
Do you not degenerate from that, and are
You not unworthy of the prerogative
Of Nature's masterpiece, when basely you
Prescribe yourself authority and law
From their examples whom you should command?
I could confute you, but the horror of
The argument confutes my understanding.—
Sir, I know you do but try me in
Your son's behalf, suspecting that
My strength
And youth of blood cannot contain themselves
With impotence.—Believe me, sir,
I never wronged him. If it be your lust,
O quench it on their prostituted flesh
Whose trade of sin can please desire with more
Delight and less offence.—The poison o' your breath,
Evaporated from so foul a soul,
Infects the air more than the damps that rise
From bodies but half rotten in their graves.

D'Am. Kiss me. I warrant thee my breath is sweet.
These dead men's bones lie here of purpose to
Invite us to supply the number of
The living. Come we'll get young bones, and do't.
I will enjoy thee. No? Nay then invoke
Your great supposed protector; I will do't.

Cast. Supposed protector! Are ye an atheist? Then
I know my prayers and tears are spent in vain.
O patient Heaven! Why dost thou not express
Thy wrath in thunderbolts to tear the frame
Of man in pieces? How can earth endure
The burden of this wickedness without
An earthquake? Or the angry face of Heaven
Be not inflamed with lightning?

D'Am.   Conjure up
The devil and his dam: cry to the graves:
The dead can hear thee: invocate their help.

Cast. O would this grave might open and my body
Were bound to the dead carcass of a man
For ever, ere it entertain the lust
Of this detested villain!

D'Am.   Tereus-like
Thus I will force my passage to—

Charl.   The Devil!

[CHARLEMONT *rises in the disguise, and frightens*
D'AMVILLE *away.*

Now, lady, with the hand of Charlemont
I thus redeem you from the arm of lust.
—My Castabella!

Cast. My dear Charlemont!

Charl. For all my wrongs I thank thee, gracious Heaven,
Th'ast made me satisfaction to reserve
Me for this blessed purpose. Now, sweet Death,
I'll bid thee welcome. Come, I'll guide thee home,
And then I'll cast myself into the arms
Of apprehension,[29] that the law may make
This worthy work the crown of all my actions,
Being the best and last.

Cast.   The last? The law?
Now Heaven forbid! What ha' you done?

Charl. Why, I have

---

[29] *i.e.* Surrender myself to justice.

Killed a man; not murdered him, my Castabella.
He would ha' murdered me.
 Cast. Then, Charlemont,
The hand of Heaven directed thy defence.
That wicked atheist! I suspect his plot.
 Charl. My life he seeks. I would he had it, since
He has deprived me of those blessings that
Should make me love it. Come, I'll give it him.
 Cast. You sha' not. I will first expose myself
To certain danger than for my defence
Destroy the man that saved me from destruction.
 Charl. Thou canst not satisfy me better than
To be the instrument of my release
From misery.
 Cast. Then work it by escape.
Leave me to this protection that still guards
The innocent. Or I will be a partner
In your destiny.
 Charl. My soul is heavy. Come, lie down to rest;
These are the pillows whereon men sleep best.

  [*They lie down, each of them with a death's head
   for a pillow.*

  Re-enter LANGUEBEAU SNUFFE, *seeking* SOQUETTE.

 Lang. Soquette, Soquette, Soquette! O art thou there?

  [*He mistakes the body of* BORACHIO *for* SOQUETTE.

Verily thou liest in a fine premeditated readiness for the
purpose. Come, kiss me, sweet Soquette.—Now purity defend me from the sin of Sodom!—This is a creature of the
masculine gender.—Verily the man is blasted.—Yea, cold
and stiff!—Murder, murder, murder!   [*Exit.*

  Re-enter D'AMVILLE *distractedly: he starts at the
   sight of a death's head.*

 D'Am. Why dost thou stare upon me? Thou art not
The soul of him I murdered. What hast thou
To do to vex my conscience? Sure thou wert
The head of a most dogged usurer,
Th'art so uncharitable. And that bawd,
The sky there: she could shut the windows and
The doors of this great chamber of the world,
And draw the curtains of the clouds between

Those lights and me, above this bed of earth,
When that same strumpet Murder and myself
Committed sin together. Then she could
Leave us i' the dark till the close deed was done.
But now that I begin to feel the loathsome horror of my
sin, and, like a lecher emptied of his lust, desire to bury
my face under my eye-brows, and would steal from my
shame unseen, she meets me
I' the face with all her light corrupted eyes
To challenge payment o' me. O behold!
Yonder's the ghost of old Montferrers, in
A long white sheet climbing yon lofty mountain
To complain to Heaven of me.—
Montferrers! pox o' fearfulness! 'Tis nothing
But a fair white cloud. Why, was I born a coward?
He lies that says so. Yet the countenance of
A bloodless worm might ha' the courage now
To turn my blood to water.
The trembling motion of an aspen leaf
Would make me, like the shadow of that leaf,
Lie shaking under 't. I could now commit
A murder were it but to drink the fresh
Warm blood of him I murdered to supply
The want and weakness o' mine own,
'Tis grown so cold and phlegmatic.

   Lang. Murder, murder, murder!   [*Within.*

   D'Am. Mountains o'erwhelm me: the ghost of old Montferrers haunts me.

   Lang. Murder, murder, murder!

   D'Am. O were my body circumvolved
Within that cloud, that when the thunder tears
His passage open, it might scatter me
To nothing in the air!

    Re-enter LANGUEBEAU SNUFFE *with the* Watch.

   Lang. Here you shall find
The murdered body.

   D'Am. Black Beelzebub,
And all his hell-hounds, come to apprehend me?

   Lang. No, my good lord, we come to apprehend
The murderer.

   D'Am. The ghost (great Pluto!) was

A fool unfit to be employed in
Any serious business for the state of hell.
Why could not he ha' suffered me to raise
The mountains o' my sins with one as damnable
As all the rest, and then ha' tumbled me
To ruin? But apprehend me e'en between
The purpose and the act before it was
Committed!

Watch. Is this the murderer? He speaks suspiciously.

Lang. No, verily. This is my Lord D'Amville. And his
distraction, I think, grows out of his grief for the loss of a
faithful servant. For surely I take him to be Borachio that is
slain.

D'Am. Hah! Borachio slain? Thou look'st like Snuffe,
dost not?

Lang. Yes, in sincerity, my lord.

D'Am. Hark thee—sawest thou not a ghost?

Lang. A ghost? Where, my lord?—I smell a fox.

D'Am. Here i' the churchyard.

Lang. Tush! tush! their walking spirits are mere imaginary fables. There's no such thing *in rerum natura*. Here is
a man slain. And with the spirit of consideration I rather
think him to be the murderer got into that disguise than
any such fantastic toy.

D'Am. My brains begin to put themselves in order. I
apprehend thee now.—'Tis e'en so.—Borachio, I will search
the centre, but I'll find the murderer.

Watch. Here, here, here.

D'Am. Stay. Asleep? so soundly,
So sweetly upon Death's heads? and in a place
So full of fear and horror? Sure there is
Some other happiness within the freedom
Of the conscience than my knowledge e'er attained to.—
          Ho, ho, ho!

Charl. Y'are welcome, uncle. Had you sooner come
You had been sooner welcome. I'm the man
You seek. You sha' not need examine me.

D'Am. My nephew and my daughter! O my dear
Lamented blood, what fate has cast you thus
Unhappily upon this accident?

Charl. You know, sir, she's as clear as chastity.

D'Am. As her own chastity. The time, the place
All circumstances argue that unclear.

Cast. Sir, I confess it; and repentantly
Will undergo the selfsame punishment
That justice shall inflict on Charlemont.

Charl. Unjustly she betrays her innocence.

Watch. But, sir, she's taken with you, and she must
To prison with you.

D'Am. There's no remedy.
Yet were it not my son's bed she abused,
My land should fly, but both should be excused.   [*Exeunt.*

SCENE IV—*An Apartment in* BELFOREST's *Mansion*

Enter BELFOREST *and a* Servant.

Bel. Is not my wife come in yet?

Ser. No, my lord.

Bel. Methinks she's very affectedly inclined
To young Sebastian's company o' late.
But jealousy is such a torment that
I am afraid to entertain it. Yet
The more I shun by circumstances to meet
Directly with it, the more ground I find
To circumvent my apprehension. First,
I know she has a perpetual appetite,
Which being so oft encountered with a man
Of such a bold luxurious freedom as
Sebastian is, and of so promising
A body, her own blood corrupted will
Betray her to temptation.

Enter FRESCO *closely.*

Fres. Precious! I was sent by his lady to see if her lord
were in bed. I should ha' done't slily without discovery, and
now I am blurted upon 'em before I was aware.   [*Exit.*

Bel. Know you not the gentlewoman my wife brought
home?

Ser. By sight, my lord. Her man was here but now.

Bel. Her man? I prithee, run and call him quickly. This

villain! I suspect him ever since I found him hid behind the tapestry.

Re-enter FRESCO.

Fresco! th'art welcome, Fresco. Leave us. [*Exit* Servant.] Dost hear, Fresco? Is not my wife at thy mistress's?

Fres. I know not, my lord.

Bel. I prithee tell me, Fresco—we are private—tell me: Is not thy mistress a good wench?

Fres. How means your lordship that? A wench o' the trade?

Bel. Yes, faith, Fresco; e'en a wench o' the trade.

Fres. O no, my lord. Those falling diseases cause baldness, and my mistress recovers the loss of hair, for she is a peri-wig maker.

Bel. And nothing else?

Fres. Sells falls, and tires, and bodies for ladies, or so.

Bel. So, sir; and she helps my lady to falls and bodies now and then, does she not?

Fres. At her ladyship's pleasure, my lord.

Bel. Her pleasure, you rogue? You are the pander to her pleasure, you varlet, are you not? You know the conveyances between Sebastian and my wife? Tell me the truth, or by this hand I'll nail thy bosom to the earth. Stir not, you dog, but quickly tell the truth.

Fres. O yes!   [*Speaks like a crier.*

Bel. Is not thy mistress a bawd to my wife?

Fres. O yes!

Bel. And acquainted with her tricks, and her plots, and her devices?

Fres. O yes! If any man, o' court, city, or country, has found my Lady Levidulcia in bed but my Lord Belforest, it is Sebastian.

Bel. What, dost thou proclaim it? Dost thou cry it, thou villain?

Fres. Can you laugh it, my lord? I thought you meant to proclaim yourself cuckold.

Enter the Watch.

Bel. The watch met with my wish. I must request the assistance of your offices.   [FRESCO *runs away.* 'Sdeath, stay that villain; pursue him!   [*Exeunt.*

SCENE V—*A Room in* Cataplasma's *House*

Enter Languebeau Snuffe, *importuning* Soquette.

Soqu. Nay, if you get me any more into the churchyard!
Lang. Why, Soquette, I never got thee there yet.
Soqu. Got me there! No, not with child.
Lang. I promised thee I would not, and I was as good
as my word.
Soqu. Yet your word was better than your deed. But
steal up into the little matted chamber o' the left hand.
Lang. I prithee let it be the right hand. Thou leftest me
before, and I did not like that.
Soqu. Precious quickly.——So soon as my mistress shall
be in bed I'll come to you.   [*Exit* Snuffe.

Enter Sebastian, Levidulcia, *and* Cataplasma.

Cata. I wonder Fresco stays so long.
Sebas. Mistress Soquette, a word with you.   [*Whispers.*
Lev. If he brings word my husband is i' bed
I will adventure one night's liberty
To be abroad.—
My strange affection to this man!—'Tis like
That natural sympathy which e'en among
The senseless creatures of the earth commands
A mutual inclination and consent.
For though it seems to be the free effect
Of mine own voluntary love, yet I can
Neither restrain it nor give reason for't.
But now 'tis done, and in your power it lies
To save my honour, or dishonour me.
Cata. Enjoy your pleasure, madam, without fear,
I never will betray the trust you have
Committed to me. And you wrong yourself
To let consideration of the sin
Molest your conscience. Methinks 'tis unjust
That a reproach should be inflicted on
A woman for offending but with one,
When 'tis light offence in husbands to
Commit with many.

Lev. So it seems to me.—
Why, how now, Sebastian, making love to that gentlewoman? How many mistresses ha' you i' faith?

Sebas. In faith, none; for I think none of 'em are faithful;
but otherwise, as many as clean shirts. The love of a woman
is like a mushroom,—it grows in one night and will serve
somewhat pleasingly next morning to breakfast, but afterwards waxes fulsome and unwholesome.

Cata. Nay, by Saint Winifred, a woman's love lasts as
long as winter fruit.

Sebas. 'Tis true—till new come in. By my experience no
longer.

Enter FRESCO *running.*

Fres. Somebody's doing has undone us, and we are like
to pay dearly for't.

Sebas. Pay dear? For what?

Fres. Will't not be a chargeable reckoning, think you,
when here are half a dozen fellows coming to call us to
account, with every man a several bill [30] in his hand that we
are not able to discharge.   [*Knock at the door.*

Cata. Passion o' me! What bouncing's that?
Madam, withdraw yourself.

Lev. Sebastian, if you love me, save my honour.
                        [*Exeunt all except* SEBASTIAN.

Sebas. What violence is this? What seek you? Zounds!
You shall not pass.

Enter BELFOREST *with the* Watch.

Bel. Pursue the strumpet [*Exit* Watch]. Villain, give me
    way,
Or I will make a passage through thy blood.

Sebas. My blood will make it slippery, my lord,
'Twere better you would take another way.
You may hap fall else.

    [*They fight. Both are slain.* SEBASTIAN *falls first. Dies.*
Sebas. I ha't, i' faith.

    [*While* BELFOREST *is staggering enter* LEVIDULCIA.
Lev. O God! my husband! my Sebastian! Husband!
Neither can speak, yet both report my shame.

---

[30] Play upon the word "bill," which meant in one sense a stout staff with
an iron blade at one end, like a partizan.

Is this the saving of my honour when
Their blood runs out in rivers, and my lust
The fountain whence it flows? Dear husband, let
Not thy departed spirit be displeased
If with adulterate lips I kiss thy cheek.
Here I behold the hatefulness of lust,
Which brings me kneeling to embrace him dead
Whose body living I did loathe to touch.
Now I can weep. But what can tears do good
When I weep only water, they weep blood.
But could I make an ocean with my tears
That on the flood this broken vessel of
My body, laden heavy with light lust,
Might suffer shipwreck and so drown my shame.
Then weeping were to purpose, but alas!
The sea wants water enough to wash away
The foulness of my name. O! in their wounds
I feel my honour wounded to the death.
Shall I out-live my honour? Must my life
Be made the world's example? Since it must,
Then thus in detestation of my deed,
To make the example move more forceably
To virtue, thus I seal it with a death
As full of horror as my life of sin.   [*Stabs herself.*

Enter the Watch *with* CATAPLASMA, FRESCO,
LANGUEBEAU SNUFFE, *and* SOQUETTE.

Watch. Hold, madam! Lord, what a strange night is this!
Lang. May not Snuffe be suffered to go out of himself?
Watch. Nor you, nor any. All must go with us.
O with what virtue lust should be withstood!
Since 'tis a fire quenched seldom without blood.   [*Exeunt.*

ACT THE FIFTH

SCENE I—*A Room in* D'AMVILLE's *Mansion*

A Servant *sleeping, with lights and money before him.
Music.*

Enter D'AMVILLE.

D'AM. What, sleep'st thou?

Ser. [*Awakening.*] No, my lord. Nor sleep nor wake;
But in a slumber troublesome to both.

D'Am. Whence comes this gold?

Ser. 'Tis part of the revenue
Due to your lordship since your brother's death.

D'Am. To bed. Leave me my gold.

Ser. And me my rest.
Two things wherewith one man is seldom blest.   [*Exit.*

D'Am. Cease that harsh music. We are not pleased with
it.   [*He handles the gold.*
Here sounds a music whose melodious touch
Like angels' voices ravishes the sense.
Behold, thou ignorant astronomer
Whose wandering speculation seeks among
The planets for men's fortunes, with amazement
Behold thine error and be planet-struck.
These are the stars whose operations make
The fortunes and the destinies of men.
Yon lesser eyes of Heaven (like subjects raised
Into their lofty houses, when their prince
Rides underneath the ambition of their loves)
Are mounted only to behold the face
Of your more rich imperious eminence
With unprevented sight. Unmask, fair queen.
    [*Unpurses the gold.*
Vouchsafe their expectations may enjoy
The gracious favour[31] they admire to see.
These are the stars, the ministers of Fate,
And man's high wisdom the superior power
To which their forces are subordinate.   [*Sleeps.*

Enter the Ghost of MONTFERRERS.

Mont. D'Amville! With all thy wisdom th'art a fool.
Not like those fools that we term innocents,
But a most wretched miserable fool
Which instantly, to the confusion of
Thy projects, with despair thou shalt behold.   [*Exit* Ghost.

D'Am. [*Starting up.*] What foolish dream dares interrupt
    my rest

---

[31] *i.e.* Countenance.

To my confusion? How can that be, since
My purposes have hitherto been borne
With prosperous judgment to secure success,
Which nothing lives to dispossess me of
But apprehended[32] Charlemont. And him
This brain has made the happy instrument
To free suspicion, to annihilate
All interest and title of his own
To seal up my assurance, and confirm
My absolute possession by the law.
Thus while the simple, honest worshipper
Of a fantastic providence, groans under
The burthen of neglected misery,
My real wisdom has raised up a state
That shall eternise my posterity.

Enter Servant *with the body of* SEBASTIAN.

What's that?
      Ser. The body of your younger son,
Slain by the Lord Belforest.
      D'Am. Slain! You lie!
Sebastian! Speak, Sebastian! He's lost
His hearing. A physician presently.
Go, call a surgeon.
      Rous. O—oh!   [*Within.*
      D'Am. What groan was that?
How does my elder son? The sound came from
His chamber.
      Ser. He went sick to bed, my lord.
      Rous. O—oh!   [*Within.*
      D'Am. The cries of mandrakes never touched the ear
With more sad horror than that voice does mine.

Enter a Servant *running.*

      Ser. Never you will see your son alive—
      D'Am. Nature forbid I e'er should see him dead.
                    [*A bed drawn forth with* ROUSARD *on it.*
Withdraw the curtains. O how does my son?
      Ser. Methinks he's ready to give up the ghost.
      D'Am. Destruction take thee and thy fatal tongue.

32 *i.e.* Arrested.

Dead! Where's the doctor?—Art not thou the face
Of that prodigious apparition stared upon
Me in my dream?

Ser. The doctor's come, my lord.

Enter Doctor.

D'Am. Doctor, behold two patients in whose cure
Thy skill may purchase an eternal fame.
If thou'st any reading in Hippocrates,
Galen, or Avicen; if herbs, or drugs,
Or minerals have any power to save,
Now let thy practice and their sovereign use
Raise thee to wealth and honour.

Doct. If any root of life remains within 'em
Capable of physic, fear 'em not, my lord.

Rous. O—oh!

D'Am. His gasping sighs are like the falling noise
Of some great building when the groundwork breaks.
On these two pillars stood the stately frame
And architecture of my lofty house.
An earthquake shakes 'em. The foundation shrinks.
Dear Nature, in whose honour I have raised
A work of glory to posterity,
O bury not the pride of that great action
Under the fall and mine of itself.

Doct. My lord, these bodies are deprived of all
The radical ability of Nature.
The heat of life is utterly extinguished.
Nothing remains within the power of man
That can restore them.

D'Am. Take this gold, extract
The spirit of it, and inspire new life
Into their bodies.

Doct. Nothing can, my lord.

D'Am. You ha' not yet examined the true state
And constitution of their bodies. Sure
You ha' not. I'll reserve their waters till
The morning. Questionless, their urines will
Inform you better.

Doct. Ha, ha, ha!

D'Am. Dost laugh,
Thou villain? Must my wisdom that has been

The object of men's admiration now
Become the subject of thy laughter?

   Rous. O—oh!   [*Dies.*

   All. He's dead.

   D'Am. O there expires the date
Of my posterity! Can Nature be
So simple or malicious to destroy
The reputation of her proper memory?
She cannot. Sure there is some power above
Her that controls her force.

   Doct. A power above
Nature? Doubt you that, my lord? Consider but
Whence man receives his body and his form.
Not from corruption like some worms and flies.
But only from the generation of
A man. For Nature never did bring forth
A man without a man; nor could the first
Man, being but the passive subject, not
The active mover, be the maker of
Himself. So of necessity there must
Be a superior power to Nature.

   D'Am. Now to myself I am ridiculous.
Nature, thou art a traitor to my soul.
Thou hast abused my trust. I will complain
To a superior court to right my wrong.
I'll prove thee a forger of false assurances.
In yon Star Chamber thou shalt answer it.
Withdraw the bodies. O the sense of death
Begins to trouble my distracted soul.   [*Exeunt.*

SCENE II—*A Hall of Justice. A scaffold at one end*

Enter Judges *and* Officers.

   1st Judge. Bring forth the malefactors to the bar.

   Enter CATAPLASMA, SOQUETTE, *and* FRESCO.

Are you the gentlewoman in whose house
The murders were committed?

   Cata. Yes, my lord.

   1st Judge. That worthy attribute of gentry which

Your habit draws from ignorant respect
Your name deserves not, nor yourself the name
Of woman, since you are the poison that
Infects the honour of all womanhood.

Cata. My lord, I am a gentlewoman; yet
I must confess my poverty compels
My life to a condition lower than
My birth or breeding.

2nd Judge. Tush, we know your birth.

1st Judge. But, under colour to profess the sale
Of tires and toys for gentlewomen's pride,
You draw a frequentation of men's wives
To your licentious house, and there abuse
Their husbands.—

Fres. Good my lord, her rent is great.
The good gentlewoman has no other thing
To live by but her lodgings. So she's forced
To let her fore-rooms out to others, and
Herself contented to lie backwards.

2nd Judge. So.

1st Judge. Here is no evidence accuses you
For accessories to the murder, yet
Since from the spring of lust, which you preserved
And nourished, ran the effusion of that blood,
Your punishment shall come as near to death
As life can bear it. Law cannot inflict
Too much severity upon the cause
Of such abhorred effects.

2nd Judge. Receive your sentence.
Your goods (since they were gotten by that means
Which brings diseases) shall be turned to the use
Of hospitals. You carted through the streets
According to the common shame of strumpets,
Your bodies whipped, till with the loss of blood
You faint under the hand of punishment.
Then that the necessary force of want
May not provoke you to your former life,
You shall be set to painful labour, whose
Penurious gains shall only give you food
To hold up Nature, mortify your flesh,
And make you fit for a repentant end.

All. O good my lord!

1st Judge. No more. Away with 'em.

[*Exeunt* CATAPLASMA, SOQUETTE, *and* FRESCO.

Enter LANGUEBEAU SNUFFE.

2nd Judge. Now, Monsieur Snuffe! A man of your profession
Found in a place of such impiety!

Lang. I grant you. The place is full of impurity. So much
the more need of instruction and reformation. The purpose
that carried me thither was with the spirit of conversion to
purify their uncleanliness, and I hope your lordship will
say the law cannot take hold o' me for that.

1st Judge. No, sir, it cannot; but yet give me leave
To tell you that I hold your wary answer
Rather premeditated for excuse
Then spoken out of a religious purpose.
Where took you your degrees of scholarship?

Lang. I am no scholar, my lord. To speak the sincere
truth, I am Snuffe the tallow-chandler.

2nd Judge. How comes your habits to be altered thus?

Lang. My Lord Belforest, taking a delight in the cleanness
of my conversation, withdrew me from that unclean life
and put me in a garment fit for his society and my present
profession.

1st Judge. His lordship did but paint a rotten post,
Or cover foulness fairly. Monsieur Snuffe,
Back to your candle-making! You may give
The world more light with that, than either with
Instruction or the example of your life.

Lang. Thus the Snuffe is put out.   [*Exit.*

Enter D'AMVILLE *distractedly with the hearses of his two
Sons borne after him.*

D'Am. Judgment! Judgment!

2nd Judge. Judgment, my lord, in what?

D'Am. Your judgment must resolve me in a case.
Bring in the bodies. Nay, I'll ha' it tried.
This is the case, my lord. By providence,
Even in a moment, by the only hurt
Of one, or two, or three at most, and those
Put quickly out o' pain, too, mark me, I
Had wisely raised a competent estate

To my posterity. And is there not
More wisdom and more charity in that
Than for your lordship, or your father, or
Your grandsire to prolong the torment and
The rack of rent from age to age upon
Your poor penurious tenants, yet perhaps
Without a penny profit to your heir?
Is't not more wise? more charitable? Speak.

   1st Judge. He is distracted.

   D'Am. How? distracted? Then
You ha' no judgment. I can give you sense
And solid reason for the very least
Distinguishable syllable I speak.
Since my thrift
Was more judicious than your grandsires', why
I would fain know why your lordship lives to make
A second generation from your father,
And the whole fry of my posterity
Extinguished in a moment. Not a brat
Left to succeed me.—I would fain know that.

   2nd Judge. Grief for his children's death distempers him.

   1st Judge. My lord, we will resolve you of your question.[33]
In the meantime vouchsafe your place with us.

   D'Am. I am contented, so you will resolve me.   [*Ascends.*

       Enter CHARLEMONT *and* CASTABELLA.

   2nd Judge. Now, Monsieur Charlemont, you are accused
Of having murdered one Borachio, that
Was servant to my Lord D'Amville. How can
You clear yourself? Guilty or not guilty?

   Charl. Guilty of killing him, but not of murder.
My lords, I have no purpose to desire
Remission for myself.—

            [D'AMVILLE *descends to* CHARLEMONT.

   D'Am. Uncivil boy!
Thou want'st humanity to smile at grief.
Why dost thou cast a cheerful eye upon
The object of my sorrow—my dead sons?

   1st Judge. O good my lord, let charity forbear
To vex the spirit of a dying man.
A cheerful eye upon the face of death

──────────

[33] Clear up the doubt conveyed in your question.

Is the true countenance of a noble mind.
For honour's sake, my lord, molest it not.

D'Am. Y'are all uncivil. O! is't not enough
That he unjustly hath conspired with Fate
To cut off my posterity, for him
To be the heir to my possessions, but
He must pursue me with his presence.
And, in the ostentation of his joy,
Laugh in my face and glory in my grief?

Charl. D'Amville, to show thee with what light respect
I value death and thy insulting pride,
Thus, like a warlike navy on the sea,
Bound for the conquest of some wealthy land,
Passed through the stormy troubles of this life,
And now arrived upon the armèd coast
In expectation of the victory
Whose honour lies beyond this exigent,[34]
Through mortal danger, with an active spirit
Thus I aspire to undergo my death.

   [*Leaps up the scaffold.* CASTABELLA *leaps after him.*

Cast. And thus I second thy brave enterprise.
Be cheerful, Charlemont. Our lives cut off
In our young prime of years are like green herbs
Wherewith we strew the hearses of our friends.
For, as their virtue, gathered when they are green,
Before they wither or corrupt, is best;
So we in virtue are the best for death
While yet we have not lived to such an age
That the increasing canker of our sins
Hath spread too far upon us.—

D'Am. A boon, my lords,
I beg a boon.

   1st Judge. What's that, my lord?

D'Am. His body when 'tis dead
For an anatomy.[35]

   2nd Judge. For what, my lord?

D'Am. Your understanding still comes short o' mine.
I would find out by his anatomy
What thing there is in Nature more exact

---

[34] Shakespeare uses this word in two senses, as "pressing business" and "extremity."
[35] *i.e.* A subject for dissection.

Than in the constitution of myself.
Methinks my parts and my dimensions are
As many, as large, as well composed as his;
And yet in me the resolution wants
To die with that assurance as he does.
The cause of that in his anatomy
I would find out.

    1st Judge. Be patient and you shall.

    D'Am. I have bethought me of a better way.
—Nephew, we must confer.—Sir, I am grown
A wondrous student now o' late. My wit
Has reached beyond the scope of Nature, yet
For all my learning I am still to seek
From whence the peace of conscience should proceed.

    Charl. The peace of conscience rises in itself.

    D'Am. Whether it be thy art or nature, I
Admire thee, Charlemont. Why, thou hast taught
A woman to be valiant. I will beg
Thy life.—My lords, I beg my nephew's life.
I'll make thee my physician. Thou shalt read
Philosophy to me. I will find out
The efficient cause of a contented mind.
But if I cannot profit in't, then 'tis
No more good being my physician,
But infuse
A little poison in a potion when
Thou giv'st me physic, unawares to me.
So I shall steal into my grave without
The understanding or the fear of death.
And that's the end I aim at. For the thought
Of death is a most fearful torment; is it not?

    2nd Judge. Your lordship interrupts the course of law.

    1st Judge. Prepare to die.

    Charl. My resolution's made.
But ere I die, before this honoured bench,
With the free voice of a departing soul,
I here protest this gentlewoman clear
Of all offence the law condemns her for.

    Cast. I have accused myself. The law wants power
To clear me. My dear Charlemont, with thee
I will partake of all thy punishments.

    Charl. Uncle, for all the wealthy benefits

My death advances you, grant me but this:
Your mediation for the guiltless life
Of Castabella, whom your conscience knows
As justly clear as harmless innocence.

D'Am. Freely. My mediation for her life
And all my interest in the world to boot;
Let her but in exchange possess me of
The resolution that she dies withal.
—The price of things is best known in their want.
Had I her courage, so I value it:
The Indies should not buy't out o' my hands.

Charl. Give me a glass of water.

D'Am. Me of wine.—
This argument of death congeals my blood.
Cold fear, with apprehension of thy end,
Hath frozen up the rivers of my veins.—

　　　　　　　[Servant *brings him a glass of wine.*

I must drink wine to warm me and dissolve
The obstruction; or an apoplexy will
Possess me.—Why, thou uncharitable knave,
Dost thou bring me blood to drink? The very glass
Looks pale and trembles at it.

Ser. 'Tis your hand, my lord.

D'Am. Canst blame me to be fearful, bearing still
The presence of a murderer about me?

　　　　　　　[Servant *gives* CHARLEMONT *a glass of water.*

Charl. Is this water?

Ser. Water, sir.

Charl. Come, thou clear emblem of cool temperance,
Be thou my witness that I use no art
To force my courage nor have need of helps
To raise my spirits, like those of weaker men
Who mix their blood with wine, and out of that
Adulterate conjunction do beget
A bastard valour. Native courage, thanks.
Thou lead'st me soberly to undertake
This great hard work of magnanimity.

D'Am. Brave Charlemont, at the reflexion of
Thy courage my cold fearful blood takes fire,
And I begin to emulate thy death.

　　　　　　　[Executioner *comes forward*

—Is that thy executioner? My lords,

You wrong the honour of so high a blood
To let him suffer by so base a hand.

Judges. He suffers by the form of law, my lord.

D'Am. I will reform it. Down, you shag-haired cur.[36]
The instrument that strikes my nephew's blood
Shall be as noble as his blood. I'll be
Thy executioner myself.

1st Judge. Restrain his fury. Good my lord, forbear.

D'Am. I'll butcher out the passage of his soul
That dares attempt to interrupt the blow.

2nd Judge. My lord, the office will impress a mark
Of scandal and dishonour on your name.

Charl. The office fits him: hinder not his hand,
But let him crown my resolution with
An unexampled dignity of death.
Strike home. Thus I submit me.

[Is made ready for execution.

    Cast. So do I.
In scorn of death thus hand in hand we die.

D'Am. I ha' the trick on't, nephew. You shall see
How easily I can put you out of pain.—Oh!

[As he raises up the axe he strikes out his own
brains, and staggers off the scaffold.

Exe. In lifting up the axe
I think he's knocked his brains out.

D'Am. What murderer was he that lifted up
My hand against my head?

1st Judge. None but yourself, my lord.

D'Am. I thought he was a murderer that did it.

1st Judge. God forbid!

D'Am. Forbid? You lie, judge. He commanded it.
To tell thee that man's wisdom is a fool.
I came to thee for judgment, and thou think'st
Thyself a wise man, I outreached thy wit
And made thy justice murder's instrument,
In Castabella's death and in Charlemont's,
To crown my murder of Montferrers with
A safe possession of his wealthy state.

Charl. I claim the just advantage of his words.

2nd Judge Descend the scaffold and attend the rest.

[36] This is addressed to the common headsman.

D'Am. There was the strength of natural understanding.
But Nature is a fool. There is a power
Above her that hath overthrown the pride
Of all my projects and posterity,
For whose surviving blood
I had erected a proud monument,
And struck 'em dead before me, for whose deaths
I called to thee for judgment. Thou didst want
Discretion for the sentence. But yon power
That struck me knew the judgment I deserved,
And gave it.—O! the lust of death commits
A rape upon me as I would ha' done
On Castabella.   [*Dies.*

   1st Judge. Strange is his death and judgment. With the
      hands
Of joy and justice I thus set you free.
The power of that eternal providence
Which overthrew his projects in their pride
Hath made your griefs the instruments to raise
Your blessings to a higher height than ever.

   Charl. Only to Heaven I attribute the work,
Whose gracious motives made me still forbear
To be mine own revenger. Now I see
That patience is the honest man's revenge.

   1st Judge. Instead of Charlemont that but e'en now
Stood ready to be dispossessed of all,
I now salute you with more titles both
Of wealth and dignity, than you were born to.
And you, sweet madam, Lady of Belforest,
You have the title by your father's death.

   Cast. With all the titles due to me, increase
The wealth and honour of my Charlemont,
Lord of Montferrers, Lord D'Amville Belforest.—
And for a close to make up all the rest—
                        [*Embraces* CHARLEMONT.
The Lord of Castabella. Now at last
Enjoy the full possession of my love,
As clear and pure as my first chastity.

   Charl. The crown of all my blessings!—I will tempt
My stars no longer, nor protract my time
Of marriage. When those nuptial rites are done,

I will perform my kinsmen's funeral.

   1st Judge. The drums and trumpets! Interchange the
      sounds
Of death and triumph. For these honoured lives,
Succeeding their deservèd tragedies.

   Charl. Thus, by the work of Heaven, the men that thought
To follow our dead bodies without tears
Are dead themselves, and now we follow theirs.   [*Exeunt.*

THE REVENGER'S TRAGEDY

THIS play was entered on the stationers' books in 1607, and was sometimes called *The Loyal Brother*. There are two quarto editions of it, one dated 1607 and one 1608, and from the care with which the text is printed it is probable that the author revised the proofs. The play has several times been reprinted.

Tourneur's plots have no known source.

DRAMATIS PERSONÆ

THE DUKE.
LUSSURIOSO, the Duke's Son.
SPURIO, a Bastard.
AMBITIOSO, the Duchess' Eldest Son.
SUPERVACUO, the Duchess' Second Son.
The Duchess' Youngest Son.
VENDICE, disguised as PIATO,
HIPPOLITO, also called CARLO, } Brothers of CASTIZA.
ANTONIO,
PIERO, } Nobles.
DONDOLO.
Judges, Nobles, Gentlemen, Officers, Keeper, Servants.

THE DUCHESS.
CASTIZA.
GRATIANA, Mother of CASTIZA.

SCENE—A CITY OF ITALY.

THE REVENGER'S TRAGEDY

ACT THE FIRST

SCENE I—*Near the House of* GRATIANA

Enter VENDICE.[1] *The* DUKE, DUCHESS, LUSSURIOSO, SPURIO,
with a train, pass over the stage with torchlight.

VEN. Duke! royal lecher! go, grey-haired adultery!
And thou his son, as impious steeped as he:
And thou his bastard, true begot in evil:
And thou his duchess, that will do with devil:
Four excellent characters! O, that marrowless age
Should stuff the hollow bones with damned desires;
And, 'stead of heat, kindle infernal fires
Within the spendthrift veins of a dry duke,
A parched and juiceless luxur.[2] O God! one,
That has scarce blood enough to live upon;
And he to riot it, like a son and heir!
O, the thought of that
Turns my abusèd heart-strings into fret.
Thou sallow picture of my poisoned love,
                  [*Views the skull in his hand.*
My study's ornament, thou shell of death,
Once the bright face of my betrothèd lady,
When life and beauty naturally filled out
These ragged imperfections;
When two heaven-pointed diamonds were set
In those unsightly rings—then 'twas a face
So far beyond the artificial shine
Of any woman's bought complexion,
That the uprightest man (if such there be,
That sin but seven times a day) broke custom,
And made up eight with looking after her.

---

[1] With a skull in his hand. That it is the skull of his mistress is evident from
the whole of the scene. He makes use of it afterwards in Act iii.—*Collier.*
[2] Luxury was the ancient term for incontinence.

O, she was able to ha' made a usurer's son
Melt all his patrimony in a kiss;
And what his father fifty years[3] told,
To have consumed, and yet his suit been cold
But, O accursèd palace!
Thee, when thou wert apparelled in thy flesh,
The old duke poisoned,
Because thy purer part would not consent
Unto his palsied lust; for old men lustful
Do show like young men angry, eager, violent,
Outbidden like their limited performances.
O, 'ware an old man hot and vicious!
"Age, as in gold, in lust is covetous."
Vengeance, thou murder's quit-rent, and whereby
Thou show'st thyself tenant to tragedy;
O keep thy day, hour, minute, I beseech,
For those thou hast determined. Hum! who e'er knew
Murder unpaid? faith, give revenge her due,
She has kept touch hitherto: be merry, merry,
Advance thee, O thou terror to fat folks,
To have their costly three-piled flesh worn off
As bare as this; for banquets, ease, and laughter
Can make great men, as greatness goes by clay;
But wise men little are more great than they.

Enter HIPPOLITO.

Hip. Still sighing o'er death's vizard?
Ven. Brother, welcome!
What comfort bring'st thou? how go things at court?
Hip. In silk and silver, brother: never braver.
Ven. Pooh!
Thou play'st upon my meaning. Prythee, say,
Has that bald madam, Opportunity,
Yet thought upon's? speak, are we happy yet?
Thy wrongs and mine are for one scabbard fit.
Hip. It may prove happiness.
Ven. What is't may prove?
Give me to taste.
Hip. Give me your hearing, then.
You know my place at court?

---

[3] Years must be read *yearès*.

Ven. Ay, the duke's chamber!
But 'tis a marvel thou'rt not turned out yet!

Hip. Faith, I've been shoved at; but 'twas still my hap
To hold by the duchess' skirt: you guess at that:
Whom such a coat keeps up, can ne'er fall flat.
But to the purpose—
Last evening, predecessor unto this,
The duke's son warily inquired for me,
Whose pleasure I attended: he began
By policy to open and unhusk me
About the time and common rumour:
But I had so much wit to keep my thoughts
Up in their built houses; yet afforded him
An idle satisfaction without danger.
But the whole aim and scope of his intent
Ended in this: conjuring me in private
To seek some strange-digested fellow forth,
Of ill-contented nature; either disgraced
In former times, or by new grooms displaced,
Since his step-mother's nuptials; such a blood,
A man that were for evil only good—
To give you the true word, some base-coined pander.

Ven. I reach you; for I know his heat is such,
Were there as many concubines as ladies,
He would not be contained; he must fly out.
I wonder how ill-featured, vile-proportioned,
That one should be, if she were made for woman,
Whom, at the insurrection of his lust,
He would refuse for once. Heart! I think none.
Next to a skull, though more unsound than one,
Each face he meets he strongly doats upon.

Hip. Brother, y' have truly spoke him.
He knows not you, but I will swear you know him.

Ven. And therefore I'll put on that knave for once,
And be a right man then, a man o' the time;
For to be honest is not to be i' the world.
Brother, I'll be that strange-composèd fellow.

Hip. And I'll prefer you, brother.

Ven. Go to, then:
The smallest advantage fattens wrongèd men:
It may point out occasion; if I meet her,
I'll hold her by the foretop fast enough;

Or, like the French mole,[4] heave up hair and all.
I have a habit that will fit it quaintly.
Here comes our mother.

   Hip. And sister.

   Ven. We must coin:
Women are apt, you know, to take false money;
But I dare stake my soul for these two creatures;
Only excuse excepted, that they'll swallow,
Because their sex is easy in belief.

Enter GRATIANA *and* CASTIZA.

   Gra. What news from court, son Carlo?

   Hip. Faith, mother,
'Tis whispered there the duchess' youngest son
Has played a rape on Lord Antonio's wife.

   Gra. On that religious lady!

   Cas. Royal blood monster! he deserves to die,
If Italy had no more hopes but he.

   Ven. Sister, y' have sentenced most direct and true,
The law's a woman, and would she were you.
Mother, I must take leave of you.

   Gra. Leave for what?

   Ven. I intend speedy travel.

   Hip. That he does, madam.

   Gra. Speedy indeed!

   Ven. For since my worthy father's funeral,
My life's unnaturally to me, e'en compelled;
As if I lived now, when I should be dead.

   Gra. Indeed, he was a worthy gentleman,
Had his estate been fellow to his mind.

   Ven. The duke did much deject him.

   Gra. Much?

   Ven. Too much:
And though disgrace oft smothered in his spirit,
When it would mount, surely I think he died
Of discontent, the noble man's consumption.

   Gra. Most sure he did.

   Ven. Did he, 'lack? you know all:—
You were his midnight secretary.

---

[4] This is not a name of syphilis, but a comparison only of it to a mole,
on account of the effects it sometimes produces in occasioning the loss of hair.
—*Pegge.*

Gra. No,
He was too wise to trust me with his thoughts.

Ven. I' faith, then, father, thou wast wise indeed;
"Wives are but made to go to bed and feed."
Come, mother, sister: you'll bring me onward, brother?

Hip. I will.

Ven. I'll quickly turn into another.   [*Aside. Exeunt.*

SCENE II—*A Hall of Justice*

Enter the DUKE, LUSSURIOSO, *the* DUCHESS, SPURIO, AMBI-
    TIOSO, *and* SUPERVACUO; *the* Duchess' Youngest Son
    brought out by Officers. *Two* Judges.

Duke. Duchess, it is your youngest son, we're sorry
His violent act has e'en drawn blood of honour,
And stained our honours;
Thrown ink upon the forehead of our state;
Which envious spirits will dip their pens into
After our death; and blot us in our tombs:
For that which would seem treason in our lives
Is laughter, when we're dead. Who dares now whisper,
That dares not then speak out, and e'en proclaim
With loud words and broad pens our closest shame?

1st Judge. Your grace hath spoke like to your silver years,
Full of confirmed gravity; for what is it to have
A flattering false insculption on a tomb,
And in men's hearts reproach? the bowelled [5] corpse
May be seared in, but (with free tongue I speak)
The faults of great men through their sear-cloths break.

Duke. They do; we're sorry for't: it is our fate
To live in fear, and die to live in hate.
I leave him to your sentence; doom him, lords—
The fact is great—whilst I sit by and sigh.

Duch. My gracious lord, I pray be merciful:
Although his trespass far exceed his years,
Think him to be your own, as I am yours;
Call him not son-in-law: the law, I fear,
Will fall too soon upon his name and him:
Temper his fault with pity.

[5] Disembowelled.

Lus. Good my lord,
Then 'twill not taste so bitter and unpleasant
Upon the judges' palate; for offences,
Gilt o'er with mercy, show like fairest women,
Good only for their beauties, which washed off,
No sin is uglier.

Amb. I beseech your grace,
Be soft and mild; let not relentless law
Look with an iron forehead on our brother.

Spu. He yields small comfort yet; hope he shall die;
And if a bastard's wish might stand in force,
Would all the court were turned into a corse!   [*Aside.*

Duch. No pity yet? must I rise fruitless then?
A wonder in a woman! are my knees
Of such low metal, that without respect—

1st Judge. Let the offender stand forth:
'Tis the duke's pleasure that impartial doom
Shall take fast hold of his unclean attempt.
A rape! why 'tis the very core of lust—
Double adultery.

Y. Son. So, sir.

2nd Judge. And which was worse,
Committed on the Lord Antonio's wife,
That general-honest lady. Confess, my lord,
What moved you to't?

Y. Son. Why, flesh and blood, my lord;
What should move men unto a woman else?

Lus. O, do not jest thy doom! trust not an axe
Or sword too far: the law is a wise serpent,
And quickly can beguile thee of thy life.
Though marriage only has made thee my brother,
I love thee so far: play not with thy death.

Y. Son. I thank you, troth; good admonitions, faith,
If I'd the grace now to make use of them.

1st Judge. That lady's name has spread such a fair wing
Over all Italy, that if our tongues
Were sparing toward the fact, judgment itself
Would be condemned, and suffer in men's thoughts.

Y. Son. Well then, 'tis done; and it would please me well,
Were it to do again: sure, she's a goddess,
For I'd no power to see her, and to live.
It falls out true in this, for I must die;

Her beauty was ordained to be my scaffold.
And yet, methinks, I might be easier 'sessed:
My fault being sport, let me but die in jest.

1st Judge. This be the sentence—

Duch. O, keep't upon your tongue; let it not slip;
Death too soon steals out of a lawyer's lip.
Be not so cruel-wise!

1st Judge. Your grace must pardon us;
'Tis but the justice of the law.

Duch. The law
Is grown more subtle than a woman should be.

Spu. Now, now he dies! rid 'em away. [*Aside.*

Duch. O, what it is to have an old cool duke,
To be as slack in tongue as in performance! [*Aside.*

1st Judge. Confirmed, this be the doom irrevocable.

Duch. O!

1st Judge. To-morrow early—

Duch. Pray be abed, my lord.

1st Judge. Your grace much wrongs yourself.

Amb. No, 'tis that tongue:
Your too much right does do us too much wrong.

1st Judge. Let that offender—

Duch. Live, and be in health.

1st Judge. Be on a scaffold—

Duke. Hold, hold, my lord!

Spu. Pox on't,
What makes my dad speak now? [*Aside.*

Duke. We will defer the judgment till next sitting:
In the meantime, let him be kept close prisoner.
Guard, bear him hence.

Amb. Brother, this makes for thee;
Fear not, we'll have a trick to set thee free. [*Aside.*

Y. Son. Brother, I will expect it from you both;
And in that hope I rest. [*Aside.*

Sup. Farewell, be merry. [*Exit with a* Guard.

Spu. Delayed! deferred! nay then, if judgment have cold
blood,
Flattery and bribes will kill it.

Duke. About it, then, my lords, with your best powers:
More serious business calls upon our hours.
  [*Exeunt, excepting the* DUCHESS.

Duch. Was't ever known step-duchess was so mild

And calm as I? some now would plot his death
With easy doctors, those loose-living men,
And make his withered grace fall to his grave,
And keep church better.
Some second wife would do this, and despatch
Her double-loathèd lord at meat or sleep.
Indeed, 'tis true, an old man's twice a child;
Mine cannot speak; one of his single words
Would quite have freed my youngest dearest son
From death or durance, and have made him walk
With a bold foot upon the thorny law,
Whose prickles should bow under him; but 'tis not,
And therefore wedlock-faith shall be forgot:
I'll kill him in his forehead; hate, there feed;
That wound is deepest, though it never bleed.
And here comes he whom my heart points unto,
His bastard son, but my love's true-begot;
Many a wealthy letter have I sent him,
Swelled up with jewels, and the timorous man
Is yet but coldly kind.
That jewel's mine that quivers in his ear,
Mocking his master's chillness and vain fear
He has spied me now!

Enter SPURIO.

Spu. Madam, your grace so private?
My duty on your hand.
Duch. Upon my hand, sir! troth, I think you'd fear
To kiss my hand too, if my lip stood there.
Spu. Witness I would not, madam.   [*Kisses her.*
Duch. 'Tis a wonder;
For ceremony has made many fools!
It is as easy way unto a duchess,
As to a hatted dame,[6] if her love answer:
But that by timorous honours, pale respects,
Idle degrees of fear, men make their ways
Hard of themselves. What, have you thought of me?
Spu. Madam, I ever think of you in duty,
Regard, and—

---

[6] She means from the highest to the lowest of her sex. At this time women of the inferior order wore hats. See Hollar's *Ornatus Muliebris Anglicanus*, 1640. —Hazlitt.

Duch. Pooh! upon my love, I mean.

Spu. I would 'twere love; but 'tis a fouler name
Than lust: you are my father's wife—your grace may
    guess now
What I could call it.

Duch. Why, th' art his son but falsely;
'Tis a hard question whether he begot thee.

Spu. I' faith, 'tis true: I'm an uncertain man
Of more uncertain woman. Maybe, his groom
O' the stable begot me; you know I know not!
He could ride a horse well, a shrewd suspicion, marry!—
He was wondrous tall: he had his length, i' faith.
For peeping over half-shut holyday windows,
Men would desire him light. When he was afoot
He made a goodly show under a pent-house;
And when he rid, his hat would check the signs,
And clatter barbers' basons.

Duch. Nay, set you a-horseback once,
You'll ne'er light off.[7]

Spu. Indeed, I am a beggar.

Duch. That's the more sign thou'rt great.—
But to our love:
Let it stand firm both in thy thought and mind,
That the duke was thy father, as no doubt then
He bid fair for't—thy injury is the more;
For had he cut thee a right diamond,
Thou had'st been next set in the dukedom's ring,
When his worn self, like age's easy slave,
Had dropped out of the collet[8] into th' grave.
What wrong can equal this? canst thou be tame,
And think upon't?

Spu. No, mad, and think upon't.

Duch. Who would not be revenged of such a father,
E'en in the worst way? I would thank that sin,
That could most injure him, and be in league with it.
O, what a grief 'tis that a man should live
But once i' the world, and then to live a bastard—
The curse o' the womb, the thief of nature,
Begot against the seventh commandment,
Half-damned in the conception by the justice

7 "Set a beggar on horseback, and he'll ride a gallop."
8 That part of a ring in which the stone is set.

Of that unbribèd everlasting law.

    Spu. O, I'd a hot-backed devil to my father.

    Duch. Would not this mad e'en patience, make blood
       rough?
Who but an eunuch would not sin? his bed,
By one false minute disinherited.

    Spu. Ay, there's the vengeance that my birth was wrapped
       in!
I'll be revenged for all: now, hate, begin;
I'll call foul incest but a venial sin.

    Duch. Cold still! in vain then must a duchess woo?

    Spu. Madam, I blush to say what I will do.

    Duch. Thence flew sweet comfort. Earnest, and farewell.
                                   [*Kisses him.*

    Spu. O, one incestuous kiss picks open hell.

    Duch. Faith, now, old duke, my vengeance shall reach
       high,
I'll arm thy brow with woman's heraldry.   [*Exit.*

    Spu. Duke, thou didst do me wrong; and, by thy act
Adultery is my nature.
Faith, if the truth were known, I was begot
After some gluttonous dinner; some stirring dish
Was my first father, when deep healths went round,
And ladies' cheeks were painted red with wine,
Their tongues, as short and nimble as their heels,
Uttering words sweet and thick; and when they rose,
Were merrily disposed to fall again.
In such a whispering and withdrawing hour,
When base male-bawds kept sentinel at stair-head,
Was I stol'n softly. O damnation meet![9]
The sin of feasts, drunken adultery!
I feel it swell me; my revenge is just!
I was begot in impudent wine and lust.
Step-mother, I consent to thy desires;
I love thy mischief well; but I hate thee
And those three cubs thy sons, wishing confusion,
Death and disgrace may be their epitaphs.
As for my brother, the duke's only son,
Whose birth is more beholding to report
Than mine, and yet perhaps as falsely sown
(Women must not be trusted with their own),

---

⁹ Old copy, "Met."

I'll loose my days upon him, hate-all-I;
Duke, on thy brow I'll draw my bastardy:
For indeed a bastard by nature should make cuckolds,
Because he is the son of a cuckold-maker.   [*Exit.*

SCENE III—*A part of the City*

Enter VENDICE *in disguise and* HIPPOLITO.

Ven. What, brother, am I far enough from myself?
Hip. As if another man had been sent whole
Into the world, and none wist how he came.
Ven. It will confirm me bold—the child o' the court;
Let blushes dwell i' the country. Impudence!
Thou goddess of the palace, mistress of mistresses.
To whom the costly perfumed people pray,
Strike thou my forehead into dauntless marble,
Mine eyes to steady sapphires. Turn my visage;
And, if I must needs glow, let me blush inward,
That this immodest season may not spy
That scholar in my cheeks, fool bashfulness;
That maid in the old time, whose flush of grace
Would never suffer her to get good clothes.
Our maids are wiser, and are less ashamed,
Save Grace the bawd, I seldom hear grace named!
Hip. Nay, brother, you reach out o' the verge now—
'Sfoot, the duke's son! settle your looks.
Ven. Pray, let me not be doubted.
Hip. My lord—

Enter LUSSURIOSO.

Lus. Hippolito—be absent, leave us!
Hip. My lord, after long search, wary inquiries,
And politic siftings, I made choice of yon fellow,
Whom I guess rare for many deep employments:
This our age swims within him; and if Time
Had so much hair, I should take him for Time,
He is so near kin to this present minute.
Lus. 'Tis enough;
We thank thee: yet words are but great men's blanks;[10]

[10] Bonds.

Gold, though it be dumb, does utter the best thanks.

[*Gives him money.*

Hip. Your plenteous honour! an excellent fellow, my lord.

Lus. So, give us leave. [*Exit* HIPPOLITO.] Welcome, be
not far off; we must be better acquainted: pish, be bold with
us—thy hand.

Ven. With all my heart, i' faith: how dost, sweet musk-
cat?
When shall we lie together?

Lus. Wondrous knave,
Gather him into boldness! 'sfoot, the slave's
Already as familiar as an ague,
And shakes me at his pleasure. Friend, I can
Forget myself in private; but elsewhere
I pray do you remember me.

Ven. O, very well, sir—I conster myself saucy.

Lus. What hast been?
Of what profession?

Ven. A bone-setter.

Lus. A bone-setter!

Ven. A bawd, my lord—
One that sets bones together.

Lus. Notable bluntness!
Fit, fit for me; e'en trained up to my hand:
Thou hast been scrivener to much knavery, then?

Ven. 'Sfoot, to abundance, sir: I have been witness
To the surrenders of a thousand virgins:
And not so little;
I have seen patrimonies washed a-pieces,
Fruit-fields turned into bastards,
And in a world of acres
Not so much dust due to the heir 'twas left to
As would well gravel[11] a petition.

Lus. Fine villain! troth, I like him wondrously:
He's e'en shaped for my purpose. [*Aside.*] Then thou
know'st
I' th' world strange lust?

Ven. O Dutch lust! fulsome lust!
Drunken procreation! which begets so many drunkards
Some fathers dread not (gone to bed in wine) to slide
from the mother,

[11] *i.e.* Sand it, to prevent it from blotting, while the ink was wet.—*Steevens.*

And cling[12] the daughter-in-law;
Some uncles are adulterous with their nieces:
Brothers with brothers' wives. O hour of incest!
Any kin now, next to the rim o' th' sister,
Is men's meat in these days; and in the morning,
When they are up and dressed, and their mask on,
Who can perceive this, save that eternal eye,
That sees through flesh and all? Well, if anything be
       damned,
It will be twelve o'clock at night; that twelve
Will never 'scape;
It is the Judas of the hours, wherein
Honest salvation is betrayed to sin.
   Lus. In troth, it is true; but let this talk glide.
It is our blood to err, though hell gape wide.
Ladies know Lucifer fell, yet still are proud.
Now, sir, wert thou as secret as thou'rt subtle,
And deeply fathomed into all estates,
I would embrace thee for a near employment;
And thou shouldst swell in money, and be able
To make lame beggars crouch to thee.
   Ven. My lord,
Secret! I ne'er had that disease o' the mother,
I praise my father: why are men made close,
But to keep thoughts in best? I grant you this,
Tell but some women a secret over night,
Your doctor may find it in the urinal i' the morning.
But, my lord—
   Lus. So thou'rt confirmed in me,
And thus I enter thee.   [*Gives him money.*
   Ven. This Indian devil
Will quickly enter any man but a usurer;
He prevents that by entering the devil first.
   Lus. Attend me. I am past my depth in lust,
And I must swim or drown. All my desires
Are levelled at a virgin not far from court,
To whom I have conveyed by messenger
Many waxed lines, full of my neatest spirit,
And jewels that were able to ravish her
Without the help of man; all which and more

12 *i.e.* Embrace.

She (foolish chaste) sent back, the messengers
Receiving frowns for answers.

Ven. Possible!
'Tis a rare Phœnix, whoe'er she be.
If your desires be such, she so repugnant,
In troth, my lord, I'd be revenged and marry her.

Lus. Pish! the dowry of her blood and of her fortunes
Are both too mean—good enough to be bad withal.
I'm one of that number can defend
Marriage is good; yet rather keep a friend.
Give me my bed by stealth—there's true delight;
What breeds a loathing in't, but night by night!

Ven. A very fine religion!

Lus. Therefore thus
I'll trust thee in the business of my heart
Because I see thee well-experienced
In this luxurious day wherein we breathe.
Go thou, and with a smooth enchanting tongue
Bewitch her ears, and cosen her of all grace:
Enter upon the portion[13] of her soul—
Her honour, which she calls her chastity,
And bring it into expense; for honesty
Is like a stock of money laid to sleep
Which, ne'er so little broke, does never keep.

Ven. You have gi'en't the tang,[14] i' faith, my lord:
Make known the lady to me, and my brain
Shall swell with strange invention: I will move it,
Till I expire with speaking, and drop down
Without a word to save me—but I'll work—

Lus. We thank thee, and will raise thee.—
Receive her name; it is the only daughter to Madam
Gratiana, the late widow.

Ven. O my sister, my sister!   [*Aside.*

Lus. Why dost walk aside?

Ven. My lord, I was thinking how I might begin:
As thus, O lady—or twenty hundred devices—
Her very bodkin will put a man in.

Lus. Ay, or the wagging of her hair.

---

[13] "Portico" has been suggested. But I see no reason to alter the text. "Portion" is here that which specially belongs to the soul as its birthright.

[14] Equivalent to hit the nail on the head. clinched the matter. Perhaps the metaphor is derived from ringing sound.

Ven. No, that shall put you in, my lord.

Lus. Shall't? why, content. Dost know the daughter then?

Ven. O, excellent well by sight.

Lus. That was her brother,
That did prefer thee to us.

Ven. My lord, I think so;
I knew I had seen him somewhere—

Lus. And therefore, prythee, let thy heart to him
Be as a virgin close.

Ven. O my good lord.

Lus. We may laugh at that simple age within him.

Ven. Ha, ha, ha!

Lus. Himself being made the subtle instrument,
To wind up a good fellow.[15]

Ven. That's I, my lord.

Lus. That's thou,
To entice and work his sister.

Ven. A pure novice!

Lus. 'Twas finely managed.

Ven. Gallantly carried!
A pretty perfumed villain!

Lus. I've bethought me,
If she prove chaste still and immovable,
Venture upon the mother; and with gifts,
As I will furnish thee, begin with her.

Ven. O, fie, fie! that's the wrong end my lord.
'Tis mere impossible that a mother, by any gifts, should
become a bawd to her own daughter!

Lus. Nay, then, I see thou'rt but a puisne[16]
In the subtle mystery of a woman.
Why, 'tis held now no dainty dish: the name
Is so in league with the age, that nowadays
It does eclipse three quarters of a mother.

Ven. Does it so, my lord?
Let me alone, then, to eclipse the fourth.

Lus. Why, well-said—come, I'll furnish thee, but first
Swear to be true in all.

Ven. True!

Lus. Nay, but swear.

[15] Put a thief upon the track.
[16] Novice.

Ven. Swear?—I hope your honour little doubts my faith.
Lus. Yet, for my humour's sake, 'cause I love swearing—
Ven. 'Cause you love swearing,—'slud,[17] I will.
Lus. Why, enough!
Ere long look to be made of better stuff.
    Ven. That will do well indeed, my lord.
    Lus. Attend me.   [*Exit.*
    Ven. O!
Now let me burst. I've eaten noble poison;
We are made strange fellows, brother, innocent villains!
Wilt not be angry, when thou hear'st on't, think'st thou?
I' faith, thou shalt: swear me to foul my sister!
Sword, I durst make a promise of him to thee;
Thou shalt disheir him; it shall be thine honour.
And yet, now angry froth is down in me,
It would not prove the meanest policy,
In this disguise, to try the faith of both.
Another might have had the selfsame office;
Some slave that would have wrought effectually,
Ay, and perhaps o'erwrought 'em; therefore I,
Being thought travelled, will apply myself
Unto the selfsame form, forget my nature,
As if no part about me were kin to 'em,
So touch 'em;—though I durst almost for good
Venture my lands in Heaven upon their blood.   [*Exit.*

SCENE IV—*A Room in* ANTONIO'S *House*

Enter ANTONIO, *whose* Wife *the* Duchess' Youngest Son
    ravished, discovering her dead body to HIPPOLITO,
    PIERO, *and* Lords.

    Ant. Draw nearer, lords, and be sad witnesses
Of a fair comely building newly fallen,
Being falsely undermined. Violent rape
Has played a glorious act: behold, my lords,
A sight that strikes man out of me.
    Piero. That virtuous lady!
    Ant. Precedent for wives!
    Hip. The blush of many women, whose chaste presence
<hr>
[17] A corruption of "God's blood."

Would e'en call shame up to their cheeks, and make
Pale wanton sinners have good colours—
   Ant. Dead!
Her honour first drank poison, and her life,
Being fellows in one house, did pledge her honour.
   Piero. O, grief of many!
   Ant. I marked not this before—
A prayer-book, the pillow to her cheek:
This was her rich confection; and another
Placed in her right hand, with a leaf tucked up,
Pointing to these words—
Melius virtute mori, quam per dedecus vivere:
True and effectual it is indeed.
   Hip. My lord, since you invite us to your sorrows,
Let's truly taste 'em, that with equal comfort,
As to ourselves, we may relieve your wrongs:
We have grief too, that yet walks without tongue;
Curæ leves loquuntur, majores stupent.
   Ant. You deal with truth, my lord;
Lend me but your attentions, and I'll cut
Long grief into short words. Last revelling night,
When torch-light made an artificial noon
About the court, some courtiers in the masque,
Putting on better faces than their own,
Being full of fraud and flattery—amongst whom
The duchess' youngest son (that moth to honour)
Filled up a room, and with long lust to eat
Into my warren, amongst all the ladies
Singled out that dear form, who ever lived
As cold in lust as she is now in death
(Which that step-duchess' monster knew too well),
And therefore in the height of all the revels,
When music was heard loudest, courtiers busiest,
And ladies great with laughter—O vicious minute!
Unfit but for relation to be spoke of:
Then with a face more impudent than his vizard,
He harried her amidst a throng of panders,
That live upon damnation of both kinds,
And fed the ravenous vulture of his lust.
O death to think on't! She, her honour forced,
Deemed it a nobler dowry for her name
To die with poison than to live with shame.

Hip. A wondrous lady! of rare fire compact;
She has made her name an empress by that act.

Piero. My lord, what judgment follows the offender?

Ant. Faith, none, my lord; it cools, and is deferred.

Piero. Delay the doom for rape!

Ant. O, you must note who 'tis should die,
The duchess' son! she'll look to be a saver:
"Judgment, in this age, is near kin to favour."

Hip. Nay, then, step forth, thou bribeless officer:

                                     [Draws his sword.
I'll bind you all in steel, to bind you surely;
Here let your oaths meet, to be kept and paid,
Which else will stick like rust, and shame the blade;
Strengthen my vow that if, at the next sitting,
Judgment speak all in gold, and spare the blood
Of such a serpent, e'en before their seats
To let his soul out, which long since was found
Guilty in Heaven—

All. We swear it, and will act it.

Ant. Kind gentlemen, I thank you in mine ire.

Hip. 'Twere pity
The ruins of so fair a monument
Should not be dipped in the defacer's blood.

Piero. Her funeral shall be wealthy; for her name
Merits a tomb of pearl. My Lord Antonio,
For this time wipe your lady from your eyes;
No doubt our grief and yours may one day court it,
When we are more familiar with revenge.

Ant. That is my comfort, gentlemen, and I joy
In this one happiness above the rest,
Which will be called a miracle at last;
That, being an old man, I'd a wife so chaste.   *[Exeunt.*

ACT THE SECOND

SCENE I—*A Room in* GRATIANA'S *House*

Enter CASTIZA.

CAS. How hardly shall that maiden be beset,
Whose only fortunes are her constant thoughts!

That has no other child's part but her honour,
That keeps her low and empty in estate;
Maids and their honours are like poor beginners;
Were not sin rich, there would be fewer sinners;
Why had not virtue a revenue? Well,
I know the cause, 'twould have impoverished hell.

Enter DONDOLO.

How now, Dondolo?

Don. Madonna, there is one as they say, a thing of flesh
and blood—a man, I take him by his beard, that would very
desirously mouth to mouth with you.

Cas. What's that?

Don. Show his teeth in your company.

Cas. I understand thee not.

Don. Why, speak with you, madonna.

Cas. Why, say so, madman, and cut off a great deal of
dirty way; had it not been better spoke in ordinary words,
that one would speak with me?

Don. Ha, ha! that's as ordinary as two shillings. I would
strive a little to show myself in my place; a gentleman-usher
scorns to use the phrase and fancy of a serving-man.

Cas. Yours be your own, sir; go, direct him hither;
　　　　　　　　　　　　　　　　　　　　[*Exit* DONDOLO.

I hope some happy tidings from my brother,
That lately travelled, whom my soul affects.
Here he comes.

Enter VENDICE, *disguised.*

Ven. Lady, the best of wishes to your sex—
Fair skins and new gowns.

Cas. O, they shall thank you, sir.
Whence this?

Ven. O, from a dear and worthy mighty friend.

Cas. From whom?

Ven. The duke's son!

Cas. Receive that.　　　　　　　　　　[*Boxes his ear.*

I swore I would put anger in my hand,
And pass the virgin limits of my sex,
To him that next appeared in that base office,
To be his sin's attorney. Bear to him
That figure of my hate upon thy cheek,

Whilst 'tis yet hot, and I'll reward thee for't;
Tell him my honour shall have a rich name,
When several harlots shall share his with shame.
Farewell; commend me to him in my hate.   [*Exit*.

    Ven. It is the sweetest box that e'er my nose came nigh;
The finest drawn-work cuff that e'er was worn;
I'll love this blow for ever, and this cheek
Shall still henceforward take the wall of this.
O, I'm above my tongue: most constant sister,
In this thou hast right honourable shown;
Many are called by[18] their honour, that have none;
Thou art approved for ever in my thoughts.
It is not in the power of words to taint thee.
And yet for the salvation of my oath,
As my resolve in that point, I will lay
Hard siege unto my mother, though I know
A syren's tongue could not bewitch her so.
Mass, fitly here she comes! thanks, my disguise—
Madam, good afternoon.

Enter GRATIANA.

    Gra. Y'are welcome, sir.
    Ven. The next[19] of Italy commends him to you,
Our mighty expectation, the duke's son.
    Gra. I think myself much honoured that he pleases
To rank me in his thoughts.
    Ven. So may you, lady:
One that is like to be our sudden duke;
The crown gapes for him every tide, and then
Commander o'er us all; do but think on him,
How blessed were they, now that could pleasure him—
E'en with anything almost!
    Gra. Ay, save their honour.
    Ven. Tut, one would let a little of that go too,
And ne'er be seen in't—ne'er be seen in't, mark you;
I'd wink, and let it go.
    Gra. Marry, but I would not.
    Ven. Marry but I would, I hope; I know you would too,
If you'd that blood now, which you gave your daughter.

---

[18] There is no reason to omit the word "by." Vendice seems to refer to "families called honourable," *i.e.*, the children of lords.
[19] *i.e.* Next heir.

To her indeed 'tis this wheel[20] comes about;
That man that must be all this, perhaps ere morning
(For his white father does but mould away),
Has long desired your daughter.

   Gra. Desired?

   Ven. Nay, but hear me;
He desires now, that will command hereafter:
Therefore be wise. I speak as more a friend
To you than him: madam, I know you're poor,
And, 'lack the day!
There are too many poor ladies already;
Why should you wax the number? 'Tis despised.
Live wealthy, rightly understand the world,
And chide away that foolish country girl
Keeps company with your daughter—Chastity.

   Gra. O fie, fie! the riches of the world cannot hire
A mother to such a most unnatural task.

   Ven. No, but a thousand angels[21] can.
Men have no power, angels must work you to't:
The world descends into such baseborn evils,
That forty angels can make fourscore devils.
There will be fools still, I perceive—still fools.
Would I be poor, dejected, scorned of greatness,
Swept from the palace, and see others' daughters
Spring with the dew o' the court, having mine own
So much desired and loved by the duke's son?
No, I would raise my state upon her breast;
And call her eyes my tenants; I would count
My yearly maintenance upon her cheeks;
Take coach upon her lip; and all her parts
Should keep men after men, and I would ride
In pleasure upon pleasure.
You took great pains for her, once when it was;
Let her requite it now, though it be but some.
You brought her forth: she may well bring you home.

   Gra. O Heavens! this o'ercomes me!

   Ven. Not, I hope, already?   [*Aside.*

   Gra. It is too strong for me; men know that know us,
We are so weak their words can overthrow us;

---

20 Wheel of fortune.
21 A play upon the double meaning of the word "angel," which was the name
of a gold coin.

He touched me nearly, made my virtues bate,[22]
When his tongue struck upon my poor estate.   [*Aside.*

Ven. I e'en quake to proceed, my spirit turns edge.
I fear me she's unmothered; yet I'll venture.
"That woman is all male, whom none can enter."   [*Aside.*
What think you now, lady? Speak, are you wiser?
What said advancement to you? Thus it said:
The daughter's fall lifts up the mother's head.
Did it not, madam? But I'll swear it does
In many places: tut, this age fears no man.
" 'Tis no shame to be bad, because 'tis common."

Gra. Ay, that's the comfort on't.

Ven. The comfort on't!
I keep the best for last—can these persuade you
To forget Heaven—and—   [*Gives her money.*

Gra. Ay, these are they—

Ven. O!

Gra. That enchant our sex. These are
The means that govern our affections—that woman
Will not be troubled with the mother long,
That sees the comfortable shine of you:
I blush to think what for your sakes I'll do.

Ven. O suffering[23] Heaven, with thy invisible finger,
E'en at this instant turn the precious side
Of both mine eyeballs inward, not to see myself.   [*Aside.*

Gra. Look you, sir.

Ven. Hollo.

Gra. Let this thank your pains.

Ven. O, you're kind, madam.

Gra. I'll see how I can move.

Ven. Your words will sting.

Gra. If she be still chaste, I'll ne'er call her mine.

Ven. Spoke truer than you meant it.

Gra. Daughter Castiza.

Re-enter CASTIZA.

Cas. Madam.

Ven. O, she's yonder;

---

[22] Decline, droop.
[23] Long suffering.

Meet her: troops of celestial soldiers guard her heart.
Yon dam has devils enough to take her part.

Cas. Madam, what makes yon evil-officed man
In presence of you?

Gra. Why?

Cas. He lately brought
Immodest writing sent from the duke's son,
To tempt me to dishonourable act.

Gra. Dishonourable act!—good honourable fool,
That wouldst be honest, 'cause thou wouldst be so,
Producing no one reason but thy will.
And't has a good report, prettily commended,
But pray, by whom? Poor people, ignorant people;
The better sort, I'm sure, cannot abide it.
And by what rule should we square out our lives,
But by our betters' actions? O, if thou knew'st
What 'twere to lose it, thou would never keep it!
But there's a cold curse laid upon all maids,
Whilst others clip[24] the sun, they clasp the shades.
Virginity is paradise locked up.
You cannot come by yourselves without fee;
And 'twas decreed that man should keep the key!
Deny advancement! treasure! the duke's son!

Cas. I cry you mercy! lady! I mistook you!
Pray did you see my mother? which way went you?
Pray God, I have not lost her.

Ven. Prettily put by!   [*Aside.*

Gra. Are you as proud to me, as coy to him?
Do you not know me now?

Cas. Why, are you she?
The world's so changed one shape into another,
It is a wise child now that knows her mother.

Ven. Most right i' faith.   [*Aside.*

Gra. I owe your cheek my hand
For that presumption now; but I'll forget it.
Come, you shall leave those childish 'haviours,
And understand your time. Fortunes flow to you;
What, will you be a girl?
If all feared drowning that spy waves ashore,
Gold would grow rich, and all the merchants poor.

[24] Embrace.

Cas. It is a pretty saying of a wicked one;
But methinks now it does not show so well
Out of your mouth—better in his!

Ven. Faith, bad enough in both,
Were I in earnest, as I'll seem no less.   [*Aside.*
I wonder, lady, your own mother's words
Cannot be taken, nor stand in full force.
'Tis honesty you urge; what's honesty?
'Tis but Heaven's beggar; and what woman is
So foolish to keep honesty,
And be not able to keep herself? No,
Times are grown wiser, and will keep less charge.
A maid that has small portion now intends
To break up house, and live upon her friends;
How blessed are you! you have happiness alone;
Others must fall to thousands, you to one,
Sufficient in himself to make your forehead
Dazzle the world with jewels, and petitionary people
Start at your presence.

Gra. O, if I were young, I should be ravished.

Cas. Ay, to lose your honour!

Ven. 'Slid, how can you lose your honour
To deal with my lord's grace?
He'll add more honour to it by his title;
Your mother will tell you how.

Gra. That I will.

Ven. O, think upon the pleasure of the palace!
Secured ease and state! the stirring meats,
Ready to move out of the dishes, that e'en now
Quicken when they are eaten!
Banquets abroad by torchlight! music! sports!
Bareheaded vassals, that had ne'er the fortune
To keep on their own hats, but let horns[25] wear 'em!
Nine coaches waiting—hurry, hurry, hurry—

Cas. Ay, to the devil.

Ven. Ay, to the devil! [*Aside.*] To the duke, by my faith.

Gra. Ay, to the duke: daughter, you'd scorn to think o'
the devil, an you were there once.

Ven. True, for most there are as proud as he for his
          heart, i' faith.   [*Aside.*

[25] Alluding to the custom of hanging hats in ancient halls upon stags' horns.
—*Steevens.*

Who'd sit at home in a neglected room,
Dealing her short-lived beauty to the pictures,
That are as useless as old men, when those
Poorer in face and fortune than herself
Walk with a hundred acres on their backs,[26]
Fair meadows cut into green foreparts? O,
It was the greatest blessing ever happened to woman
When farmers' sons agreed and met again,
To wash their hands, and come up gentlemen!
The commonwealth has flourished ever since:
Lands that were mete[27] by the rod, that labour's spared:
Tailors ride down, and measure 'em by the yard.
Fair trees, those comely foretops of the field,
Are cut to maintain head-tires—much untold.
All thrives but chastity; she lies a-cold.
Nay, shall I come nearer to you? mark but this:
Why are there so few honest women, but because 'tis the
poorer profession? that's accounted best that's best followed;
least in trade, least in fashion; and that's not honesty, be-
lieve it; and do but note the love and dejected price of it—
Lose but a pearl, we search, and cannot brook it:
But that[28] once gone, who is so mad to look it?
   Gra. Troth, he says true.
   Cas. False! I defy you both:
I have endured you with an ear of fire;
Your tongues have struck hot irons on my face.
Mother, come from that poisonous woman there.
   Gra. Where?
   Cas. Do you not see her? she's too inward, then!
Slave, perish in thy office! you Heavens, please
Henceforth to make the mother a disease,
Which first begins with me: yet I've outgone you.   [*Exit.*
   Ven. O angels, clap your wings upon the skies,
And give this virgin crystal plaudites!   [*Aside.*
   Gra. Peevish, coy, foolish!—but return this answer,
My lord shall be most welcome, when his pleasure
Conducts him this way. I will sway mine own.
Women with women can work best alone.   [*Exit.*
   Ven. Indeed, I'll tell him so.

---

[26] This allusion to farms sold for a court-wardrobe is common in our drama.
[27] *i.e.* Measured.
[28] *i.e.* Honesty.

O, more uncivil, more unnatural,
Than those base-titled creatures that look downward;
Why does not Heaven turn black, or with a frown
Undo the world? Why does not earth start up,
And strike the sins that tread upon't? O,
Were't not for gold and women, there would be no damna-
        tion.
Hell would look like a lord's great kitchen without fire in't.
But 'twas decreed, before the world began,
That they should be the hooks to catch at man.   [*Exit.*

SCENE II—*An Apartment in the* DUKE's *Palace*

Enter LUSSURIOSO, *with* HIPPOLITO.

Lus. I much applaud
Thy judgment; thou art well-read in a fellow
And 'tis the deepest art to study man.
I know this, which I never learnt in schools,
The world's divided into knaves and fools.
    Hip. Knave in your face, my lord—behind your back—
                                    [*Aside.*
Lus. And I much thank thee, that thou hast preferred
A fellow of discourse, well-mingled,
And whose brain time hath seasoned.
    Hip. True, my lord,
We shall find season once, I hope. O villain!
To make such an unnatural slave of me—but—   [*Aside.*
Lus. Mass, here he comes.
    Hip. And now shall I have free leave to depart.   [*Aside.*
Lus. Your absence, leave us.
    Hip. Are not my thoughts true?   [*Aside.*
I must remove; but, brother, you may stay.
Heart! we are both made bawds a new-found way!   [*Exit.*

Enter VENDICE, *disguised.*

Lus. Now we're an even number, a third man's dangerous,
Especially her brother;—say, be free,
Have I a pleasure toward—
    Ven. O my lord!
Lus. Ravish me in thine answer; art thou rare?

Hast thou beguiled her of salvation,
And rubbed hell o'er with honey? Is she a woman?

Ven. In all but in desire.

Lus. Then she's in nothing—I bate[29] in courage now.

Ven. The words I brought
Might well have made indifferent honest naught.
A right good woman in these days is changed
Into white money with less labour far;
Many a maid has turned to Mahomet
With easier working: I durst undertake,
Upon the pawn and forfeit of my life,
With half those words to flat a Puritan's wife.
But she is close and good; yet 'tis a doubt
By this time.—O, the mother, the mother!

Lus. I never thought their sex had been a wonder,
Until this minute. What fruit from the mother?

Ven. How must I blister my soul, be forsworn,
Or shame the woman that received me first!
I will be true: thou liv'st not to proclaim.
Spoke to a dying man, shame has no shame.   [*Aside.*
My lord.

Lus. Who's that?

Ven. Here's none but I, my lord.

Lus. What would thy haste utter?

Ven. Comfort.

Lus. Welcome.

Ven. The maid being dull, having no mind to travel
Into unknown lands, what did I straight,
But set spurs to the mother? golden spurs
Will put her to a false gallop in a trice.

Lus. Is't possible that in this
The mother should be damned before the daughter?

Ven. O, that's good manners, my lord; the mother for
her age must go foremost, you know.

Lus. Thou'st spoke that true! but where comes in this
comfort?

Ven. In a fine place, my lord,—the unnatural mother
Did with her tongue so hard beset her honour,
That the poor fool was struck to silent wonder;
Yet still the maid, like an unlighted taper,
Was cold and chaste, save that her mother's breath

²⁹ Decline.

Did blow fire on her cheeks. The girl departed;
But the good ancient madam, half mad, threw me
These promising words, which I took deeply note of:
"My lord shall be most welcome"—

Lus. Faith, I thank her.

Ven. "When his pleasure conducts him this way"—

Lus. That shall be soon, i' faith.

Ven. "I will sway mine own"—

Lus. She does the wiser: I commend her for't.

Ven. "Women with women can work best alone."

Lus. By this light, and so they can; give 'em their due,
men are not comparable to 'em.

Ven. No, that's true; for you shall have one woman knit
more in an hour, than any man can ravel again in seven-and-
twenty years.

Lus. Now my desires are happy; I'll make 'em freemen
         now.
Thou art a precious fellow; faith, I love thee;
Be wise and make it thy revenue; beg, beg;
What office couldst thou be ambitious for?

Ven. Office, my lord! marry, if I might have my wish, I
would have one that was never begged yet.

Lus. Nay, then, thou canst have none.

Ven. Yes, my lord, I could pick out another office yet;
nay, and keep a horse and drab upon't.

Lus. Prythee, good bluntness, tell me.

Ven. Why, I would desire but this, my lord—to have all
the fees behind the arras, and all the farthingales that fall
plump about twelve o'clock at night upon the rushes.

Lus. Thou'rt a mad, apprehensive knave; dost think to
make any great purchase of that?

Ven. O, 'tis an unknown thing, my lord; I wonder't has
been missed so long.

Lus. Well, this night I'll visit her, and 'tis till then
A year in my desires—farewell, attend
Trust me with thy preferment.

Ven. My loved lord!   [*Exit* LUSSURIOSO.
O, shall I kill him o' th' wrong side now? no!
Sword, thou wast never a backbiter yet.
I'll pierce him to his face; he shall die looking upon me.
Thy veins are swelled with lust, this shall unfill 'em.

Great men were gods, if beggars could not kill 'em.
Forgive me, Heaven, to call my mother wicked!
O, lessen not my days upon the earth,
I cannot honour her. By this, I fear me,
Her tongue has turned my sister unto use.
I was a villain not to be forsworn
To this our lecherous hope, the duke's son;
For lawyers, merchants, some divines, and all,
Count beneficial perjury a sin small.
It shall go hard yet, but I'll guard her honour,
And keep the ports sure.   [*Exit.*

SCENE III—*A Corridor in the Palace*

Enter VENDICE, *still disguised, and* HIPPOLITO.

Hip. Brother, how goes the world? I would know news
       of you.
But I have news to tell you.
    Ven. What, in the name of knavery?
    Hip. Knavery, faith;
This vicious old duke's worthily abused;
The pen of his bastard writes him cuckold?
    Ven. His bastard?
    Hip. Pray, believe it; he and the duchess
By night meet in their linen;[30] they have been seen
By stair-foot panders.
    Ven. O, sin foul and deep!
Great faults are winked at when the duke's asleep.
See, see, here comes the Spurio.
    Hip. Monstrous luxur!
    Ven. Unbraced! two of his valiant bawds with him!
O, there's a wicked whisper; hell's in his ear.
Stay, let's observe his passage—

Enter SPURIO *and* Servants.

    Spu. O, but are you sure on't?
    1st Ser. My lord, most sure on't; for 'twas spoke by one,
That is most inward with the duke's son's lust,

30 *i.e.* Nightdresses.

That he intends within this hour to steal
Unto Hippolito's sister, whose chaste life
The mother has corrupted for his use.

   Spu. Sweet word! sweet occasion! faith, then, brother,
I'll disinherit you in as short time
As I was when I was begot in haste.
I'll damn you at your pleasure: precious deed!
After your lust, O, 'twill be fine to bleed.
Come, let our passing out be soft and wary.

                           [*Exeunt* SPURIO *and* Servants.

   Ven. Mark! there; there; that step; now to the duchess!
This their second meeting writes the duke cuckold
With new additions—his horns newly revived.
Night! thou that look'st like funeral heralds' fees,
Torn down betimes i' the morning, thou hang'st fitly
To grace those sins that have no grace at all.
Now 'tis full sea abed over the world:
There's juggling of all sides; some that were maids
E'en at sunset, are now perhaps i' the toll-book.[31]
This woman in immodest thin apparel
Lets in her friend by water; here a dame
Cunning nails leather hinges to a door,
To avoid proclamation.
Now cuckolds are coining, apace, apace, apace, apace!
And careful sisters spin that thread i' the night,
That does maintain them and their bawds i' the day.

   Hip. You flow well, brother.

   Ven. Pooh! I'm shallow yet;
Too sparing and too modest; shall I tell thee?
If every trick were told that's dealt by night,
There are few here that would not blush outright.

   Hip. I am of that belief too. Who's this comes?

   Ven. The duke's son up so late? Brother, fall back,
And you shall learn some mischief. My good lord!

              Enter LUSSURIOSO.

   Lus. Piato! why, the man I wished for! Come,
I do embrace this season for the fittest
To taste of that young lady.

   Ven. Heart and hell.   [*Aside.*

[31] Alluding to the custom of entering horses sold at fairs in a book called the "Toll-book."

Hip. Damned villain!   [*Aside.*
Ven. I have no way now to cross it, but to kill him.
                                                         [*Aside.*

Lus. Come, only thou and I.
Ven. My lord! my lord!
Lus. Why dost thou start us?
Ven. I'd almost forgot—the bastard!
Lus. What of him?
Ven. This night, this hour, this minute, now—
Lus. What? what?
Ven. Shadows the duchess—
Lus. Horrible word!
Ven. And (like strong poison) eats
Into the duke your father's forehead.
Lus. O!
Ven. He makes horn-royal.
Lus. Most ignoble slave!
Ven. This is the fruit of two beds.
Lus. I am mad.
Ven. That passage he trod warily.
Lus. He did?
Ven. And hushed his villains every step he took.
Lus. His villains! I'll confound them.
Ven. Take 'em finely—finely, now.
Lus. The duchess' chamber-door shall not control me.
                               [*Exeunt* Lussurioso *and* Vendice.

Hip. Good, happy, swift: there's gunpowder i' the court,
Wildfire at midnight. In this heedless fury
He may show violence to cross himself.
I'll follow the event.   [*Exit.*

SCENE IV—*The* Duke's *Bedchamber.*—*The* Duke
                   and Duchess *in bed*

Enter Lussurioso *and* Vendice, *disguised.*

Lus. Where is that villain?
Ven. Softly, my lord, and you may take 'em twisted.
Lus. I care not how.
Ven. O! 'twill be glorious
To kill 'em doubled, when they're heaped. Be soft, my lord

Lus. Away! my spleen is not so lazy: thus and thus
I'll shake their eyelids ope, and with my sword
Shut 'em again for ever. Villain! strumpet!

Duke. You upper guard, defend us!

Duch. Treason! treason!

Duke. O, take me not in sleep!
I have great sins; I must have days,
Nay, months, dear son, with penitential heaves,
To lift 'em out, and not to die unclear.
O, thou wilt kill me both in Heaven and here.

Lus. I am amazed to death.

Duke. Nay, villain, traitor,
Worse than the foulest epithet; now I'll gripe thee
E'en with the nerves of wrath, and throw thy head
Amongst the lawyers!—guard!

Enter AMBITIOSO, SUPERVACUO, *and* Lords.

1st Lord. How comes the quiet of your grace disturbed?

Duke. This boy, that should be myself after me,
Would be myself before me; and in heat
Of that ambition bloodily rushed in,
Intending to depose me in my bed.

2nd Lord. Duty and natural loyalty forfend!

Duch. He called his father villain, and me strumpet,
A word that I abhor to file[32] my lips with.

Amb. That was not so well-done, brother.

Lus. I am abused—I know there's no excuse can do me
good.   [*Aside.*

Ven. 'Tis now good policy to be from sight;
His vicious purpose to our sister's honour
I crossed beyond our thought.   [*Aside.*

Hip. You little dreamt his father slept here.

Ven. O, 'twas far beyond me:
But since it fell so—without frightful words,
Would he had killed him, 'twould have eased our swords.

Duke. Be comforted, our duchess, he shall die.

             [*Exeunt* VENDICE *and* HIPPOLITO.

Lus. Where's this slave-pander now? out of mine eye,
Guilty of this abuse.

32 Defile.

Enter Spurio *with* Servants.

Spu. Y' are villains, fablers! [33]
You have knaves' chins and harlots' tongues; you lie;
And I will damn you with one meal a day.

1st Ser. O good my lord!

Spu. 'Sblood, you shall never sup.

2nd Ser. O, I beseech you, sir!

Spu. To let my sword catch cold so long, and miss him!

1st. Ser. Troth, my lord, 'twas his intent to meet there.

Spu. Heart! he's yonder.
Ha, what news here? is the day out o' the socket,
That it is noon at midnight? the court up?
How comes the guard so saucy with his elbows?

Lus. The bastard here?
Nay, then the truth of my intent shall out;
My lord and father hear me.

Duke. Bear him hence.

Lus. I can with loyalty excuse.

Duke. Excuse? to prison with the villain!
Death shall not long lag after him.

Spu. Good, i' faith: then 'tis not much amiss.

Lus. Brothers, my best release lies on your tongues;
I pray, persuade for me.

Amb. It is our duties; make yourself sure of us.

Sup. We'll sweat in pleading.

Lus. And I may live to thank you.   [*Exit with* Lords.

Amb. No, thy death shall thank me better.

Spu. He's gone; I'll after him,
And know his trespass; seem to bear a part
In all his ills, but with a puritan heart. [*Exit with* Servants.

Amb. Now, brother, let our hate and love be woven
So subtlely together, that in speaking one word for his life,
We may make three for his death:
The craftiest pleader gets most gold for breath.

Sup. Set on, I'll not be far behind you, brother.

Duke. Is't possible a son should be disobedient as far as
the sword? It is the highest: he can go no farther.

Amb. My gracious lord, take pity—

Duke. Pity, boys!

[33] Liars.

Amb. Nay, we'd be loth to move your grace too much;
We know the trespass is unpardonable,
Black, wicked, and unnatural.

Sup. In a son! O, monstrous!

Amb. Yet, my lord,
A duke's soft hand strokes the rough head of law,
And makes it lie smooth.

Duke. But my hand shall ne'er do't.

Amb. That as you please, my lord.

Sup. We must needs confess.
Some fathers would have entered into hate
So deadly-pointed, that before his eyes
He would ha' seen the execution sound[34]
Without corrupted favour.

Amb. But, my lord,
Your grace may live the wonder of all times,
In pardoning that offence, which never yet
Had face to beg a pardon.

Duke. Hunny, how's this?

Amb. Forgive him, good my lord; he's your own son:
And I must needs say, 'twas the viler done.

Sup. He's the next heir: yet this true reason gathers,
None can possess that dispossess their fathers.
Be merciful!—

Duke. Here's no step-mother's wit;
I'll try them both upon their love and hate.   [*Aside.*

Amb. Be merciful—although—

Duke. You have prevailed.
My wrath, like flaming wax, hath spent itself;
I know 'twas but some peevish moon[35] in him;
Go, let him be released.

Sup. 'Sfoot, how now, brother?   [*Aside.*

Amb. Your grace doth please to speak beside your spleen;
I would it were so happy.

Duke. Why, go, release him.

Sup. O my good lord! I know the fault's too weighty
And full of general loathing: too inhuman,
Rather by all men's voices worthy death.

Duke. 'Tis true too; here, then, receive this signet.
Doom shall pass;

[34] Stable.
[35] Some lune or frenzy.

Direct it to the judges; he shall die
Ere many days. Make haste.
 Amb. All speed that may be.
We could have wished his burden not so sore:
We knew your grace did but delay before.
      [*Exeunt* AMBITIOSO *and* SUPERVACUO.
 Duke. Here's envy with a poor thin cover o'er't;
Like scarlet hid in lawn, easily spied through.
This their ambition by the mother's side
Is dangerous, and for safety must be purged.
I will prevent their envies; sure it was
But some mistaken fury in our son,
Which these aspiring boys would climb upon:
He shall be released suddenly.

     Enter Nobles.

 1st Noble. Good morning to your grace.
 Duke. Welcome, my lords.
 2nd Noble. Our knees shall take
Away the office of our feet for ever,
Unless your grace bestow a father's eye
Upon the clouded fortunes of your son,
And in compassionate virtue grant him that,
Which makes e'en mean men happy—liberty.
 Duke. How seriously their loves and honours woo
For that which I am about to pray them do!
Arise, my lord; your knees sign his release.
We freely pardon him.
 1st Noble. We owe your grace much thanks, and he much
  duty.   [*Exeunt* Nobles.
 Duke. It well becomes that judge to nod at crimes,
That does commit greater himself, and lives.
I may forgive a disobedient error,
That expect pardon for adultery,
And in my old days am a youth in lust.
Many a beauty have I turned to poison
In the denial, covetous of all.
Age hot is like a monster to be seen;
My hairs are white, and yet my sins are green.

ACT THE THIRD

SCENE I—*A Room in the Palace*

Enter AMBITIOSO *and* SUPERVACUO.

Sup. Brother, let my opinion sway you once;
I speak it for the best, to have him die
Surest and soonest; if the signet come
Unto the judge's hand, why then his doom
Will be deferred till sittings and court-days,
Juries, and further. Faiths are bought and sold;
Oaths in these days are but the skin of gold.

Amb. In troth, 'tis true too.

Sup. Then let's set by the judges,
And fall to the officers; 'tis but mistaking
The duke our father's meaning; and where he named
"Ere many days"—'tis but forgetting that,
And have him die i' the morning.

Amb. Excellent!
Then am I heir! duke in a minute!

Sup. [*Aside.*] Nay,
An he were once puffed out, here is a pin
Should quickly prick your bladder.

Amb. Blessed occasion!
He being packed we'll have some trick and wile
To wind our younger brother out of prison,
That lies in for the rape. The lady's dead,
And people's thoughts will soon be buried.

Sup. We may with safety do't, and live and feed;
The duchess' sons are too proud to bleed.

Amb. We are, i' faith, to say true—come, let's not linger:
I'll to the officers; go you before,
And set an edge upon the executioner.

Sup. Let me alone to grind.   [*Exit.*

Amb. Meet farewell!
I am next now; I rise just in that place,
Where thou'rt cut off; upon thy neck, kind brother;
The falling of one head lifts up another.   [*Exit.*

SCENE II—*The Courtyard of a Prison*

Enter LUSSURIOSO *with* Nobles.

Lus. My lords, I am so much indebted to your loves
For this, O, this delivery—
  1st Noble. Put your duties, my lord, unto the hopes that
    grow in you.
  Lus. If e'er I live to be myself, I'll thank you.
O liberty, thou sweet and heavenly dame!
But hell for prison is too mild a name.   [*Exeunt.*

Enter AMBITIOSO *and* SUPERVACUO, *with* Officers.

Amb. Officers, here's the duke's signet, your firm warrant,
Brings the command of present death along with it
Unto our brother, the duke's son; we are sorry
That we are so unnaturally employed
In such an unkind office, fitter far
For enemies than brothers.
  Sup. But, you know,
The duke's command must be obeyed.
  1st Off. It must and shall, my lord. This morning, then—
So suddenly?
  Amb. Ay, alas! poor, good soul!
He must breakfast betimes; the executioner
Stands ready to put forth his cowardly valour.
  2nd Off. Already?
  Sup. Already, i' faith. O sir, destruction hies,
And that is least imprudent,[36] soonest dies.
  1st Off. Troth, you say true. My lord, we take our leaves:
Our office shall be sound; we'll not delay
The third part of a minute.
  Amb. Therein you show
Yourselves good men and upright. Officers,
Pray, let him die as private as he may;
Do him that favour; for the gaping people
Will but trouble him at his prayers,

---

[36] Edits., "Impudent." The least imprudent is equivalent to the most farsighted or wary.

And make him curse and swear, and so die black.
Will you be so far kind?

1st Off. It shall be done, my lord.

Amb. Why, we do thank you; if we live to be—
You shall have a better office.

2nd Off. Your good lordship—

Sup. Commend us to the scaffold in our tears.

1st Off. We'll weep, and do your commendations.

Amb. Fine fools in office!   [*Exeunt* Officers.

Sup. Things fall out so fit!

Amb. So happily! come, brother! ere next clock,
His head will be made serve a bigger block.[37]   [*Exeunt.*

SCENE III—*Inside a Prison*

Enter the Duchess' Youngest Son *and* Keeper.

Y. Son. Keeper!

Keep. My lord.

Y. Son. No news lately from our brothers?
Are they unmindful of us?

Keep. My lord, a messenger came newly in,
And brought this from 'em.

Y. Son. Nothing but paper-comforts?
I looked for my delivery before this,
Had they been worth their oaths.—Prythee, be from us.
                                                    [*Exit* Keeper.
Now what say you, forsooth? speak out, I pray.
    [*Reads the letter.*] "Brother, be of good cheer";
'Slud, it begins like a whore with good cheer.
"Thou shalt not be long a prisoner."
Not six-and-thirty years, like a bankrupt—I think so.
"We have thought upon a device to get thee out by a trick."
By a trick! pox o' your trick, an' it be so long a playing.
"And so rest comforted, be merry, and expect it suddenly!"
Be merry! hang merry, draw and quarter merry; I'll be
mad. Is't not strange that a man should lie-in a whole month
for a woman? Well, we shall see how sudden our brothers
will be in their promise. I must expect still a trick: I
shall not be long a prisoner. How now, what news?

37 *i.e.* Hat.

Re-enter Keeper.

Keep. Bad news, my lord; I am discharged of you.

Y. Son. Slave! call'st thou that bad news? I thank you, brothers.

Keep. My lord, 'twill prove so. Here come the officers,
Into whose hands I must commit you.

Y. Son. Ha, officers! what? why?

Enter Officers.

1st. Off. You must pardon us, my lord:
Our office must be sound: here is our warrant,
The signet from the duke; you must straight suffer.

Y. Son. Suffer! I'll suffer you to begone; I'll suffer you
To come no more; what would you have me suffer?

2nd Off. My lord, those words were better changed to
prayers.
The time's but brief with you: prepare to die.

Y. Son. Sure, 'tis not so!

3rd Off. It is too true, my lord.

Y. Son. I tell you 'tis not; for the duke my father
Deferred me till next sitting; and I look,
E'en every minute, threescore times an hour,
For a release, a trick wrought by my brothers.

1st Off. A trick, my lord! if you expect such comfort,
Your hope's as fruitless as a barren woman:
Your brothers were the unhappy messengers
That brought this powerful token for your death.

Y. Son. My brothers? no, no.

2nd Off. 'Tis most true, my lord.

Y. Son. My brothers to bring a warrant for my death!
How strange this shows!

3rd Off. There's no delaying time.

Y. Son. Desire 'em hither: call 'em up—my brothers!
They shall deny it to your faces.

1st Off. My lord,
They're far enough by this; at least at court;
And this most strict command they left behind 'em.
When grief swam in their eyes, they showed like brothers,
Brimful of heavy sorrow—but the duke
"Must have his pleasure."

Y. Son. His pleasure!

1st Off. These were the last words, which my memory
    bears,
"Commend us to the scaffold in our tears."

Y. Son. Pox dry their tears! what should I do with tears?
I hate 'em worse than any citizen's son
Can hate salt water. Here came a letter now,
New-bleeding from their pens, scarce stinted yet:
Would I'd been torn in pieces when I tore it:
Look, you officious whoresons, words of comfort,
"Not long a prisoner."

1st Off. It says true in that, sir; for you must suffer
    presently.

Y. Son. A villainous Duns[38] upon the letter, knavish ex-
    position!
Look you then here, sir: "we'll get thee out by a trick,"
    says he.

2nd Off. That may hold too, sir; for you know a trick is
commonly four cards,[39] which was meant by us four officers.

Y. Son. Worse and worse dealing.

1st Off. The hour beckons us.
The headsman waits: lift up your eyes to Heaven.

Y. Son. I thank you, faith; good pretty wholesome counsel!
I should look up to Heaven, as you said,
Whilst he behind me cosens me of my head.
Ay, that's the trick.

3rd Off. You delay too long, my lord.

Y. Son. Stay, good authority's bastards; since I must,
Through brothers' perjury, die, O, let me venom
Their souls with curses.

3rd Off. Come, 'tis no time to curse.

Y. Son. Must I bleed then without respect of sign? well—
My fault was sweet sport which the world approves,
I die for that which every woman loves.   [*Exeunt.*

[38] Alluding to Duns Scotus, who commented upon "The Master of the Sen-
tences."
[39] In the game of Primero.

SCENE IV—*A Lodge in the Ducal Grounds*

Enter VENDICE, *disguised, and* HIPPOLITO.

Ven. O, sweet, delectable, rare, happy, ravishing!

Hip. Why, what's the matter, brother?

Ven. O, 'tis able to make a man spring up and knock his
    forehead

Against yon silver ceiling.

Hip. Prythee, tell me;

Why may not I partake with you? you vowed once

To give me share to every tragic thought.

Ven. By the mass, I think I did too;

Then I'll divide it too thee. The old duke,

Thinking my outward shape and inward heart

Are cut out of one piece (for he that prates his secrets,

His heart stands o' the outside), hires me by price

To greet him with a lady

In some fit place, veiled from the eyes o' the court,

Some darkened, blushless angle, that is guilty

Of his forefather's lust and great folks' riots;

To which I easily (to maintain my shape)

Consented, and did wish his impudent grace

To meet her here in this unsunnèd lodge,

Wherein 'tis night at noon; and here the rather

Because, unto the torturing of his soul,

The bastard and the duchess have appointed

Their meeting too in this luxurious circle;

Which most afflicting sight will kill his eyes,

Before we kill the rest of him.

Hip. 'Twill, i' faith! Most dreadfully digested!

I see not how you could have missed me, brother.

Ven. True; but the violence of my joy forgot it.

Hip. Ay, but where's that lady now?

Ven. O! at that word

I'm lost again; you cannot find me yet:

I'm in a throng of happy apprehensions.

He's suited for a lady; I have took care

For a delicious lip, a sparkling eye—

You shall be witness, brother:
Be ready; stand with your hat off.   [*Exit.*

Hip. Troth, I wonder what lady it should be!
Yet 'tis no wonder, now I think again,
To have a lady stoop to a duke, that stoops unto his men.
'Tis common to be common through the world:
And there's more private common shadowing vices,
Than those who are known both by their names and prices.
'Tis part of my allegiance to stand bare
To the duke's concubine; and here she comes.

Re-enter VENDICE, *with the skull of his* Betrothed *dressed
up in tires.*

Ven. Madam, his grace will not be absent long.[40]
Secret! ne'er doubt us, madam; 'twill be worth
Three velvet gowns to your ladyship. Known!
Few ladies respect that disgrace: a poor thin shell!
'Tis the best grace you have to do it well.
I'll save your hand that labour: I'll unmask you!

Hip. Why, brother, brother!

Ven. Art thou beguiled now? tut, a lady can,
As such all hid, beguile a wiser man.
Have I not fitted the old surfeiter
With a quaint piece of beauty? Age and bare bone
Are e'er allied in action. Here's an eye,
Able to tempt a great man—to serve God:
A pretty hanging lip, that has forgot now to dissemble.
Methinks this mouth should make a swearer tremble;
A drunkard clasp his teeth, and not undo 'em,
To suffer wet damnation to run through 'em.
Here's a cheek keeps her colour, let the wind go whistle:
Spout, rain, we fear thee not: be hot or cold,
All's one with us; and is not he absurd,
Whose fortunes are upon their faces set,
That fear no other god but wind and wet?

Hip. Brother, you've spoke that right:
Is this the form that, living, shone so bright?

Ven. The very same.
And now methinks I could e'en chide myself
For doating on her beauty, though her death
Shall be revenged after no common action.

40 He imagines her to be speaking, and answers her.

Does the silkworm expend her yellow labours
For thee? For thee does she undo herself?
Are lordships sold to maintain ladyships,
For the poor benefit of a bewildering minute?
Why does yon fellow falsify highways,
And put his life between the judge's lips,
To refine such a thing—keeps horse and men
To beat their valours for her?
Surely we are all mad people, and they
Whom we think are, are not: we mistake those;
'Tis we are mad in sense, they but in clothes.
   Hip. Faith, and in clothes too we, give us our due.
   Ven. Does every proud and self-affecting dame
Camphire her face for this, and grieve her Maker
In sinful baths of milk, when many an infant starves
For her superfluous outside—all for this?
Who now bids twenty pounds a night? prepares
Music, perfumes, and sweetmeats? All are hushed.
Thou may'st lie chaste now! it were fine, methinks,
To have thee seen at revels, forgetful feasts,
And unclean brothels! sure, 'twould fright the sinner,
And make him a good coward: put a reveller
Out of his antic amble,
And cloy an epicure with empty dishes.
Here might a scornful and ambitious woman
Look through and through herself. See, ladies, with false
      forms
You deceive men, but cannot deceive worms.—
Now to my tragic business. Look you, brother,
I have not fashioned this only for show
And useless property; no, it shall bear a part
E'en in its own revenge. This very skull,
Whose mistress the duke poisoned, with this drug,
The mortal curse of the earth, shall be revenged
In the like strain, and kiss his lips to death.
As much as the dumb thing can, he shall feel:
What fails in poison, we'll supply in steel.
   Hip. Brother, I do applaud thy constant vengeance—
The quaintness of thy malice—above thought.
   Ven. So, 'tis laid on [*He poisons the lips of the skull*]:
      now come and welcome, duke,
I have her for thee. I protest it, brother,

Methinks she makes almost as fair a fine,
As some old gentlewoman in a periwig.
Hide thy face now for shame; thou hadst need have a
    mask now:
'Tis vain when beauty flows; but when it fleets,
This would become graves better than the streets.

Hip. You have my voice in that: hark, the duke's come.

Ven. Peace, let's observe what company he brings,
And how he does absent 'em; for you know
He'll wish all private. Brother, fall you back a little
With the bony lady.

Hip. That I will.   [*Retires.*

Ven. So, so; now nine years' vengeance crowd into a
minute!

Enter DUKE *and* Gentlemen.

Duke. You shall have leave to leave us, with this charge
Upon your lives, if we be missed by the duchess
Or any of the nobles, to give out,
We're privately rid forth.

Ven. O happiness!

Duke. With some few honourable gentlemen, you may
    say—
You may name those that are away from court.

Gen. Your will and pleasure shall be done, my lord.
                             [*Exeunt* Gentlemen.

Ven. "Privately rid forth!"
He strives to make sure work on't. Your good grace!
                                 [*Advances.*

Duke. Piato, well done, hast brought her! what lady is't?

Ven. Faith, my lord, a country lady, a little bashful at
first, as most of them are; but after the first kiss, my lord,
the worst is past with them. Your grace knows now what
you have to do; she has somewhat a grave look with her—
but—

Duke. I love that best; conduct her.

Ven. Have at all.   [*Aside.*

Duke. In gravest looks the greatest faults seem less.
Give me that sin that's robed in holiness.

Ven. Back with the torch! brother, raise the perfumes.
                                   [*Aside.*

Duke. How sweet can a duke breathe! Age has no fault.

Pleasure should meet in a perfumèd mist.
Lady, sweetly encountered: I came from court,
I must be bold with you. O, what's this? O!

Ven. Royal villain! white devil!

Duke. O!

Ven. Brother, place the torch here, that his affrighted eyeballs
May start into those hollows. Duke, dost know
Yon dreadful vizard? View it well; 'tis the skull
Of Gloriana, whom thou poisonedst last.

Duke. O! 't has poisoned me.

Ven. Didst not know that till now?

Duke. What are you two?

Ven. Villains all three! the very ragged bone
Has been sufficiently revenged.

Duke. O, Hippolito, call treason!   [*He sinks down.*

Hip. Yes, my lord; treason! treason! treason!
                    [*Stamping on him.*

Duke. Then I'm betrayed.

Ven. Alas! poor lecher: in the hands of knaves,
A slavish duke is baser than his slaves.

Duke. My teeth are eaten out.

Ven. Hadst any left?

Hip. I think but few.

Ven. Then those that did eat are eaten.

Duke. O my tongue!

Ven. Your tongue? 'twill teach you to kiss closer,
Not like a slobbering Dutchman. You have eyes still:
Look, monster, what a lady hast thou made me
                    [*Discovers himself.*
My once betrothèd wife.

Duke. Is it thou, villain? nay, then—

Ven. 'Tis I, 'tis Vendice, 'tis I.

Hip. And let this comfort thee: our lord and father
Fell sick upon the infection of thy frowns,
And died in sadness: be that thy hope of life.

Duke. O!

Ven. He had his tongue, yet grief made him die speechless.
Pooh! 'tis but early yet; now I'll begin
To stick thy soul with ulcers. I will make
Thy spirit grievous sore; it shall not rest,

But like some pestilent man toss in thy breast. Mark me,
    duke:
Thou art a renownèd, high and mighty cuckold.
    Duke. O!
    Ven. Thy bastard, thy bastard rides a-hunting in thy
brow.
    Duke. Millions of deaths!
    Ven. Nay, to afflict thee more,
Here in this lodge they meet for damnèd clips.[41]
Those eyes shall see the incest of their lips.
    Duke. Is there a hell besides this, villains?
    Ven. Villain!
Nay, Heaven is just; scorns are the hire of scorns;
I ne'er knew yet adulterer without horns.
    Hip. Once, ere they die, 'tis quitted.
    Ven. Hark! the music:
Their banquet is prepared, they're coming—
    Duke. O, kill me not with that sight!
    Ven. Thou shalt not lose that sight for all thy dukedom.
    Duke. Traitors! murderers!
    Ven. What! is not thy tongue eaten out yet?
Then we'll invent a silence. Brother, stifle the torch.
    Duke. Treason! murder!
    Ven. Nay, faith, we'll have you hushed. Now with thy
    dagger
Nail down his tongue, and mine shall keep possession
About his heart; if he but gasp, he dies;
We dread not death to quittance injuries.
Brother, if he but wink, not brooking the foul object,
Let our two other hands tear up his lids,
And make his eyes like comets shine through blood.
When the bad bleeds, then is the tragedy good.
    Hip. Whist, brother! the music's at our ear; they come.

Enter Spurio, *meeting the* Duchess.

    Spu. Had not that kiss a taste of sin, 'twere sweet.
    Duch. Why, there's no pleasure sweet, but it is sinful.
    Spu. True, such a bitter sweetness fate hath given;
Best side to us is the worst side to Heaven.
    Duch. Pish! come: 'tis the old duke, thy doubtful father:

[41] Embraces

The thought of him rubs Heaven in thy way.
But I protest by yonder waxen fire,
Forget him, or I'll poison him.

    Spu. Madam, you urge a thought which ne'er had life.
So deadly do I loathe him for my birth,
That if he took me hasped within his bed,
I would add murder to adultery,
And with my sword give up his years to death.

    Duch. Why, now thou'rt sociable; lets in and feast:
Loud'st music sound; pleasure is banquet's guest.

                        [Exeunt DUCHESS *and* SPURIO.

    Duke. I cannot brook—   *[Dies.*

    Ven. The brook is turned to blood.

    Hip. Thanks to loud music.

    Ven. 'Twas our friend, indeed.
'Tis state in music for a duke to bleed.
The dukedom wants a head, though yet unknown;
As fast as they peep up, let's cut 'em down.   *[Exeunt.*

SCENE V—*A Room in the Palace*

Enter AMBITIOSO *and* SUPERVACUO.

    Amb. Was not his execution rarely plotted?
We are the duke's sons now.

    Sup. Ay, you may thank my policy for that.

    Amb. Your policy for what?

    Sup. Why, was't not my invention, brother,
To slip the judges? and in lesser compass
Did I not draw the model of his death;
Advising you to sudden officers
And e'en extemporal execution?

    Amb. Heart! 'twas a thing I thought on too.

    Sup. You thought on't too! 'sfoot, slander not your
        thoughts
With glorious untruth; I know 'twas from you.

    Amb. Sir, I say, 'twas in my head.

    Sup. Ay, like your brains then,
Ne'er to come out as long as you lived.

    Amb. You'd have the honour on't, forsooth, that your wit
Led him to the scaffold.

Sup. Since it is my due,
I'll publish't, but I'll ha't in spite of you.

Amb. Methinks, y'are much too bold; you should a little
Remember us, brother, next to be honest duke.

Sup. Ay, it shall be as easy for you to be duke
As to be honest; and that's never, i' faith.   [*Aside.*

Amb. Well, cold he is by this time; and because
We're both ambitious, be it our amity,
And let the glory be shared equally.

Sup. I am content to that.

Amb. This night our younger brother shall out of prison:
I have a trick.

Sup. A trick! prythee, what is't?

Amb. We'll get him out by a wile.

Sup. Prythee, what wile?

Amb. No, sir; you shall not know it, till it be done;
For then you'd swear 'twere yours.

Enter an Officer.

Sup. How now, what's he?

Amb. One of the officers.

Sup. Desired news.

Amb. How now, my friend?

Off. My lords, under your pardon, I am allotted
To that desertless office, to present you
With the yet bleeding head—

Sup. Ha, ha! excellent.

Amb. All's sure our own: brother, canst weep, think'st
    thou?
'Twould grace our flattery much; think of some dame;
'Twill teach thee to dissemble.

Sup. I have thought;—now for yourself.

Amb. Our sorrows are so fluent,
Our eyes o'erflow our tongues; words spoke in tears
Are like the murmurs of the waters—the sound
Is loudly heard, but cannot be distinguished.

Sup. How died he, pray?

Off. O, full of rage and spleen.

Sup. He died most valiantly, then; we're glad to hear it.

Off. We could not woo him once to pray.

Amb. He showed himself a gentleman in that:
Give him his due.

Off. But, in the stead of prayer,
He drew forth oaths.

Sup. Then did he pray, dear heart,
Although you understood him not?

Off. My lords,
E'en at his last, with pardon be it spoke,
He cursed you both.

Sup. He cursed us? 'las, good soul!

Amb. It was not in our powers, but the duke's pleasure.
Finely dissembled a both sides, sweet fate;
O happy opportunity!   [*Aside.*

Enter LUSSURIOSO.

Lus. Now, my lords.

Amb. and Sup. O!—

Lus. Why do you shun me, brothers?
You may come nearer now:
The savour of the prison has forsook me.
I thank such kind lords as yourselves, I'm free.

Amb. Alive!

Sup. In health!

Amb. Released!
We were both e'en amazed with joy to see it.

Lus. I am much to thank to you.

Sup. Faith, we spared no tongue unto my lord the duke.

Amb. I know your delivery, brother,
Had not been half so sudden but for us.

Sup. O, how we pleaded!

Lus. Most deserving brothers!
In my best studies I will think of it.   [*Exit.*

Amb. O death and vengeance!

Sup. Hell and torments!

Amb. Slave, cam'st thou to delude us?

Off. Delude you, my lords?

Sup. Ay, villain, where's his head now?

Off. Why here, my lord;
Just after his delivery, you both came
With warrant from the duke to behead your brother.

Amb. Ay, our brother, the duke's son.

Off. The duke's son, my lord, had his release before you
came.

Amb. Whose head's that, then?

Off. His whom you left command for, your own brother's.
Amb. Our brother's? O furies.
Sup. Plagues!
Amb. Confusions!
Sup. Darkness!
Amb. Devils!
Sup. Fell it out so accursedly?
Amb. So damnedly?
Sup. Villain, I'll brain thee with it.
Off. O my good lord!
Sup. The devil overtake thee!
Amb. O fatal!
Sup. O prodigious to our bloods!
Amb. Did we dissemble?
Sup. Did we make our tears women for thee?
Amb. Laugh and rejoice for thee?
Sup. Bring warrant for thy death?
Amb. Mock off thy head?
Sup. You had a trick: you had a wile, forsooth.
Amb. A murrain meet 'em; there's none of these wiles
that ever come to good: I see now, there's nothing sure in
mortality, but mortality.
Well, no more words: shalt be revenged, i' faith.
Come, throw off clouds; now, brother, think of vengeance,
And deeper-settled hate; sirrah, sit fast,
We'll pull down all, but thou shalt down at last.   [*Exeunt.*

ACT THE FOURTH

SCENE I—*The precincts of the Palace*

Enter LUSSURIOSO *with* HIPPOLITO.

Lus. Hippolito!
  Hip. My lord,
Has your good lordship aught to command me in?
  Lus. I prythee, leave us!
  Hip. How's this? come and leave us!
  Lus. Hippolito!
  Hip. Your honour, I stand ready for any duteous employment.

Lus. Heart! what mak'st thou here?

Hip. A pretty lordly humour!
He bids me be present to depart; something
Has stung his honour.

Lus. Be nearer; draw nearer:
Ye're not so good, methinks; I'm angry with you.

Hip. With me, my lord? I'm angry with myself for't.

Lus. You did prefer a goodly fellow to me:
'Twas wittily elected; 'twas. I thought
He had been a villain, and he proves a knave—
To me a knave.

Hip. I chose him for the best, my lord:
'Tis much my sorrow, if neglect in him
Breed discontent in you.

Lus. Neglect! 'twas will. Judge of it.
Firmly to tell of an incredible act,
Not to be thought, less to be spoken of,
'Twixt my step-mother and the bastard; oh!
Incestuous sweets between 'em.

Hip. Fie, my lord!

Lus. I, in kind loyalty to my father's forehead,
Made this a desperate arm; and in that fury
Committed treason on the lawful bed,
And with my sword e'en rased my father's bosom,
For which I was within a stroke of death.

Hip. Alack! I'm sorry. 'Sfoot, just upon the stroke,
Jars in my brother; 'twill be villainous music.   [*Aside.*

Enter VENDICE, *disguised.*

Ven. My honoured lord.

Lus. Away! prythee, forsake us: hereafter we'll not know
thee.

Ven. Not know me, my lord! your lordship cannot choose.

Lus. Begone, I say: thou art a false knave.

Ven. Why, the easier to be known, my lord.

Lus. Pish! I shall prove too bitter, with a word
Make thee a perpetual prisoner,
And lay this iron age upon thee.

Ven. Mum!
For there's a doom would make a woman dumb.
Missing the bastard—next him—the wind's come about:

Now 'tis my brother's turn to stay, mine to go out.
                                              [*Aside. Exit.*

   Lus. He has greatly moved me.
   Hip. Much to blame, i' faith.
   Lus. But I'll recover, to his ruin. 'Twas told me lately,
I know not whether falsy, that you'd a brother.
   Hip. Who, I? yes, my good lord, I have a brother.
   Lus. How chance the court ne'er saw him? of what
     nature?
How does he apply his hours?
   Hip. Faith, to curse fates
Who, as he thinks, ordained him to be poor—
Keeps at home, full of want and discontent.
   Lus. There's hope in him; for discontent and want
Is the best clay to mould a villain of.   [*Aside.*
Hippolito, wish him repair to us:
If there be ought in him to please our blood,
For thy sake we'll advance him, and build fair
His meanest fortunes; for it is in us
To rear up towers from cottages.
   Hip. It is so, my lord: he will attend your honour;
But he's a man in whom much melancholy dwells.
   Lus. Why, the better; bring him to court.
   Hip. With willingness and speed:
Whom he cast off e'en now, must now succeed.
Brother, disguise must off;
In thine own shape now I'll prefer thee to him:
How strangely does himself work to undo him!
                                              [*Aside. Exit.*
   Lus. This fellow will come fitly; he shall kill
That other slave, that did abuse my spleen,
And made it swell to treason. I have put
Much of my heart into him; he must die.
He that knows great men's secrets, and proves slight,[42]
That man ne'er lives to see his beard turn white.
Ay, he shall speed him: I'll employ the brother;
Slaves are but nails to drive out one another.
He being of black condition, suitable
To want and ill-content, hope of preferment
Will grind him to an edge.

[42] Weak, treacherous.

Enter Nobles.

1st Noble. Good days unto your honour.

Lus. My kind lords, I do return the like.

2nd Noble. Saw you my lord the duke?

Lus. My lord and father! is he from court?

1st Noble. He's sure from court;
But where—which way his pleasure took, we know not,
Nor can we hear on't.

Lus. Here come those should tell.
Saw you my lord and father?

3rd Noble. Not since two hours before noon, my lord,
And then he privately rode forth.

Lus. O, he's rid forth.

1st Noble. 'Twas wondrous privately.

2nd Noble. There's none i' th' court had any knowledge
on't.

Lus. His grace is old and sudden: 'tis no treason
To say the duke, my father, has a humour,
Or such a toy about him; what in us
Would appear light, in him seems virtuous.

3rd Noble. 'Tis oracle, my lord.   [*Exeunt.*

SCENE II—*An Apartment in the Palace*

Enter VENDICE, *out of his disguise, and* HIPPOLITO.

Hip. So, so, all's as it should be, y'are yourself.

Ven. How that great villain puts me to my shifts!

Hip. He that did lately in disguise reject thee,
Shall, now thou art thyself, as much respect thee.

Ven. 'Twill be the quainter fallacy. But, brother,
'Sfoot, what use will he put me to now, think'st thou?

Hip. Nay, you must pardon me in that: I know not.
He has some employment for you: but what 'tis,
He and his secretary (the devil) know best.

Ven. Well, I must suit my tongue to his desires,
What colour soe'er they be; hoping at last
To pile up all my wishes on his breast.

Hip. Faith, brother, he himself shows the way.

Ven. Now the duke is dead, the realm is clad in clay.

His death being not yet known, under his name
The people still are governed. Well, thou his son
Art not long-lived: thou shalt not joy his death.
To kill thee, then, I should most honour thee;
For 'twould stand firm in every man's belief,
Thou'st a kind child, and only died'st with grief.

    Hip. You fetch about well; but let's talk in present.
How will you appear in fashion different,
As well as in apparel, to make all things possible?
If you be but once tripped, we fall for ever.
It is not the least policy to be doubtful;
You must change tongue: familiar was your first.

    Ven. Why, I'll bear me in some strain of melancholy,
And string myself with heavy-sounding wire,
Like such an instrument, that speaks merry things sadly.

    Hip. Then 'tis as I meant;
I gave you out at first in discontent.

    Ven. I'll tune myself, and then—

    Hip. 'Sfoot, here he comes. Hast thought upon't?

    Ven. Salute him; fear not me.

Enter LUSSURIOSO.

    Lus. Hippolito!

    Hip. Your lordship—

    Lus. What's he yonder?

    Hip. 'Tis Vendice, my discontented brother,
Whom, 'cording to your will, I've brought to court.

    Lus. Is that thy brother? Beshrew me, a good presence;
I wonder he has been from the court so long.
Come nearer.

    Hip. Brother! Lord Lussurioso, the duke's son.

    Lus. Be more near to us; welcome; nearer yet.

    Ven. How don you? gi' you good den.

                      [Takes off his hat and bows.

    Lus. We thank thee.
How strangely such a coarse homely salute
Shows in the palace, where we greet in fire,
Nimble and desperate tongues! should we name
God in a salutation, 'twould ne'er be stood on;—Heaven!
Tell me, what has made thee so melancholy?

    Ven. Why, going to law.

    Lus. Why, will that make a man melancholy?

Ven. Yes, to look long upon ink and black buckram. I went me to law in *anno quadragesimo secundo,* and I waded out of it in *anno sexagesimo tertio.*

Lus. What, three-and-twenty years in law?

Ven. I have known those that have been five-and-fifty, and all about pullen[43] and pigs.

Lus. May it be possible such men should breathe,
To vex the terms so much?

Ven. 'Tis food to some, my lord. There are old men at the present, that are so poisoned with the affectation of law-words (having had many suits canvassed), that their common talk is nothing but Barbary Latin. They cannot so much as pray but in law, that their sins may be removed with a writ of error, and their souls fetched up to Heaven with a sasarara.[44]

Lus. It seems most strange to me;
Yet all the world meets round in the same bent:
Where the heart's set, there goes the tongue's consent.
How dost apply thy studies, fellow?

Ven. Study? why, to think how a great rich man lies a-dying, and a poor cobbler tolls the bell for him. How he cannot depart the world, and see the great chest stand before him; when he lies speechless, how he will point you readily to all the boxes; and when he is past all memory, as the gossips guess, then thinks he of forfeitures and obligations; nay, when to all men's hearings he whurls and rattles in the throat, he's busy threatening his poor tenants. And this would last me now some seven years' thinking, or thereabouts. But I have a conceit a-coming in picture upon this; I draw it myself, which, i' faith, la, I'll present to your honour; you shall not choose but like it, for your honour shall give me nothing for it.

Lus. Nay, you mistake me, then,
For I am published bountiful enough.
Let's taste of your conceit.

Ven. In picture, my Lord?

Lus. Ay, in picture.

Ven. Marry, this it is—"A usuring father to be boiling in hell, and his son and heir with a whore dancing over him."

---

[43] Poultry.
[44] A corruption of *certiorari.*

Hip. He has pared him to the quick.   [*Aside.*

Lus. The conceit's pretty, i' faith;
But, take't upon my life, 'twill ne'er be liked.

Ven. No? why I'm sure the whore will be liked well
enough.

Hip. Aye, if she were out o' the picture, he'd like her
then himself.   [*Aside.*

Ven. And as for the son and heir, he shall be an eyesore
to no young revellers, for he shall be drawn in cloth-of-gold
breeches.

Lus. And thou hast put my meaning in the pockets,
And canst not draw that out? My thought was this:
To see the picture of a usuring father
Boiling in hell—our rich men would never like it.

Ven. O, true, I cry you heartily mercy,
I know the reason, for some of them had rather
Be damned in deed than damned in colours.

Lus. A parlous melancholy! he has wit enough
To murder any man, and I'll give him means.   [*Aside.*
I think thou art ill-moneyed?

Ven. Money! ho, ho!
'T has been my want so long, 'tis now my scoff:
I've e'en forgot what colour silver's of.

Lus. It hits as I could wish.   [*Aside.*

Ven. I get good clothes
Of those that dread my humour; and for table-room
I feed on those that cannot be rid of me.

Lus. Somewhat to set thee up withal.   [*Gives him money.*

Ven. O mine eyes!

Lus. How now, man?

Ven. Almost struck blind;
This bright unusual shine to me seems proud;
I dare not look till the sun be in a cloud.

Lus. I think I shall affect[45] his melancholy,
How are they now?

Ven. The better for your asking.

Lus. You shall be better yet, if you but fasten
Truly on my intent. Now y'are both present,
I will unbrace such a close private villain
Unto your vengeful swords, the like ne'er heard of,
Who hath disgraced you much, and injured us.

45 Like

Hip. Disgraced us, my lord?

Lus. Ay, Hippolito.
I kept it here till now, that both your angers
Might meet him at once.

Ven. I'm covetous
To know the villain.

Lus. You know him: that slave-pander,
Piato, whom we threatened last
With irons in perpetual 'prisonment.

Ven. All this is I.   [*Aside.*

Hip. Is't he, my lord?

Lus. I'll tell you; you first preferred him to me.

Ven. Did you, brother?

Hip. I did indeed.

Lus. And the ungrateful villain,
To quit that kindness, strongly wrought with me—
Being, as you see, a likely man for pleasure—
With jewels to corrupt your virgin sister.

Hip. O villain!

Ven. He shall surely die that did it.

Lus. I, far from thinking any virgin harm,
Especially knowing her to be as chaste
As that part which scarce suffers to be touched—
The eye—would not endure him.

Ven. Would you not, my lord?
'Twas wondrous honourably done.

Lus. But with some fine frowns kept him out.

Ven. Out, slave!

Lus. What did me he, but in revenge of that,
Went of his own free will to make infirm
Your sister's honour (whom I honour with my soul
For chaste respect) and not prevailing there
(As 'twas but desperate folly to attempt it),
In mere spleen, by the way, waylays your mother,
Whose honour being a coward as it seems,
Yielded by little force.

Ven. Coward indeed!

Lus. He, proud of this advantage (as he thought),
Brought me this news for happy. But I, Heaven forgive
    me for't!—

Ven. What did your honour?

Lus. In rage pushed him from me,

Trampled beneath his throat, spurned him, and bruised:
Indeed I was too cruel, to say troth.

Hip. Most nobly managed!

Ven. Has not Heaven an ear? is all the lightning wasted?
[*Aside.*

Lus. If I now were so impatient in a modest cause,
What should you be?

Ven. Full mad: he shall not live
To see the moon change.

Lus. He's about the palace;
Hippolito, entice him this way, that thy brother
May take full mark of him.

Hip. Heart! that shall not need, my lord:
I can direct him so far.

Lus. Yet for my hate's sake,
Go, wind him this way. I'll see him bleed myself.

Hip. What now, brother?   [*Aside.*

Ven. Nay, e'en what you will—y'are put to't, brother.
[*Aside.*

Hip. An impossible task, I'll swear,
To bring him hither, that's already here. [*Aside and Exit.*

Lus. Thy name? I have forgot it.

Ven. Vendice, my lord.

Lus. 'Tis a good name that.

Ven. Ay, a revenger.

Lus. It does betoken courage; thou shouldst be valiant,
And kill thine enemies.

Ven. That's my hope, my lord.

Lus. This slave is one.

Ven. I'll doom him.

Lus. Then I'll praise thee.
Do thou observe me best, and I'll best raise thee.

Re-enter HIPPOLITO.

Ven. Indeed, I thank you.

Lus. Now, Hippolito, where's the slave-pander?

Hip. Your good lordship
Would have a loathsome sight of him, much offensive.
He's not in case now to be seen, my lord.
The worst of all the deadly sins is in him—
That beggarly damnation, drunkenness.

Lus. Then he's a double slave.

Ven. 'Twas well conveyed upon a sudden wit.   [*Aside.*

Lus. What, are you both
Firmly resolved? I'll see him dead myself.

Ven. Or else let not us live.

Lus. You may direct your brother to take note of him.

Hip. I shall.

Lus. Rise but in this, and you shall never fall.

Ven. Your honour's vassals.

Lus. This was wisely carried.   [*Aside.*
Deep policy in us makes fools of such:
Then must a slave die, when he knows too much.   [*Exit.*

Ven. O thou almighty patience! 'tis my wonder
That such a fellow, impudent and wicked,
Should not be cloven as he stood;
Or with a secret wind burst open!
Is there no thunder left: or is't kept up
In stock for heavier vengeance? [*Thunder*] there it goes!

Hip. Brother, we lose ourselves.

Ven. But I have found it;
'Twill hold, 'tis sure; thanks, thanks to any spirit,
That mingled it 'mongst my inventions.

Hip. What is't?

Ven. 'Tis sound and good; thou shalt partake it;
I'm hired to kill myself.

Hip. True.

Ven. Prythee, mark it;
And the old duke being dead, but not conveyed,
For he's already missed too, and you know
Murder will peep out of the closest husk—

Hip. Most true.

Ven. What say you then to this device?
If we dressed up the body of the duke?

Hip. In that disguise of yours?

Ven. Y'are quick, y' have reached it.

Hip. I like it wondrously.

Ven. And being in drink, as you have published him.
To lean him on his elbow, as if sleep had caught him
Which claims most interest in such sluggy men?

Hip. Good yet; but here's a doubt;
We, thought by the duke's son to kill that pander,
Shall, when he is known, be thought to kill the duke.

Ven. Neither, O thanks! it is substantial:

For that disguise being on him which I wore,
It will be thought I, which he calls the pander, did kill
the duke, and fled away in his apparel, leaving him so
disguised to avoid swift pursuit.

Hip. Firmer and firmer.

Ven. Nay, doubt not, 'tis in grain: I warrant it holds
    colour.

Hip. Let's about it.

Ven. By the way, too, now I think on't, brother,
Let's conjure that base devil out of our mother.   [*Exeunt.*

SCENE III—*A Corridor in the Palace*

Enter the DUCHESS, *arm in arm with* SPURIO, *looking
lasciviously on her. After them, enter* SUPERVACUO,
with a rapier, running; AMBITIOSO *stops him.*

Spu. Madam, unlock yourself;
Should it be seen, your arm would be suspected.

Duch. Who is't that dares suspect or this or these?
May not we deal our favours where we please?

Spu. I'm confident you may.

                   [*Exeunt* DUCHESS *and* SPURIO.

Amb. 'Sfoot, brother, hold.

Sup. Wouldst let the bastard shame us?

Amb. Hold, hold, brother! there's fitter time than now.

Sup. Now, when I see it!

Amb. 'Tis too much seen already.

Sup. Seen and known;
The nobler she's, the baser is she grown.

Amb. If she were bent lasciviously (the fault
Of mighty women, that sleep soft)—O death!
Must she needs choose such an unequal sinner,
To make all worse?—

Sup. A bastard! the duke's bastard! shame heaped on
    shame!

Amb. O our disgrace!
Most women have small waists the world throughout;
But their desires are thousand miles about.

Sup. Come, stay not here, let's after, and prevent,
Or else they'll sin faster than we'll repent.   [*Exeunt.*

SCENE IV—*A Room in* GRATIANA'S *House*

Enter VENDICE *and* HIPPOLITO, *bringing out* GRATIANA *by the shoulders, and with daggers in their hands.*

Ven. O thou, for whom no name is bad enough!
Gra. What mean my sons? what, will you murder me?
Ven. Wicked, unnatural parent!
Hip. Fiend of women!
Gra. O! are sons turned monsters? help!
Ven. In vain.
Gra. Are you so barbarous to set iron nipples
Upon the breast that gave you suck?
    Ven. That breast
Is turned to quarled[46] poison.
    Gra. Cut not your days for't! am not I your mother?[47]
    Ven. Thou dost usurp that title now by fraud,
For in that shell of mother breeds a bawd.
    Gra. A bawd! O name far loathsomer than hell!
    Hip. It should be so, knew'st thou thy office well.
    Gra. I hate it.
    Ven. Ah! is't possible? thou only? Powers on high,
That women should dissemble when they die!
    Gra. Dissemble!
    Ven. Did not the duke's son direct
A fellow of the world's condition hither,
That did corrupt all that was good in thee?
Made thee uncivilly forget thyself,
And work our sister to his lust?
    Gra. Who, I?
That had been monstrous. I defy that man
For any such intent! none lives so pure,
But shall be soiled with slander. Good son, believe it not.
    Ven. O, I'm in doubt,
Whether I am myself, or no—   [*Aside.*

---

[46] It has been suggested that *quarled* is equivalent to *guarelled;* and that it alludes to poison put on arrows. The sound of the word seems to point at some synonym for *curdled.*
[47] Alluding to the 5th Commandment.

Stay, let me look again upon this face.
Who shall be saved, when mothers have no grace?
   Hip. 'Twould make one half despair.
   Ven. I was the man.
Defy me now; let's see, do't modestly.
   Gra. O hell unto my soul!
   Ven. In that disguise, I, sent from the duke's son,
Tried you, and found you base metal,
As any villain might have done.
   Gra. O, no,
No tongue but yours could have bewitched me so.
   Ven. O nimble in damnation, quick in tune!
There is no devil could strike fire so soon:
I am confuted in a word.
   Gra. O sons, forgive me! to myself I'll prove more true;
You that should honour me, I kneel to you.

[Kneels and weeps.

   Ven. A mother to give aim to her own daughter![48]
   Hip. True, brother; how far beyond nature 'tis.
   Ven. Nay, an you draw tears once, go you to bed;
We will make iron blush and change to red.
Brother, it rains. 'Twill spoil your dagger: house it.
   Hip. 'Tis done.
   Ven. I' faith, 'tis a sweet shower, it does much good.
The fruitful grounds and meadows of her soul
Have been long dry: pour down, thou blessèd dew!
Rise, mother; troth, this shower has made you higher!
   Gra. O you Heavens! take this infectious spot out of my
     soul,
I'll rinse it in seven waters of mine eyes!
Make my tears salt enough to taste of grace.
To weep is to our sex naturally given:
But to weep truly, that's a gift from Heaven.
   Ven. Nay, I'll kiss you now. Kiss her, brother:
Let's marry her to our souls, wherein's no lust,
And honourably love her.
   Hip. Let it be.
   Ven. For honest women are so seld and rare,
'Tis good to cherish those poor few that are.
O you of easy wax! do but imagine

---

[48] *i.e.* Incite, encourage her.

Now the disease has left you, how leprously
That office would have clinged unto your forehead!
All mothers that had any graceful hue
Would have worn masks to hide their face at you:
It would have grown to this—at your foul name,
Green-coloured maids would have turned red with shame.

Hip. And then our sister, full of hire and baseness—

Ven. There had been boiling lead again,
The duke's son's great concubine!
A drab of state, a cloth-o'-silver slut,
To have her train borne up, and her soul trail i' the dirt!

Hip. Great, to be miserably great; rich, to be eternally
wretched.

Ven. O common madness!
Ask but the thrivingest harlot in cold blood,
She'd give the world to make her honour good.
Perhaps you'll say, but only to the duke's son
In private; why she first begins with one,
Who afterward to thousands prove a whore:
"Break ice in one place, it will crack in more."

Gra. Most certainly applied!

Hip. O brother, you forget our business.

Ven. And well-remembered; joy's a subtle elf,
I think man's happiest when he forgets himself.
Farewell, once dry, now holy-watered mead;
Our hearts wear feathers, that before wore lead.

Gra. I'll give you this—that one I never knew
Plead better for and 'gainst the devil than you.

Ven. You make me proud on't.

Hip. Commend us in all virtue to our sister.

Ven. Ay, for the love of Heaven, to that true maid.

Gra. With my best words.

Ven. Why, that was motherly said.[49]

[*Exeunt* VENDICE *and* HIPPOLITO.

Gra. I wonder now, what fury did transport me!
I feel good thoughts begin to settle in me.

[49] The reality and life of this dialogue passes any scenical illusion I ever felt.
I never read it but my ears tingle, and I feel a hot flush spread my cheeks,
as if I were presently about to "proclaim" some such "malefactions" of myself
as the brothers here rebuke in this unnatural parent, in words more keen and
dagger-like than those which Hamlet speaks to his mother. Such power has the
passion of shame, truly personated, not only to "strike guilty creatures unto
the soul," but to "appal" even those that are "free."—*Lamb.*

O, with what forehead can I look on her,
Whose honour I've so impiously beset?
And here she comes—

Enter CASTIZA.

 Cas. Now, mother, you have wrought with me so strongly,
That what for my advancement, as to calm
The trouble of your tongue, I am content.
 Gra. Content, to what?
 Cas. To do as you have wished me;
To prostitute my breast to the duke's son;
And put myself to common usury.
 Gra. I hope you will not so!
 Cas. Hope you I will not?
That's not the hope you look to be saved in.
 Gra. Truth, but it is.
 Cas. Do not deceive yourself;
I am as you, e'en out of marble wrought.
What would you now? are ye not pleased yet with me?
You shall not wish me to be more lascivious
Than I intend to be.
 Gra. Strike not me cold.
 Cas. How often have you charged me on your blessing
To be a cursèd woman? When you knew
Your blessing had no force to make me lewd,
You laid your curse upon me; that did more,
The mother's curse is heavy; where that fights,
Suns set in storm, and daughters lose their lights.
 Gra. Good child, dear maid, if there be any spark
Of heavenly intellectual fire within thee,
O, let my breath revive it to a flame!
Put not all out with woman's wilful follies.
I am recovered of that foul disease,
That haunts too many mothers; kind, forgive me.
Make me not sick in health! If then
My words prevailed, when they were wickedness,
How much more now, when they are just and good?
 Cas. I wonder what you mean! are not you she,
For whose infect persuasions I could scarce
Kneel out my prayers, and had much ado
In three hours' reading to untwist so much
Of the black serpent as you wound about me?

Gra. 'Tis unfruitful, child, and tedious to repeat
What's past; I'm now your present mother.

Cas. Tush! now 'tis too late.

Gra. Bethink again: thou know'st not what thou say'st.

Cas. No! deny advancement? treasure? the duke's son?

Gra. O, see! I spoke those words, and now they poison
me!
What will the deed do then?
Advancement? true; as high as shame can pitch!
For treasure; who e'er knew a harlot rich?
Or could build by the purchase of her sin
An hospital to keep her bastards in?
The duke's son! O, when women are young courtiers,
They are sure to be old beggars;
To know the miseries most harlots taste,
Thou'dst wish thyself unborn, when thou art unchaste.

Cas. O mother, let me twine about your neck,
And kiss you, till my soul melt on your lips!
I did but this to try you.

Gra. O, speak truth!

Cas. Indeed I did but; for no tongue has force
To alter me from honest.
If maidens would, men's words could have no power;
A virgin's honour is a crystal tower
Which (being weak) is guarded with good spirits;
Until she basely yields, no ill inherits.

Gra. O happy child! faith, and thy birth hath saved me.
'Mong thousand daughters, happiest of all others:
Be thou a glass for maids, and I for mothers.   [*Exeunt.*

ACT THE FIFTH

SCENE I—*A Room in the Lodge. The* DUKE'S *corpse, dressed
in* VENDICE'S *disguise, lying on a couch*

Enter VENDICE *and* HIPPOLITO.

VEN. So, so, he leans well; take heed you wake him not,
brother.

Hip. I warrant you my life for yours.

Ven. That's a good lay, for I must kill myself.

Brother, that's I, that sits for me: do you mark it? And
I must stand ready here to make away myself yonder. I
must sit to be killed, and stand to kill myself. I could vary
it not so little as thrice over again; 't has some eight returns,
like Michaelmas term.[50]

Hip. That's enow, o' conscience.

Ven. But, sirrah, does the duke's son come single?

Hip. No; there's the hell on't: his faith's too feeble to
go alone. He brings flesh-flies after him, that will buzz
against supper-time, and hum for his coming out.

Ven. Ah, the fly-flap of vengeance beat 'em to pieces!
Here was the sweetest occasion, the fittest hour, to have
made my revenge familiar with him; show him the body of
the duke his father, and how quaintly he died, like a
politician, in hugger-mugger,[51] made no man acquainted
with it; and in catastrophe slay him over his father's breast.
O, I'm mad to lose such a sweet opportunity!

Hip. Nay, tush! prythee, be content! there's no remedy
present; may not hereafter times open in as fair faces as
this?

Ven. They may, if they can paint so well.

Hip. Come now: to avoid all suspicion, let's forsake this
room, and be going to meet the duke's son.

Ven. Content: I'm for any weather. Heart! step close: here
he comes.

Enter Lussurioso.

Hip. My honoured lord!

Lus. O me! you both present?

Ven. E'en newly, my lord, just as your lordship entered
now: about this place we had notice given he should be,
but in some loathsome plight or other.

Hip. Came your honour private?

Lus. Private enough for this; only a few
Attend my coming out.

Hip. Death rot those few!   [*Aside.*

Lus. Stay, yonder's the slave.

Ven. Mass, there's the slave, indeed, my lord.

---

[50] Michaelmas term now has but four returns.
[51] In secret.

'Tis a good child: he calls his father a slave!   [*Aside.*

Lus. Ay, that's the villain, the damned villain.
Softly. Tread easy.

Ven. Pah! I warrant you, my lord, we'll stifle-in our
breaths.

Lus. That will do well:
Base rogue, thou sleepest thy last; 'tis policy
To have him killed in's sleep; for if he waked,
He would betray all to them.

Ven. But, my lord—

Lus. Ha, what say'st?

Ven. Shall we kill him now he's drunk?

Lus. Ay, best of all.

Ven. Why, then he will ne'er live to be sober.

Lus. No matter, let him reel to hell.

Ven. But being so full of liquor, I fear he will put out
all the fire.

Lus. Thou art a mad beast.

Ven. And leave none to warm your lordship's golls[52]
withal; for he that dies drunk falls into hell-fire like a
bucket of water—qush, qush!

Lus. Come, be ready: nake[53] your swords: think of your
wrongs; this slave has injured you.

Ven. Troth, so he has, and he has paid well for't.

Lus. Meet with him now.

Ven. You'll bear us out, my lord?

Lus. Pooh! am I a lord for nothing, think you? quickly
now!

Ven. Sa, sa, sa, thump [*Stabs the* DUKE's *corpse*]—there
he lies.

Lus. Nimbly done.—Ha! O villains! murderers! 'Tis the
old duke, my father.

Ven. That's a jest.

Lus. What stiff and cold already!
O, pardon me to call you from your names:
'Tis none of your deed. That villain Piato,
Whom you thought now to kill, has murdered
And left him thus disguised.

Hip. And not unlikely.

---

[52] Hands.
[53] *i.e.* Unsheathe.

Ven. O rascal! was he not ashamed
To put the duke into a greasy doublet?

Lus. He has been stiff and cold—who knows how long?

Ven. Marry, that I do.   [*Aside.*

Lus. No words, I pray, of anything intended.

Ven. O my lord.

Hip. I would fain have your lordship think that we have
small reason to prate.

Lus. Faith, thou say'st true; I'll forthwith send to court
For all the nobles; bastard, duchess; tell,
How here by miracle we found him dead,
And in his raiment that foul villain fled.

Ven. That will be the best way, my lord,
To clear us all; let's cast about to be clear.

Lus. Ho! Nencio, Sordido, and the rest!

Enter all of them.

1st Ser. My lord.

2nd Ser. My lord.

Lus. Be witnesses of a strange spectacle.
Choosing for private conference that sad room,
We found the duke my father gealed in blood.

1st Ser. My lord the duke! run, hie thee, Nencio.
Startle the court by signifying so much.

Ven. Thus much by wit a deep revenger can,
When murder's known, to be the clearest man.
We're farthest off, and with as bold an eye
Survey his body as the standers-by.   [*Aside.*

Lus. My royal father, too basely let blood
By a malevolent slave!

Hip. Hark! he calls thee slave again.   [*Aside.*

Ven. He has lost: he may.   [*Aside.*

Lus. O sight! look hither, see, his lips are gnawn
With poison.

Ven. How! his lips? by the mass, they be.
O villain! O rogue! O slave! O rascal!

Hip. O good deceit! he quits him with like terms.
                                                 [*Aside.*

Amb. [*Within.*] Where?

Sup. [*Within.*] Which way?

Enter AMBITIOSO *and* SUPERVACUO, *with* Nobles *and*
Gentlemen.

Amb. Over what roof hangs this prodigious comet
In deadly fire?

Lus. Behold, behold, my lords, the duke my father's
murdered by a vassal that owes this habit, and here left
disguised.

Enter DUCHESS *and* SPURIO.

Duch. My lord and husband!

1st Noble. Reverend majesty!

2nd Noble. I have seen these clothes often attending on
him.

Ven. That nobleman has been i' th' country, for he does
    not lie.   [*Aside.*

Sup. Learn of our mother; let's dissemble too:
I am glad he's vanished; so, I hope, are you.

Amb. Ay, you may take my word for't.

Spu. Old dad dead!
I, one of his cast sins, will send the Fates
Most hearty commendations by his own son;
I'll tug in the new stream, till strength be done.

Lus. Where be those two that did affirm to us,
My lord the duke was privately rid forth?

1st Gent. O, pardon us, my lords; he gave that charge—
Upon our lives, if he were missed at court,
To answer so; he rode not anywhere;
We left him private with that fellow here.

Ven. Confirmed.   [*Aside.*

Lus. O Heavens! that false charge was his death.
Impudent beggars! durst you to our face
Maintain such a false answer? Bear him straight
To execution.

1st Gent. My lord!

Lus. Urge me no more in this!
The excuse may be called half the murder.

Ven. You've sentenced well.   [*Aside.*

Lus. Away; see it be done.

Ven. Could you not stick? See what confession doth!
Who would not lie, when men are hanged for truth?
                                  [*Aside.*

Hip. Brother, how happy is our vengeance!   [*Aside.*
Ven. Why, it hits past the apprehension of
Indifferent wits.   [*Aside.*
Lus. My lord, let post-horses be sent
Into all places to entrap the villain.
Ven. Post-horses, ha, ha!   [*Aside.*
1st Noble. My lord, we're something bold to know our
        duty.
Your father's accidentally departed;
The titles that were due to him meet you.
Lus. Meet me! I'm not at leisure, my good lord.
I've many griefs to despatch out o' the way.
Welcome, sweet titles!—   [*Aside.*
Talk to me, my lords,
Of sepulchres and mighty emperors' bones;
That's thought for me.
Ven. So one may see by this
How foreign markets go;
Courtiers have feet o' the nines, and tongues o' the twelves;
They flatter dukes, and dukes flatter themselves.   [*Aside.*
2nd Noble. My lord, it is your shine must comfort us.
Lus. Alas! I shine in tears, like the sun in April.
1st Noble. You're now my lord's grace.
Lus. My lord's grace! I perceive you'll have it so.
2nd Noble. 'Tis but your own.
Lus. Then, Heavens, give me grace to be so!
Ven. He prays well for himself.   [*Aside.*
1st Noble. Madam, all sorrows
Must run their circles into joys. No doubt but time
Will make the murderer bring forth himself.
Ven. He were an ass then, i' faith.   [*Aside.*
1st Noble. In the mean season,
Let us bethink the latest funeral honours
Due to the duke's cold body. And withal,
Calling to memory our new happiness
Speed in his royal son: lords, gentlemen,
Prepare for revels.
Ven. Revels!   [*Aside.*
1st Noble. Time hath several falls.
Griefs lift up joys: feasts put down funerals.
Lus. Come then, my lords, my favour's to you all.
The duchess is suspected foully bent;

I'll begin dukedom with her banishment.   [*Aside.*
                [*Exeunt* LUSSURIOSO, DUCHESS, *and* Nobles.

Hip. Revels!

Ven. Ay, that's the word: we are firm yet;
Strike one strain more, and then we crown our wit.
                        [*Exeunt* VENDICE *and* HIPPOLITO.

Spu. Well, have at the fairest mark—so said the duke
        when he begot me;
And if I miss his heart, or near about,
Then have at any; a bastard scorns to be out.   [*Exit.*

Sup. Notest thou that Spurio, brother?

Ant. Yes, I note him to our shame.

Sup. He shall not live: his hair shall not grow much
longer. In this time of revels, tricks may be set afoot. Seest
thou yon new moon? it shall outlive the new duke by much;
this hand shall dispossess him. Then we're mighty.
    A mask is treason's licence, that build upon:
        'Tis murder's best face, when a vizard's on.   [*Exit.*

Amb. Is't so? 'tis very good!
And do you think to be duke then, kind brother?
I'll see fair play; drop one, and there lies t'other.   [*Exit.*

SCENE II—*A Room in* PIERO's *House*

Enter VENDICE *and* HIPPOLITO, *with* PIERO *and other* Lords.

Ven. My lords, be all of music, strike old griefs into other
        countries
That flow in too much milk, and have faint livers,
Not daring to stab home their discontents.
Let our hid flames break out as fire, as lightning,
To blast this villainous dukedom, vexed with sin;
Wind up your souls to their full height again.

Piero. How?

1st Lord. Which way?

2nd Lord. Any way: our wrongs are such,
We cannot justly be revenged too much.

Ven. You shall have all enough. Revels are toward,
And those few nobles that have long suppressed you,
Are busied to the furnishing of a masque,
And do affect to make a pleasant tale on't:

The masquing suits are fashioning: now comes in
That which must glad us all. We too take pattern
Of all those suits, the colour, trimming, fashion,
E'en to an undistinguished hair almost:
Then entering first, observing the true form,
Within a strain or two we shall find leisure
To steal our swords out handsomely;
And when they think their pleasure sweet and good,
In midst of all their joys they shall sigh blood.

   Piero. Weightily, effectually!

   3rd Lord. Before the t'other maskers come—

   Ven. We're gone, all done and past.

   Piero. But how for the duke's guard?

   Ven. Let that alone;
By one and one their strengths shall be drunk down.

   Hip. There are five hundred gentlemen in the action,
That will apply themselves, and not stand idle.

   Piero. O, let us hug your bosoms!

   Ven. Come, my lords,
Prepare for deeds: let other times have words.   [*Exeunt.*

SCENE III—*Hall of State in the Palace*

In a dumb show, the possessing[54] *of the* YOUNG DUKE *with
all his* Nobles; *sounding music. A furnished table is
brought forth; then enter the* DUKE *and his* Nobles
to the banquet. A blazing star appeareth.

   1st Noble. Many harmonious hours and choicest pleasures
Fill up the royal number of your years!

   Lus. My lords, we're pleased to thank you, though we
know
'Tis but your duty now to wish it so.

   1st Noble. That shine makes us all happy.

   3rd Noble. His grace frowns.

   2nd Noble. Yet we must say he smiles.

   1st Noble. I think we must.

   Lus. That foul incontinent duchess we have banished;
The bastard shall not live. After these revels,
I'll begin strange ones: he and the step-sons

[54] *i.e.* The installation or putting in possession.

Shall pay their lives for the first subsidies;
We must not frown so soon, else't had been now. [*Aside.*

  1st Noble. My gracious lord, please you prepare for
    pleasure.
The masque is not far off.

  Lus. We are for pleasure.
Beshrew thee, what art thou? thou mad'st me start!
Thou hast committed treason. A blazing star!

  1st Noble. A blazing star! O, where, my lord?

  Lus. Spy out.

  2nd Noble. See, see, my lords, a wondrous dreadful one!

  Lus. I am not pleased at that ill-knotted fire,
That bushing, staring star. Am I not duke?
It should not quake me now. Had it appeared
Before, it I might then have justly feared;
But yet they say, whom art and learning weds,
When stars wear locks, they threaten great men's heads:
Is it so? you are read, my lords.

  1st Noble. May it please your grace,
It shows great anger.

  Lus. That does not please our grace.

  2nd Noble. Yet here's the comfort, my lord: many times,
When it seems most near, it threatens farthest off.

  Lus. Faith, and I think so too.

  1st Noble. Beside, my lord,
You're gracefully established with the loves
Of all your subjects; and for natural death,
I hope it will be threescore years a-coming.

  Lus. True? no more but threescore years?

  1st Noble. Fourscore, I hope, my lord.

  2nd Noble. And fivescore, I.

  3rd Noble. But 'tis my hope, my lord, you shall ne'er die.

  Lus. Give me thy hand; these others I rebuke:
He that hopes so is fittest for a duke:
Thou shalt sit next me; take your places, lords;
We're ready now for sports; let 'em set on:
You thing! we shall forget you quite anon!

  3rd Noble. I hear 'em coming, my lord.

Enter the Masque of revengers: VENDICE *and* HIPPOLITO,
with two Lords.

  Lus. Ah, 'tis well!

Brothers and bastard, you dance next in hell!   [*Aside.*
[*They dance; at the end they steal out their swords, and
    kill the four seated at the table. Thunder.*
    Ven. Mark, thunder!
Dost know thy cue, thou big-voiced crier?
Dukes' groans are thunder's watchwords.
    Hip. So, my lords, you have enough.
    Ven. Come, let's away, no lingering.
    Hip. Follow! go!   [*Exeunt except* VENDICE.
    Ven. No power is angry when the lustful die;
When thunder claps, heaven likes the tragedy.   [*Exit.*
    Lus. O, O!

Enter the Masque of intended murderers: AMBITIOSO, SUPER-
    VACUO, SPURIO, *and a* Lord, *coming in dancing.*
    LUSSURIOSO *recovers a little in voice, groans, and calls,*
    "A guard! treason!" *at which the* Dancers *start out of
    their measure, and, turning towards the table, find
    them all to be murdered.*

    Spu. Whose groan was that?
    Lus. Treason! a guard!
    Amb. How now? all murdered!
    Sup. Murdered!
    3rd Lord. And those his nobles?
    Amb. Here's a labour saved;
I thought to have sped him. 'Sblood, how came this?
    Spu. Then I proclaim myself; now I am duke.
    Amb. Thou duke! brother, thou liest.
    Spu. Slave! so dost thou.   [*Kills* AMBITIOSO.
    3rd Lord. Base villain! hast thou slain my lord and
        master?   [*Stabs* SPURIO.

Re-enter VENDICE *and* HIPPOLITO *and the two* Lords.

    Ven. Pistols! treason! murder! Help! guard my lord the
    duke!

Enter ANTONIO *and* Guard.

    Hip. Lay hold upon this traitor.
    Lus. O!
    Ven. Alas! the duke is murdered.
    Hip. And the nobles.

Ven. Surgeons! surgeons! Heart! does he breathe so long?

                                     [*Aside.*

Ant. A piteous tragedy! able to make
An old man's eyes bloodshot.

   Lus. O!

Ven. Look to my lord the duke. A vengeance throttle
    him!   [*Aside.*
Confess, thou murderous and unhallowed man,
Didst thou kill all these?

   3rd Lord. None but the bastard, I.

Ven. How came the duke slain, then?

   3rd Lord. We found him so.

   Lus. O villain!

   Ven. Hark!

   Lus. Those in the masque did murder us.

   Ven. La you now, sir—
O marble impudence! will you confess now?

   3rd Lord. 'Sblood, 'tis all false.

   Ant. Away with that foul monster,
Dipped in a prince's blood.

   3rd Lord. Heart! 'tis a lie.

   Ant. Let him have bitter execution.

   Ven. New marrow! no, I cannot be expressed.
How fares my lord the duke?

   Lus. Farewell to all;
He that climbs highest has the greatest fall.
My tongue is out of office.

   Ven. Air, gentlemen, air.
Now thou'lt not prate on't, 'twas Vendice murdered thee.

                           [*Whispers in his ear.*

   Lus. O!

   Ven. Murdered thy father.   [*Whispers.*

   Lus. O!   [*Dies.*

   Ven. And I am he—tell nobody: [*Whispers*] So, so, the
    duke's departed.

   Ant. It was a deadly hand that wounded him.
The rest, ambitious who should rule and sway
After his death, were so made all away.

   Ven. My lord was unlikely—

   Hip. Now the hope
Of Italy lies in your reverend years.

   Ven. Your hair will make the silver age again,
When there were fewer, but more honest men.
   Ant. The burthen's weighty, and will press age down;
May I so rule, that Heaven may keep the crown!
   Ven. The rape of your good lady has been quitted
With death on death.
   Ant. Just is the law above.
But of all things it put me most to wonder
How the old duke came murdered!
   Ven. O my lord!
   Ant. It was the strangeliest carried: I've not heard of the
     like.
   Hip. 'Twas all done for the best, my lord.
   Ven. All for your grace's good. We may be bold to speak
     it now,
'Twas somewhat witty carried, though we say it—
'Twas we two murdered him.
   Ant. You two?
   Ven. None else, i' faith, my lord. Nay, 'twas well-man-
     aged.
   Ant. Lay hands upon those villains!
   Ven. How! on us?
   Ant. Bear 'em to speedy execution.
   Ven. Heart! was't not for your good, my lord?
   Ant. My good! Away with 'em: such an old man as he!
You, that would murder him, would murder me.
   Ven. Is't come about?
   Hip. 'Sfoot, brother, you begun.
   Ven. May not we set as well as the duke's son?
Thou hast no conscience, are we not revenged?
Is there one enemy left alive amongst those?
'Tis time to die, when we're ourselves our foes:
When murderers shut deeds close, this curse does seal 'em:
If none disclose 'em, they themselves reveal 'em!
This murder might have slept in tongueless brass
But for ourselves, and the world died an ass.
Now I remember too, here was Piato
Brought forth a knavish sentence once;
No doubt (said he), but time
Will make the murderer bring forth himself.
'Tis well he died; he was a witch.
And now, my lord, since we are in for ever,